THE COGNITIVE SCIENCE OF RELIGION

The field of study called the Cognitive Science of Religion provides interesting and informative theories about the cognitive and evolutionary origins of human religion. However, most of these theories include the unnecessary assumption that religion is "nothing but" the chance outcome of a random evolutionary walk. In this very useful book, James Van Slyke provides a thoughtful review of this field, while also arguing for a more balanced view of the human aspects of religion that takes seriously the embodiment of human nature and cognition, modern philosophy of mind, and theology.

Warren S. Brown, Fuller Graduate School of Psychology, USA

The cognitive science of religion is a relatively new academic field in the study of the origins and causes of religious belief and behavior. The focal point of empirical research is the role of basic human cognitive functions in the formation and transmission of religious beliefs. However, many theologians and religious scholars are concerned that this perspective will reduce and replace explanations based in religious traditions, beliefs, and values. This book attempts to bridge the reductionist divide between science and religion through examination and critique of different aspects of the cognitive science of religion and offers a conciliatory approach that investigates the multiple causal factors involved in the emergence of religion.

Ashgate Science and Religion Series

Series Editors:

Roger Trigg, *Emeritus Professor, University of Warwick, and Academic Director of the Centre for the Study of Religion in Public Life, Kellogg College, Oxford*

J. Wentzel van Huyssteen, *Princeton Theological Seminary, USA*

Science and religion have often been thought to be at loggerheads but much contemporary work in this flourishing interdisciplinary field suggests this is far from the case. The *Ashgate Science and Religion Series* presents exciting new work to advance interdisciplinary study, research and debate across key themes in science and religion, exploring the philosophical relations between the physical and social sciences on the one hand and religious belief on the other. Contemporary issues in philosophy and theology are debated, as are prevailing cultural assumptions arising from the 'post-modernist' distaste for many forms of reasoning. The series enables leading international authors from a range of different disciplinary perspectives to apply the insights of the various sciences, theology and philosophy and look at the relations between the different disciplines and the rational connections that can be made between them. These accessible, stimulating new contributions to key topics across science and religion will appeal particularly to individual academics and researchers, graduates, postgraduates and upper-undergraduate students.

Other titles in the series:

Naturalism, Theism and the Cognitive Study of Religion
Religion Explained?
Aku Visala
978-1-4094-2426-0 (hbk)

Science and Faith within Reason
Reality, Creation, Life and Design
Edited by Jaume Navarro
978-1-4094-2608-0 (hbk)

Human Identity at the Intersection of Science, Technology and Religion
Edited by Nancey Murphy and Christopher C. Knight
978-1-4094-1050-8 (hbk)

The Cognitive Science of Religion

JAMES A. VAN SLYKE
Fuller Theological Seminary, USA

ASHGATE

© James A. Van Slyke 2011

All rights reserved. No part of this publication may be reproduced, stored in a retrieval system or transmitted in any form or by any means, electronic, mechanical, photocopying, recording or otherwise without the prior permission of the publisher.

James A. Van Slyke has asserted his right under the Copyright, Designs and Patents Act, 1988, to be identified as the author of this work.

Published by
Ashgate Publishing Limited
Wey Court East
Union Road
Farnham
Surrey, GU9 7PT
England

Ashgate Publishing Company
Suite 420
101 Cherry Street
Burlington
VT 05401-4405
USA

www.ashgate.com

British Library Cataloguing in Publication Data
Van Slyke, James A.
 The cognitive science of religion. -- (Ashgate science and religion series)
 1. Psychology, Religious. 2. Faith and reason. 3. Cognitive neuroscience.
 I. Title II. Series
 200.1'9-dc22

Library of Congress Cataloging-in-Publication Data
Van Slyke, James A.
 The cognitive science of religion / James A. Van Slyke.
  p. cm. -- (Ashgate science and religion series)
 Includes bibliographical references and index.
 ISBN 978-1-4094-2123-8 (hardcover) -- ISBN 978-1-4094-2124-5 (ebook)
 1. Psychology, Religious. 2. Cognitive science. I. Title.

BL53.V283 2011
200.1'9--dc22

ISBN 9781409421238 (hbk)
ISBN 9781409421245 (ebk)

Printed and bound in Great Britain by the
MPG Books Group, UK

Contents

List of Figures	vii
Acknowledgments	ix

	Introduction	1
1	The Standard Model and the Problem of Causal Reductionism	5
	Cognitive Science of Religion	5
	Understanding Reductionism	13
	Defining Emergence	17
	Defining Top-down Constraints	19
	Eliminative Reduction	21
	Differentiating Science from Metaphysics	25
	Integrating a Theological Worldview	27
	Conclusion	30
2	Counterintuitive Religious Concepts and Emergent Cognition	31
	Counterintuitive Religious Concepts	31
	Defining Emergence	39
	Emergent Cognition	42
	Evidence of Emergence from Neuroscience	51
	Conclusion	58
3	Theological Incorrectness and the Causal Relevance of Religious Beliefs and Theological Reasoning	61
	Theologically Correct or Incorrect?	62
	Understanding Bottom-up and Top-down Processing	65
	Cognition and External Scaffolding	72
	Beliefs as Causes	74
	Philosophical Issues	77
	Computational Modeling and Top-down Processing	81
	Recurrent Neural Networks	84
	Conclusion	90

4 Evolutionary Psychology and the Emergence of the Symbolic Mind 91
    Evolutionary Psychology 92
    Imitation and Mirror Neurons 101
    Shared Intentions 103
    Co-Evolution of the Symbolic Mind 107
    Conclusion 118

5 Evolution, Cognition, and Religion: Toward a Multi-level Perspective
    on the Emergence of Religious Beliefs 121
    Counterintuitive Concepts 122
    Hyperactive Agency Detection 124
    Emotion and Religion 126
    God as Attachment Figure 134
    Religion and Group Processes 144
    Conclusion 153

Postscript 155
Bibliography 157
Index 177

List of Figures

1.1	Hierarchy of the sciences	13
3.1	The cat—word superiority effect	66
3.2	Old/young woman	86

Acknowledgments

This book is based on my dissertation, which I completed in June 2008 at Fuller Theological Seminary in Pasadena, California. So I would first like to thank my two primary mentors, Nancey Murphy and Warren Brown. My ability to write is really a result of many years of working with Nancey. Through discussion and critique (sometimes difficult but always filled with grace) Nancey made me the writer I am today. Plus, her clarity in philosophical method and analysis helped me to think much more clearly and incisively. Much of what I know about cognitive neuroscience comes from Warren. Through sitting in on his classes and many personal discussions, I learned the basics of neuropsychology, physiological psychology and cognitive science. Warren also has a way of parsing philosophical problems into the important ingredients that must be addressed, which helped me to figure out what philosophical problems to address in this book.

I also want to thank Wentzel van Huyssteen whose encouragement over a brief meeting one day helped me to focus on the task of getting the book proposal completed and pushed me forward towards completing the book. I owe a debt of gratitude to many scholars and scientists working in the cognitive science of religion for different discussions and disagreements over the nature of cognition and its ability to explain different facets of religion, which includes D. Jason Slone, Justin Barrett, Robert N. McCauley, Donald Wiebe, Luther Martin, Joseph Bulbulia, Edward Slingerland, and Ann Taves. Our discussions helped to clarify the relevant issues and helped me to understand the basics of the cognitive science of religion.

At a conference in Oxford, discussions with David Leech and Aku Visala were particularly helpful, as well as their comments on an early draft of the first chapter. Portions of Chapter 1 come from the article, James A. Van Slyke, "Challenging the By-Product Theory of Religion in the Cognitive Science of Religion," *Theology & Science* 8, no. 2 (2010): 163-180; and portions of Chapter 5 come from the article James A. Van Slyke, "Evolutionary and Cognitive Factors in the Emergence of Human Altruism," *Zygon* 45, no. 4 (2010): 841-860. My research would not have been possible without the support of a grant from the Cognition, Religion and Theology Project at the University of Oxford, funded by the John Templeton Foundation. The views expressed in this book are not necessarily those of the Cognition, Religion and Theology Project, the University of Oxford or the John Templeton Foundation.

Most of all, I want to thank my family. My daughters, Kail and Abby, who let me be away from home to work on this book and had to deal with a distracted father when I was contemplating some new theory. And to my wife, who is the sole person responsible for giving me the time, resources, and support necessary to complete this book. Thank you for 12 wonderful years together filled with love.

Introduction

The cognitive science of religion is a relatively new academic field in the study of the origins and causes of religious belief and behavior. The focal point of empirical research is the role of basic human cognitive functions in the formation and transmission of religious beliefs. These cognitive functions are universal and applicable to the study of religious concepts, rituals and behaviors across cultural contexts and historical time periods. The cognitive science of religion is a highly interdisciplinary project composed of scholars from various fields including religious studies, cognitive psychology, neuroscience, philosophy, human anthropology, and evolutionary science. The field continues to expand across North America and Europe with centers and programs located at various universities such as the University of Michigan, University of Oxford, Aarhus University in Denmark, and the University of British Columbia.

The cognitive science of religion has received a mixed reception among religious scholars and theologians. Reduction is the primary issue of contention for many of the critics of this new area of study. Kelly Bulkeley, in a book review of *Religion Explained* and *How Religion Works*, describes the concern for reductionism that this new field seems to generate.[1]

> Beliefs, doctrines, practices, rituals, mystical experiences, moral systems, communal structures—everything about religion can be explained, according to Boyer and Pysiainen, by using the latest advances in evolutionary theory and cognitive science.[2]

As Gregory Peterson explains, religious scholars and theologians are concerned that explanations from religious studies, anthropology, sociology, and theology will simply be reduced and replaced with explanations from the biological sciences.

> Many scholars in the field understand that these biological explanations will also be exhaustive and consequently reductive, that is, showing that religion is

---

[1] Pascal Boyer, *Religion Explained: The Evolutionary Origins of Religious Thought* (New York: Basic Books, 2001); Ilkka Pyysiäinen, *How Religion Works: Toward a New Cognitive Science of Religion* (Leiden: Brill 2003).

[2] Kelly Bulkeley, "Review of Religion Explained: The Evolutionary Origins of Religious Thought, by Pascal Boyer and How Religion Works: Towards a New Cognitive Science of Religion, by Ilkka Pyysianien," *Journal of the American Academy of Religion* 71, no. 3 (2003): 671.

nothing but a result of biological pressures and therefore, in the words of Pascal Boyer, an "airy nothing" that has no proper domain and whose claims can be safely dismissed.[3]

The wide range of religious beliefs and behaviors can now simply be explained by some of the basic principles of human cognition and the evolution of the human species.

As demonstrated by Bulkeley's review, most of the criticism has been focused on Boyer's *Religion Explained*, which is the most identifiable trade book associated with the cognitive science of religion. Paul J. Griffiths contends that *Religion Explained* is not just an explanation of religion, but that Boyer intends to explain religion away.[4] John Haught expresses similar concerns over the apparent reductionism implied by Boyer's work.

> Not only does Boyer believe that we can dispense completely with ideas of God, revelation, and the sacred when trying to explain why people are religious, we can now also see that even cultural causes are secondary to biological factors in the genesis of our long affair with the gods.[5]

John Polkinghorne contends that Boyer has simply gone too far in his claims about religion; although there are many helpful insights to religion, religion has not been explained.[6]

This sentiment is very common in many circles investigating the relationship between religion and science. Yet, is Boyer's work representative of the cognitive science of religion as a whole? Is it possible to construct a cognitive science of religion without the reductionist baggage and apparent elimination of religion and theology as important areas of study? This book attempts to bridge the reductionist divide between cognitive/evolutionary science and religion/theological studies. Through examination and critique of different aspects of the cognitive science of religion, this book offers a competing, and yet conciliatory approach to the relationship between cognitive and evolutionary descriptions of religion and the corresponding descriptions offered by religious scholars and theologians.

There are several possible explanations for the causes and development of religious belief and behavior associated with the cognitive science of religion. Religion may have evolved as a by-product of cognitive adaptations that served

---

[3] Gregory R. Peterson, "Theology and the Science Wars: Who Owns Human Nature?," *Zygon* 41, no. 4 (2006): 860.

[4] Paul J. Griffiths, "'Faith Seeking Explanation. Review of *Religion Explained: The Evolutionary Origins of Religious Thought*, by Pascal Boyer," *First Things*, no. 119 (2002): 53-57.

[5] John Haught, "The Darwinian Universe: Isn't There Room for God?," *Commonweal* 129, no. 2 (2002).

[6] John Polkinghorne, "Some of the Truth," *Science* 28 (2001): 2400.

an adaptive function in the evolution of the human species during the Pleistocene era.[7] The original adaptation caused a secondary, unintended effect in human cognitive systems, which promoted beliefs in supernatural agents and religious rituals. A by-product can be characterized as a kind of spandrel, which is the space created by two adjoining arches.[8] Although the spandrel has no direct function in the architecture of a cathedral, it can still have an artistic role that was not a part of the original design. Consequently, certain products of human evolution can fulfill a role they were not originally intended to fill, like a nose that can hold up a pair of glasses.[9]

Other explanations describe religion as a type of adaptation, which evolved as a consequence of its effectiveness in fostering communication and cooperation in early human groups.[10] The social brain hypothesis suggests that many of the cognitive advances in the evolution of the human brain are the result of the selection pressures created by living in groups.[11] Adaptive theories suggest that religious rituals, beliefs, or behaviors may have contributed to enhancing the formation of different types of social relationships. At the individual level, religious commitment serves as a proxy for ascertaining the reliability of potential cooperative partners.[12] At the group level, religion promoted beliefs and behaviors that allowed groups of early humans to outcompete with others.[13] For example, religious morality helps to unite a group for a common purpose and monitor individual behavior for possible benefits or detriments.

The cognitive science of religion is not necessarily hostile to the descriptions of religion offered by theology or other branches of religious study. My critique of the cognitive science of religion focuses on the standard model of human cognition used to describe the formation of religious beliefs and behaviors, which has been the dominate model used to describe religious cognition. The standard model primarily describes religion as a by-product of cognitive adaptations, which spreads in human culture because of the exploitation of default properties

---

[7] Pascal Boyer, "Religious Thought and Behavior as By-Products of Brain Function," *Trends in Cognitive Sciences* 7, no. 3 (2003): 119-124.

[8] Stephen J. Gould and Richard C. Lewontin, "The Spandrels of San Marco and the Panglossian Paradigm: A Critique of the Adaptionist Programme," *Proceedings of the Royal Society of London* 205, no. 1161 (1979): 581-598.

[9] David Sloan Wilson, *Darwin's Cathedral: Evolution, Religion, and the Nature of Society* (Chicago: University of Chicago Press, 2002), 44.

[10] Richard Sosis and Candace Alcorta, "Signaling, Solidarity, and the Sacred: The Evolution of Religious Behavior," *Evolutionary Anthropology* 12 (2003): 264-274.

[11] R. I. M. Dunbar, "The Social Brain Hypothesis," *Evolutionary Anthropology* 6 (1998): 178-190.

[12] Joseph Bulbulia, "Religion as Evolutionary Cascade: On Scott Atran, *in Gods We Trust* (2002)," in *Contemporary Theories of Religion: A Critical Companion*, ed. Michael Stausberg (New York: Routledge, 2009).

[13] Wilson, *Darwin's Cathedral*.

of human cognition. Thus, the primary cause of religious belief and behavior is reduced to a by-product of evolved cognitive adaptations. This book attempts to offer evidence from cognitive neuroscience and philosophy that critiques some of the assumptions in the standard model while preserving and promoting others. My work attempts to enrich the picture of cognition offered in the cognitive science of religion and promotes a different model of religious cognition for further empirical investigation and analysis.

Philosophically, I introduce the concepts of emergence and top-down constraints in order to bridge the multitude of disciplines involved in the study of religion. This is not to say that these terms are merely of philosophical interest, for these concepts have seen an upswing in usage in a number of scientific disciplines. Rather the book focuses on two types of explanation: (1) how human cognition works based in the sciences of evolution, neuroscience, and cognition and (2) philosophical issues in regard to the causes and explanations for religious thought and behavior. These two types of explanation are not mutually exclusive but highly intertwined based on the interdisciplinary character of attempting to understand religion. Yet, the focus is primarily about how the cognitive and evolutionary sciences contribute to our understanding of religion.

Understanding religious cognition requires a multi-level approach that incorporates different facets of scientific explanation. Aspects of religious concepts and beliefs are by-products of certain features of human cognition, but the by-product theory is insufficient as a full explanation of religion. The role of emergent processes and top-down constraints presents a more dynamic and interactional picture of the formation and evolution of religious concepts, beliefs and behaviors. Religion is not simply an unintended by-product, but contains adaptive elements at the level of individual and group selection. As empirical investigation continues, the scientific explanation of religion will demonstrate multiple adaptive and nonadaptive processes that contributed to the evolution and formation of religion in the human species. Thus, multiple areas of investigation in science, philosophy, and the humanities are necessary to develop a clear picture of the scope and function of religion and theology.

Chapter 1
The Standard Model and the Problem of Causal Reductionism

The standard model in the cognitive science of religion defines religion as a by-product of cognitive adaptations that occurred during the evolution of the human species. Religious beliefs, rituals, and practices exploit different features of cognitive adaptations, which make them easy to remember and transmit to others based on a shared universal cognitive architecture. Although aspects of religious cognition are by-products of cognitive adaptations, this theory is insufficient as an explanation of religion for two reasons. First, evidence from a wide range of sources in the cognitive neurosciences demonstrates that the by-product theory is unable to account for a number of important causal processes in the formation and function of religious beliefs. The by-product theory characterizes religious phenomena from a causally reductive perspective that assumes that causation is primarily bottom-up from part to whole. However, an emergent view of cognition and top-down constraints provide a better account of the multiple causal factors involved in religion.

Secondly, the by-product theory is often assumed to indicate that any theological explanation of religious belief is invalidated through the process of eliminative reduction. Thus, the real explanation for religious beliefs is at the level of cognitive and evolutionary science, not higher-level descriptions offered by religious studies or theology. The problem here lies in a lack of discrimination between scientific and metaphysical statements. Metaphysical propositions about the existence or non-existence of gods are inherently multi-level, meaning that they rely on argumentation from multiple areas of knowledge, not just the empirical evidence offered by one level in the hierarchy of science. Thus, empirical evidence from the cognitive science of religion is insufficient to simply eliminate a theological explanation of religion beliefs. Theology is one option that can offer a competing perspective on the interpretation of findings from the cognitive science of religion.

Cognitive Science of Religion

During the 1990s, the success of the cognitive sciences and evolutionary biology led to a new research program in religion called the cognitive science of religion, which has flourished throughout the new century. This research program began in the work of several scholars including Pascal Boyer, Harvey Whitehouse, Stewart Guthrie, Scott Atran, Justin Barrett, Robert N. McCauley, and E. Thomas Lawson.

Since the year 2000, research and publication has significantly increased as well as the formation of several research centers and programs in Europe and North America such as the Institute for Cognition and Culture at Queen's University, Belfast and the Institute for the Biocultural Study of Religion at Boston University.[1] Popular books focused on the cognitive science of religion such as Pascal Boyer's *Religion Explained: The Evolutionary Origins of Religious Thought* and Scott Atran's *In Gods We Trust: The Evolutionary Landscape of Religion* have received a great deal of attention across several academic disciplines.[2]

From this perspective, religion is not an ineffable construct, experience, or feeling; instead it is a set of research questions that can be understood through cognitive and evolutionary science.

> ... although bookshelves may be overflowing with treatises on religion, histories of religion, religious people's account of their ideas, and so on, it makes sense to add to this and show the intractable mystery that was religion is now just another set of difficult but manageable problems.[3]

The cognitive science of religion attempts to identify the aspects of cognition that are universal to the human species, which provide constraints on the way religious concepts are processed and transmitted.

> What unifies the various projects in CSR is the commitment that human conceptual structures are not merely a product of cultural contingencies but that they inform and constrain cultural expression, including religious thought and action.[4]

Based on this theoretical orientation, several hypotheses have emerged as the primary focal points for research on religious beliefs, rituals, and practices.

Current Hypotheses

Several years before the formation and popularity of cognitive approaches to religion, Stewart Guthrie introduced an anthropomorphic theory of religion, which was partially based on new research in the cognitive sciences.[5] Although

---

[1] www.iacsr.com/CSR_Links.html.

[2] Scott Atran, *In Gods We Trust: The Evolutionary Landscape of Religion* (New York: Oxford University Press, 2002); Pascal Boyer, *Religion Explained: The Evolutionary Origins of Religious Thought* (New York: Basic Books, 2001).

[3] Boyer, *Religion Explained*, 2.

[4] Justin L. Barrett, "Cognitive Science of Religion: What Is It and Why Is It?," *Religion Compass* 1, no. 6 (2007): 768-786.

[5] Stewart Guthrie, "A Cognitive Theory of Religion, " *Current Anthropology* 21, no. 2 (1980): 181-203.

the work of Ludwig Feuerbach and Sigmund Freud had already introduced a view of the origins of religion based on anthropomorphism, Guthrie was one of the first to argue that cognitive science may provide evidence for this tendency in human beings.[6] Guthrie later developed this theory in *Faces in the Clouds*, which argued that certain aspects of a shared universal human cognitive structure predispose us to anthropomorphosize different aspects of the world, which is primarily seen in religion.[7] One illustration of this phenomenon is that persons often mistake the rustling of trees branches outside a window late at night as a potential burglar; persons assume some sort of agent is responsible for the rustling first, and then may later entertain a more benign explanation for the rustling.[8]

Based on Guthrie's theory, the detection of agency has been suggested as one of the primary cognitive foundations of belief in supernatural beings. Justin Barrett proposes that supernatural belief is a result of a hyperactive agency detection device (HADD), which is a cognitive default in human perceptual processes.[9] In the process of evolution it was adaptive to assume that unidentified movements or sounds were produced by potential predators and the organism should move quickly to avoid being attacked. Those who moved quickly were more likely to survive, while those who reacted slowly were much less likely to avoid being eaten. Thus, humans tend to find agents everywhere even if they are not actually present. Fritz Heider and Mary-Ann Simmel performed the classic psychological experiment that demonstrates this phenomenon.[10] Persons will use descriptions and narratives that assume some form of agency is present while watching movies of geometrical shapes moving on a screen.

E. Thomas Lawson and Robert N. McCauley developed a theory of different cognitive functions involved in religious practices called the ritual form hypothesis.[11] Religious rituals are processed by an "action representation system" that represents different aspects of the ritual such as agents, the action

---

[6] Ludwig Feuerbach, *The Essence of Religion*, trans. Alexander Loos (Amherst: Prometheus Books, 1873/2004); Sigmund Freud, *The Psychopathology of Everyday Life*, trans. Anthea Bell (New York: Penguin Books, 1901/2002).

[7] Stewart Guthrie, *Faces in the Clouds: A New Theory of Religion* (Oxford: Oxford University Press, 1993).

[8] Benson Saler, "Anthropomorphism and Animism: On Stewart E. Guthrie, *Faces in the Clouds* (1993)," in *Contemporary Theories of Religion: A Critical Companion*, ed. Michael Stausberg (New York: Routledge, 2009).

[9] Justin L. Barrett, "Exploring the Natural Foundations of Religion," *Trends in Cognitive Sciences* 4, no. 1 (2000): 29-34.

[10] Fritz Heider and Mary-Ann Simmel, "An Experimental Study of Apparent Behavior," *American Journal of Psychology* 57 (1944): 243-249.

[11] E. Thomas Lawson and Robert N. McCauley, *Rethinking Religion: Connecting Cognition and Culture* (Cambridge: Cambridge University Press, 1990).

performed, and the objects used during the ritual.[12] The defining characteristic of religious rituals is that some type of supernatural agency is involved in the ritual. Since supernatural agency is difficult to directly observe it is often assessed by the intentions of the person performing the ritual, which is more of a product of cognitive programs that assess social information and relationships. Some religious rituals involve elaborate costumes and artifacts that serve as sensory pageantry and arouse different emotional systems, which convey the message that this particular ritual is especially important.

Harvey Whitehouse also analyses religious rituals but from a different cognitive angle. Whitehouse argues that rituals can be distinguished according to two different modes: the doctrinal and imagistic.[13] In the doctrinal mode, religious concepts and values tend to be more complex and difficult to transmit so there is a focus on repetition and routine where rituals and teaching occurs weekly (or more often) to facilitate the dissemination of larger chunks of information in semantic memory. In contrast, in the imagistic mode religious rituals are more focused on highly arousing experiences that occur less frequently but are so dramatic that they access flash-bulb memory systems, which are associated with highly emotional and often traumatic events. The best examples of the imagistic mode include initiation rites and ecstatic religious rituals, which may involve violent acts such as the evulsion of fingernails, whipping, burning with hot coals, mutilation, circumcision, or other acts of physical deprivation.[14]

One of the most important hypotheses in the cognitive science of religion is the counterintuitive hypothesis, which asserts that religious concepts are a combination of intuitive ontological categories about everyday objects in the environment and some *violation* of those categories, which contributes to their memorability.[15] For example, a ghost would be a combination of the person category plus the ability to walk through walls, which violates the intuitive properties of the person category or reincarnation, which is a combination of the person category plus no death and several future bodies.[16] Counterintuitive concepts will spread faster because they exploit certain default processing assumptions of intuitive categories in human cognition making them easier to process, understand, and transmit to others. Religious concepts that violate too

---

[12] Justin L. Barrett, "Bringing Data to Mind: Empirical Claims of Lawson and McCauley's Theory of Religious Ritual," in *Religion as Human Capacity: A Festscrift in Honor of E. Thomas Lawson*, ed. T. Light and B. C. Wilson (Cambridge: Cambridge University Press, 2004), 207.

[13] Harvey Whitehouse, *Modes of Religiosity: A Cognitive Theory of Religious Transmission* (Walnut Creek: AltaMira Press, 2004).

[14] Ibid., 111.

[15] Pascal Boyer and Charles Ramble, "Cognitive Templates for Religious Concepts: Cross-Cultural Evidence for Recall of Counter-Intuitive Representations," *Cognitive Science* 25 (2001): 535-564.

[16] Boyer, *Religion Explained*, 63-64.

many aspects of intuitive categories will be more difficult to process and not spread as easily in human cultures.

This is not an exhaustive account of the hypotheses currently under investigation in the cognitive science of religion, but provides a brief overview of some of the important hypotheses and their history. Later chapters will investigate other important hypotheses such as costly signaling theory, theological incorrectness, and group selection. Since the cognitive science of religion is such a new field, hypotheses continue to be generated and investigated by a diverse group of scholars. The aforementioned hypotheses are most closely associated with the standard model of reduction in the cognitive science of religion. Although aspects of the standard model are helpful in describing religion, reductionism becomes a problem in this model in the causal explanation of religion and the distorted picture of how cognition works.

Standard Model in the Cognitive Science of Religion

The investigation of the primary hypotheses in the cognitive science of religion has fostered the development of a standard model of cognition based on the universal mental processes involved in religion. These universal mental processes are the product of a shared cognitive architecture that promotes the spread and persistence of certain religious concepts and rituals despite the distorting effects of individual and cultural transmission.[17] Universal properties of human cognition facilitate similar inferences about religion, which constrain the formation of religious concepts and rituals. Those features of religion that most successfully exploit the universal aspects of religious cognition have the largest probability of survival and transmission across generations. Thus, the standard model attempts to understand and categorize the universal cognitive properties that facilitate religion, which play the most important role in the formation and endurance of religion.

Boyer describes the three most important aspects of the standard model.[18] First, cognitive explanations are *general*, meaning that they are cross-cultural and would apply in any religious or cultural environment. The focus is on cognitive systems that process religious information, not the social contexts in which they are embedded. Secondly, cognitive accounts are probabilistic, meaning that the probability of a particular religious concept remaining in a culture is dependent upon how much those concepts match up with the way cognitive inference systems process information. Thirdly, cognitive accounts are "experience distant," meaning that the experiential and explicit accounts of religion are different from

---

[17] Pascal Boyer, "A Reductionistic Model of Distinct Modes of Religious Transmission," in *Mind and Religion: Psychological and Cognitive Foundations of Religiosity*, ed. Harvey Whitehouse and Robert N. McCauley (Walnut Creek: AltaMira Press, 2005).

[18] Ibid., 7.

the actual processes that make them memorable.[19] The implicit cognitive systems that are used are unconscious and work automatically, providing constraints on the processing of religious information.

The standard model is based on the by-product theory of religion. The human cognitive architecture that propagates certain religious concepts, beliefs, and rituals is a product of human evolution. Religion, as a cultural or individual phenomenon, has no specific adaptive value in the history of evolution, but the cognitive adaptations that facilitate the development of the current universal human cognitive architecture did have adaptive value in the ancient past for the survival and reproduction of the human race.[20] Thus, the origin and development of religion is a by-product or secondary effect of the evolution of human cognition. Religion is parasitic on the functions and structures of the evolved tendencies of human cognition. Human cognition was originally designed for a different set of adaptive problems, but has been recruited for its usefulness in spreading and disseminating religion.

The by-product theory in the standard model of religious cognition is based on two primary theories of human cognition: evolutionary psychology and cultural epidemiology.[21] Evolutionary psychology suggests that the human mind/brain is comprised of many different adaptive cognitive modules.[22] These modules contain cognitive programs specific to the prehistory evolutionary environment, which required adaptive solutions to problems faced by our ancient Pleistocene ancestors. Thus, human cognition can be modeled after a Swiss army knife; cognitive problems in our contemporary environment approximate problems of our evolutionary ancestors, which triggers a particular module that processes the problem according to a pre-set series of computations (similar to an algorithm) that leads to a cognitive solution.[23] Cultural epidemiology models the spread of beliefs and concepts as analogous to the spread of a pathogen in a particular population.[24] Thus, certain types of religious beliefs

---

[19] Ibid

[20] Pascal Boyer, "Religious Thought and Behavior as By-Products of Brain Function," *Trends in Cognitive Sciences* 7, no. 3 (2003): 119-124.

[21] Jeppe Sinding Jensen, "Religion as the Unintended Product of Brain Functions in the 'Standard Cognitive Science of Religion Model': On Pascal Boyer, *Religion Explained* (2001) and Ilkka Pyysiäinen, *How Religion Works* (2003)," in *Contemporary Theories of Religion: A Critical Companion*, ed. Michael Stausberg (New York: Routledge, 2009).

[22] David Buss, ed., *The Handbook of Evolutionary Psychology* (New Jersey: John Wiley & Sons, Inc., 2005); John Tooby and Leda Cosmides, "Mapping the Evolved Functional Organization of the Mind and Brain," in *The Cognitive Neurosciences*, ed. Michael Gazzaniga (Cambridge: The MIT Press, 1995).

[23] Leda Cosmides and John Tooby, "Evolutionary Psychology: A Primer" www.psych.ucsb.edu/research/cep/-primer.html (accessed August 2004).

[24] Dan Sperber, *Explaining Culture: A Naturalistic Approach* (Oxford: Blackwell Publishers, 1996).

are more contagious in cultural populations than others and will spread readily by exploiting certain default inferences afforded by cognitive adaptations. The architecture of the human mind/brain is predisposed to fixate on certain types of religious concepts because they are easily processed and remembered, whereas others are more cognitively costly (require more time and processing power) and do not spread as easily.

Reduction is an important element of the standard model. In the past, the study of religion focused on sociological, ethnographic, historical, and theoretical models of religion, which were more descriptive rather than explanatory in that they failed to demonstrate the origins and purpose of religion in human society. But the development of cognitive and evolutionary science provides a new perspective on the origins of human culture and offers a naturalistic explanation for the existence of religion. Thus, the study of religion can be reduced to the cognitive and evolutionary foundations of religious thought and behavior.

> The explanation for religious beliefs and behaviors is to be found in the way all human minds work. I really mean all human minds, not just the minds of religious people or of some of them. I am talking about human minds, because what matters here are properties of minds that are found in all members of our species with normal brains.[25]

Reducing religion to a by-product of cognitive and evolutionary functions enables the possibility of a new science of religion and circumvents all the disagreement over method in the study of religion and the postmodern critique of meaning and explanation.

Critiques of Standard Model

The standard model has been criticized for its narrow focus on particular facets of cognitive and evolutionary theory. Mathew Day cites several areas of anthropology, cognitive science, and theoretical biology that show a larger network of causes in the development of religious cognition. The standard model may lead to an "abnormal" view of religion and cognition.

> [B]y treating the cumulative effects of social structures, cultural practices, material artifacts, and historical trends as extraneous features of a biologically fixed cognitive system, we may actually end up with an abnormal portrait of what a normal human mind actually is.[26]

---

[25] Boyer, *Religion Explained*, 2.
[26] Matthew Day, "Rethinking Naturalness: Modes of Religiosity and Religion in the Round," in *Mind and Religion: Psychological and Cognitive Foundations of Religiosity*, ed. Harvey Whitehouse and Robert N. McCauley (Walnut Creek: AltaMira Press, 2005), 88.

Robert Hinde argues that multiple levels of complexity influence religion, including society, groups, interactions, and individuals, in which each level influences and is influenced by the other levels.

> The multiplicity of causation and the ubiquitous influence of a variety of social processes, including dialectical influences between what people do or believe and what they are supposed to do or believe, must always be borne in mind in considering complex human activities.[27]

Each of these critiques indicate that the standard model used in the cognitive science of religion might not be the best overall representation of how cognitive explanations influence the formation of religious concepts.

The standard model in the cognitive science of religion is problematic as a result of two separate but interrelated types of reduction: epistemological and causal. Epistemological reductionism is concerned with the question of whether theories from a higher-level science can be reduced to theories from a lower-level science. For example, a theory about the social or psychological causes of schizophrenia is reduced to a theory about the neurological causes that occur during neural communication. Causal reductionism assumes that the primary explanation for any phenomena lies in the causal relationships among the parts of a whole. Thus, causation is mainly understood as bottom-up from part to whole and the best explanation for any particular phenomena is based on the functions of the parts in contrast to the whole.

The standard model in the cognitive science of religion claims that religious beliefs and behaviors are ultimately reducible to a by-product of evolutionary cognitive adaptations. This view of religion is problematic on two counts. First, evidence from a wide range of sources in the cognitive neurosciences demonstrates that the by-product theory is unable to account for a number of important causal processes in the formation and function of religious beliefs. The by-product theory characterizes religious phenomena from a causally reductive perspective that assumes that causation is primarily bottom-up from part to whole. Thus, although aspects of religious cognition may be by-products, the theory is insufficient as a large-scale explanation for religion. An emergent view of cognition incorporating top-down constraints provides a better account of the multiple causal factors involved in the evolution and formation of religious beliefs.

Secondly, some proponents of the standard model assume that any theological explanation of religious belief is invalidated through the process of epistemological reduction. Thus, the real explanation for religious beliefs is at the level of cognitive and evolutionary science, not higher-level descriptions offered by religious studies or theology. However, the problem here lies in a lack of demarcation between

---

[27] Robert A. Hinde, "Modes Theory: Some Theoretical Considerations," in *Mind and Religion: Psychological and Cognitive Foundations of Religiosity*, ed. Harvey Whitehouse and Robert N. McCauley (Walnut Creek: Alta Mira Press, 2005), 51.

scientific and metaphysical statements. Metaphysical propositions about the existence or non-existence of gods are inherently multi-level, meaning that they rely on argumentation from multiple areas of knowledge, not just the empirical evidence offered by one level in the hierarchy of science. Thus, empirical evidence from the cognitive science of religion is insufficient to simply eliminate a theological explanation of religion beliefs. Theology is one option that can offer a competing perspective on the interpretation of empirical findings.

Understanding Reductionism

Science is organized according to different disciplines that study phenomena in nature according to a hierarchy based on levels of complexity.[28] Each level has its own laws and processes within a particular science; lower-level sciences, such as physics and chemistry, are the foundational sciences, while the higher-level sciences such as psychology, sociology, and anthropology are the sciences of larger complex systems. Thus, a rough sketch of the hierarchy of the sciences may look something like this (Figure 1.1):

Philosophy
Literature
Anthropology
Sociology
Psychology
Cognitive Science
Neuroscience
Human Physiology
Zoology
Cellular Biology
Genetics
Chemistry
Physics

Figure 1.1   Hierarchy of the sciences

Paul Oppenheim and Hillary Putnam suggested that this hierarchy could act as the basis for unity among the sciences, which raised the issue of reduction among different levels in the sciences.[29]

---

[28]   Francisco J. Ayala and Theodosius Dobzhansky, eds., *Studies in the Philosophy of Biology: Reduction and Related Problems* (Berkeley and Los Angeles: University of California Press, 1974).

[29]   Paul Oppenheim and Hillary Putnam, "The Unity of Science as a Working Hypothesis," in *Concepts, Theories, and the Mind-Body Problem*, ed. Herbert Feigel,

Reduction is notoriously difficult to define because of its wide usage in many different scientific and philosophical contexts. Many of the problems in definition arise from the lack of distinction between the use of the term in scientific practice and its use in philosophical discussion and argumentation. The current philosophical debates can be traced back to the logical empiricists of the early 1900s who attempted to move philosophy away from metaphysical speculation and focus on epistemic knowledge in logical propositions based on observational "sense-data."[30] This raised the issue of the epistemic limitations of scientific explanation generally and the role of reduction specifically in the relationship between different concepts and theories used in science. During the 1960s, Paul Feyerabend raised the problem of incommensurability in scientific theories while Thomas Kuhn demonstrated the historicity of scientific progress and the fissures between competing paradigms.[31]

Ernst Nagel developed the standard model for reduction in terms of the logical derivation of one theory from another lower-level theory via bridge principles that specify the epistemic links between the reducing theory and the reduced theory.[32] This later became known as epistemological reductionism and was primarily concerned with the reduction of theories or laws. The two other types of reductionism currently debated and discussed are ontological and methodological.[33] Methodological reduction is defined as the technique by which scientists study a particular phenomenon by reducing it to its parts; the functioning of the parts is empirically researched to understand the functioning of the whole.[34] Ontological reductionism is concerned with the issue of what substances or processes constitute a phenomenon studied at a particular level in the hierarchy of science. For example, vitalism considered different biological systems to be composed of nonmaterial forces such as an *élan vital* that played an important role in evolution.[35] In this case, most contemporary biologists would endorse an

---

Michael Scriven, and Grover Maxwell, *Minnesota Studies in Philosophy of Science* (Minneapolis: University of Minnesota Press, 1958).

[30] Rudolph Carnap, *The Logical Structure of the World and Pseudoproblems in Philosophy* (Chicago: Open Court, 1928/2003); Bertrand Russell, *Logical Atomism* (Chicago: Open Court, 1918/1985).

[31] Paul Feyerabend, *Against Method* (London: Verso, 1975/1988); Thomas Kuhn, *The Structure of Scientific Revolutions* (Chicago: Chicago University Press, 1962).

[32] Ernst Nagel, *The Structure of Science* (New York/Indianapolis: Harcourt, Brace and World/Hackett, 1961/1979).

[33] Ingo Brigandt and Alan Love, "Reductionism in Biology," in *The Stanford Encyclopedia of Philosophy*, ed. Edward N. Zalta (Stanford: The Metaphysics Research Lab, 2008).

[34] Francisco J. Ayala, "Introduction," in *Studies in the Philosophy of Biology: Reduction and Related Problems*, ed. Francisco J. Ayala and Theodosius Dobzhansky (Berkeley and Los Angeles: University of California Press, 1974).

[35] Henry Bergson, *Creative Evolution*, trans. Arthur Mitchell (New York: Dover, 1911/1998).

ontological reduction in that biological systems are composed simply of physical material rather than any type of additional force.

As a corollary to the ontological definition of reduction, Nancey Murphy has identified causal reductionism as a problematic formulation of the relationship between systemic wholes and their constituent parts.[36] This is the view that the parts of the system determine the behavior of the entire system. From this perspective, causation is primarily defined in terms of causal relations between the parts of something while the whole does not perform any processes that contribute to its causal outcome. Thus, there is often a distinction between bottom-up and top-down causation. Epistemological reduction is associated with causal reductionism to the extent that if a theory at one level in the hierarchy of science is reduced to a theory at a lower level than the causal relations and laws pertinent to the reduced theory would no longer be relevant to the explanation of the phenomenon in question. However, if it could be shown that causal processes or relations studied at a particular level play an indispensible role in the function of some phenomenon then epistemological or causal reduction would not be applicable.

Causal reductionism involves a unique combination of conceptual assumptions and ontological questions about the relationship between a structure and the arrangement of the pieces that constitutes the formation of that structure. This particular view of reduction has an interesting conceptual history beginning with the transition from the medieval to the modern worldview. Prior to the rise of science during the modern period, most medieval scholars accepted a hylomorphic view of matter based on the work of Aristotle.[37] This view stipulated that things are composed of matter (physical constituents) and form (the particular function or telos of the object). Modern science rejected hylomorphism in favor of reviving the atomism of ancient Greek philosophy in the work of Leucippus and Democritus.[38] Thus, causal relations between atoms became the primary model for understanding causation at the higher level of composite wholes. Whole objects were epiphenomenal aggregates of micro-level processes or secondary effects of the primary causal interactions between the parts.[39] This led to the general practice of describing any particular whole

---

[36] Nancey Murphy, "Supervenience and the Downward Efficacy of the Mental: A Nonreductive Physicalist Account of Human Action," in *Neuroscience and the Person: Scientific Perspectives on Divine Action*, ed. Robert John Russell et al. (Vatican City State and Berkeley: Vatican Observatory Publications and the Center for Theology and the Natural Sciences, 1999).

[37] Graham White, "Medieval Theories of Causation," in *The Stanford Encyclopedia of Philosophy*, ed. Edward N. Zalta (Stanford: The Metaphysics Research Lab, 2009).

[38] Louis P. Pojman, "The Pre-Socratics," in *Classics of Philosophy*, ed. Louis P. Pojman and Lewis Vaughn (New York: Oxford University Press, 2011).

[39] Nancey Murphy and Warren S. Brown, *Did My Neurons Make Me Do It? Philosophical and Neurobiological Perspectives on Moral Responsibility and Free Will* (Oxford: Oxford University Press, 2007).

phenomenon by simply referring to processes and functions of its parts one rung down in the hierarchy of sciences.

The primary problem with causal reductionism in the standard model is the focus on constituent parts to explain complex systems. Thus, the causal explanation for religious cognition is reduced to the functions of cognitive adaptations, which produces misleading statements about the nature of religious beliefs. Religious beliefs are defined as a "mere consequence or side effect of having the brains we have" and an "airy nothing."[40] Or religion may simply be an accident caused by the misuse of adaptations:

> ... enthusiasm is building among scientists for the view that religion emerged not to serve a purpose—not as an opiate or a social glue—but by accident. It is a by-product of biological adaptations gone awry.[41]

Thus, the real cause for religious beliefs will be explained by scientific investigation in the cognitive and evolutionary sciences. "The explanation for religious beliefs and behaviors is to be found in the way all human minds work."[42]

Religious concepts and beliefs are not reducible to by-products of cognitive adaptations because certain aspects of cognition are emergent and involve top-down constraints. The theory of emergence recognizes that not all of the causal factors involved in the formation of religious concepts can be described by bottom-up causation alone. Certain aspects of the human capacity and practice of religion occur at different levels of complexity, which are not reducible to the laws and processes of the lower levels. With the incorporation of an account of emergent complex systems, it can be argued that aspects of religious concepts are not reducible to by-products of cognitive adaptations. The concept of a top-down constraint refers to the way a systemic whole can have a causal influence on the parts that constitute the whole. Hence, systemic configurations can constrain the functions of the parts of the system. The causal explanation of the development of religious concepts is at least partially determined by top-down constraints when emergent complex levels act as a causal factor in certain types of processes.

In later chapters, I shall argue that several cognitive systems involved in religious cognition are emergent systems and top-down constraints play an important role in their functioning. Although aspects of religion may be explained by looking at the ways in which cognitive universals process information, the standard model does not offer an account of how larger religious systems and individual beliefs influence religious thought. The problem in the standard model is that the cause of religious cognition is reduced to the functioning of evolutionary cognitive adaptations. The problem, to put it simply, is that *cognition does not work that way*. The formation of many important aspects of religion is dependent on several

---

[40] Boyer, *Religion Explained*, 330.
[41] Paul Bloom, "Is God an Accident?" *Atlantic Monthly*, December 2005, 2.
[42] Boyer, *Religion Explained*, 2.

emergent and top-down processes. Cognitive representations of religious concepts and beliefs are composed of emergent patterns of neural activation dependent upon environmental feedback. These representations are influenced by the top-down constraints of cultural information, experience, and abstract goals and concepts.

Defining Emergence

To overcome the problems of causal reductionism in the standard model of reduction in the cognitive science of religion, it is necessary to incorporate aspects of the theory of emergence as a general principle that specifies processes involved in the formation of religious beliefs. Most definitions of emergence presuppose some form of top-down causation or constraints, which is discussed in the following section, but I will begin by discussing the definition of emergence. Generally speaking, emergence is the *antithesis* to reductionism.[43] Emergence theories were born in a historical context that witnessed several successful predictions in quantum physics. Therefore, it was assumed that physics could simply build on Newton's laws, Maxwell's equations, and Einstein's theories to construct a complete explanation of quantum phenomena.[44] However, quantum indeterminacy demonstrated that predictions at the quantum level were inherently unpredictable and could only be ascertained to a certain percentage.[45]

Emergence theories tend to agree that an exhaustive reductive explanation of natural phenomena is ultimately not possible and emergence is an important aspect of the process of evolution. Harold Morowitz argues that emergence is a part of many natural processes including the formation of stars and other planetary structures, multicellular organisms, as well as the formation of the numerous animal species and even the human cultural advancements of tool making, language, and agriculture.[46] Emergence has also been defined according to particular themes such as self-organization, which is illustrated in the formation and maintenance of ant colonies and feedback processes that characterize the flow of information in media and the Internet.[47]

---

[43] Robert Van Gulick, "Reduction, Emergence and Other Recent Options on the Mind/Body Problem," *Journal of Consciousness Studies* 8, no. 9-10 (2001): 16.

[44] Philip Clayton, *Mind and Emergence: From Quantum to Consciousness* (Oxford: Oxford University Press, 2004), 2.

[45] Robert John Russell, "Special Providence and Genetic Mutation: A New Defense of Theistic Evolution," in *Evolutionary and Molecular Biology*, ed. Robert John Russell, William R. Stoeger SJ, and Francisco J. Ayala (Berkeley and Vatican City State: Vatican Observatory Publications and Center for Theology and the Natural Sciences, 1998), 200-205.

[46] Harold J. Morowitz, *The Emergence of Everything: How the World Became Complex* (Oxford: Oxford University Press, 2002).

[47] Steven Johnson, *Emergence: The Connected Lives of Ants, Brains, Cities, and Software* (New York: Scribner, 2001).

Although most theories of emergence run counter to certain forms of reductionism, there are differences of opinion on the definition of emergence. Currently, the most distinctive divergence is between forms of weak and strong emergence or nonreductive and radical forms of emergence.[48] In general, weak or nonreductive forms of emergence specify that there are particular emergent properties of systemic wholes that are not reducible to the constituent parts, but different levels of complexity are not necessarily ontologically distinct. It is the formation, organization, or pattern of constituent parts that makes the crucial difference. Strong or radical emergence claims that certain systemic wholes not only have properties that are nonreducible but that in certain cases there is an ontological distinction between certain levels of complexity. Thus, strong forms of emergence argue that in certain circumstances something novel, unique, or distinct emerges through the interaction of the components that produces a type of emergent entity.

The debate between weak and strong emergence is an important issue and involves several different perspectives in the dialogue between theology and science.[49] However, for the present discussion, weak emergence provides the necessary resources for contradicting causal reductionism in the cognitive science of religion. This type of emergence refutes certain assumptions about the nature of causation in the sphere of causal reductionism, especially the understanding of causation as primarily bottom-up. Emergence provides a positive account of the causal role of systemic wholes in the various processes that involve whole part relations.

> ... what the emergentist needs to show is that as we go up the hierarchy of complex systems we find entities that exhibit new causal powers (or, perhaps better, participate in new causal processes or fulfill new causal roles) that cannot be reduced to the combined effects of lower-level causal processes.[50]

---

[48] Mark A. Bedau, "Downward Causation and Autonomy in Weak Emergence," in *Emergence: Contemporary Readings in Philosophy and Science*, ed. Mark A. Bedau and Paul Humphreys (Cambridge: The MIT Press, 2008); Gregory R. Peterson, "Species of Emergence," *Zygon* 41, no. 3 (2006): 689-712.

[49] Mark A. Bedau and Paul Humphreys, eds., *Emergence: Contemporary Readings in Philosophy and Science* (Cambridge: The MIT Press, 2008); Philip Clayton and Paul Davies, eds., *The Re-Emergence of Emergence: The Emergentist Hypothesis from Science to Religion* (Oxford: Oxford University Press, 2006); Nancey Murphy and William R. Stoeger SJ, eds., *Evolution & Emergence: Systems, Organisms, Persons* (Oxford: Oxford University Press, 2007).

[50] Nancey Murphy, "Reductionism: How Did We Fall into It and Can We Emerge from It?" in *Evolution & Emergence: Systems, Organisms, Persons*, ed. Nancey Murphy and William R. Stoeger, SJ (Oxford: Oxford University Press, 2007), 27.

According to William Bechtel emergence "simply recognizes that whole systems exhibit behaviors that go beyond the behaviors of their parts."[51] This does not mean that wholes contain some type of separate ontological substance to separate wholes from their parts, but simply shows that the operations of a phenomenon at the level of a whole system contain a wider range of possible functional states than the parts themselves. Thus, investigation of systemic properties requires a different level of analysis appropriate to the complexity of the phenomenon in question.

Bechtel argues that descriptions of the mind/brain in cognitive neuroscience and philosophy of mind require the use of descriptions that include "component parts, component operations, and their organization."[52] Thus, causally reductionistic explanations of any phenomena (in this case a religious belief), which describe the contributions of the components parts in a bottom-up fashion, are insufficient to address the complexity of causal processes at work in their formation.

> ... reductionistic research that focuses on the contributions of the parts and operation of a mechanism typically needs to be complemented by approaches geared to appreciating systemic properties such as how the parts and operations are organized and the difference that organization makes to the behavior of the components.[53]

Additionally, complex systems such as the human mind/brain are embedded in environments, which include shifting parameters that affect different properties and constrain some of the possibilities for cognition and behavior.

Defining Top-down Constraints

Alicia Juarrero argues that a new understanding of causation is necessary in light of recent developments in systems theory and nonequilibrium thermodynamics.[54] Causation is not fully explainable through standard descriptions of causation but requires an account of inter-level causality where the whole is able to act as a constraint on its parts. This form of causation operates by limiting the degrees of freedom of potential actions of the parts.[55] Once a system has been organized

---

[51] William Bechtel, *Mental Mechanisms: Philosophical Perspectives on Cognitive Neuroscience* (New York: Routledge, 2008), 129.

[52] William Bechtel and Adele Abrahamsen, "Explanation: A Mechanist Alternative" *Studies in History and Philosophy of Biological and Biomedical Sciences* 36 (200A): 421-441.

[53] Bechtel, *Mental Mechanisms*, 17.

[54] Alicia Juarrero, *Dynamics in Action: Intentional Behavior as a Complex System* (Cambridge: The MIT Press, 1999), 75.

[55] Ibid., 128.

into a particular configuration, the possibility of the parts operating in way that is inconsistent with the original configuration becomes highly unlikely. The behavior of the parts of a system is limited by the overall configuration of the system. Robert Van Gulick referred to this process as "selective activation," which is not the alteration of component parts, but that the systemic configuration selects the types of constituent parts that play a role in the current processes.[56]

The idea of top-down causation may be misleading for some definitions of causal relations. Top-down causation is not in competition with bottom-up accounts of causation. Thus, a better name is top-down *constraints*, rather than causation, to show that we are talking about something that amends certain accounts of causation. Certain features of cognitive systems of representation contained in neural networks settle into attractor states similar to a topographical map with different valleys and groves.[57] When the cognitive system is activated, the valleys and groves act as attractor states that constrain the potential representational states of the system.

In cognitive science this process is often referred to as top-down processing, where larger conceptual schemas are employed to perceive different objects in the world in contrast to bottom-up processing.[58] Joaquín Fuster argues that as cognitive representational networks get farther from basic forms of representation in the primary sensory areas there is a higher level of reliance upon top-down processing.[59] Top-down cognitive constraints play an active role in processing incoming information especially in terms of concepts and language processing. Cognitive science has shown several examples of top-down processing in perception such as the word superiority effect where identical symbols are perceived differently depending on the context or phoneme restoration where missing sounds are inserted depending on the context.[60]

Based on the evidence from emergence and top-down constraints, it seems highly unlikely that religious beliefs can simply be reduced to a by-product of cognitive adaptations. The formation of religious beliefs includes environmental feedback in terms of cultural and contextual variables that aid in the formation of specific religious beliefs. Additionally, religious beliefs can be conceptualized as a type of cognitive attractor state, which constraints how information is ultimately processed. Thus, religious beliefs may also function as a particular constraint in certain situations where top-down processing is activated in the processing of

---

[56] Robert Van Gulick, "Who's in Charge Here? And Who's Doing All the Work?" in *Mental Causation*, ed. John Heil and Alfred Mele (Oxford: Clarendon, 1995), 252.

[57] Juarrero, *Dynamics in Action*, 156.

[58] Edward Smith and Stephen Kosslyn, *Cognitive Psychology: Mind and Brain* (Upper Saddle River: Pearson Prentice Hall, 2007), 55.

[59] Joaquín M. Fuster, *Cortex and Mind* (Oxford: Oxford University Press, 2003), 51.

[60] O. Selfridge, "Pattern Recognition and Modern Computers," in *Proceedings of the Western Joint Computer Conference* (Los Angeles, CA: Institute of Electrical and Electronics Engineers, 1955); R. M. Warren and R. P. Warren, "Auditory Illusions and Confusions," *Scientific American* 223, no. 6 (1970): 30-36.

incoming information. Religious beliefs are not causally reducible to an "airy nothing" or "biological adaptations gone awry," in that several other causal processes at many different levels of complexity are involved in the formation and function of religious beliefs in individual persons and cultures.

Eliminative Reduction

The previous section demonstrated problems with causal reductionism and argued that the concepts of emergence and top-down constraints illustrate certain causal processes that are not reducible to by-products of cognitive adaptations. For this section, a further argument is made that certain aspects of the by-product theory may be shown to be philosophically objectionable. Certain uses of the by-product theory do not clearly differentiate between metaphysical and scientific statements. This mainly relates to the problem of eliminative reductionism and the relationship between different theories at different levels in the hierarchy of the sciences. The by-product theory and other theories about religion from the cognitive science of religion does not necessitate the elimination of theological explanations of religious beliefs. A theological perspective can be used as a competing interpretative framework in contrast to the assumed connection between the cognitive science of religion and philosophical naturalism. Eliminative reduction is the thesis that the success of lower-level theories in explaining some phenomenon will ultimately lead to the elimination of higher-level theories in favor of the explanation offered at the lower level, which is related to the earlier discussion of epistemological reduction. The best example of this type of reduction is eliminative materialism, which claims that psychological folk concepts used in everyday language will ultimately be replaced with a comprehensive established neuroscience.[61]

In the case of theological explanations, the issue is whether a lower-level science (such as evolutionary or cognitive science) can provide a sufficient explanation of religious phenomena such that the principles and explanations presented by theology can be mapped onto a lower-level description, which offers a more penetrating account of religion. Thus, theology (or some other religious explanation) can be eliminated in favor of an explanation offered by the evolutionary or cognitive sciences or, even if theology is not fully reduced, enough of the theories from that paradigm are reduced such that it serves merely as a placeholder for the aggregate effects that are studied by the lower-level sciences and does not offer any important contributions to the true causes of religious beliefs. If religion is an airy nothing or a by-product of biological adaptations gone awry it seems to be the case that theological explanations for the formation of religious beliefs are eliminated in favor of evolutionary and cognitive explanations because the evolution of these features of human society is accidental and without purpose.

---

[61] Paul M. Churchland, *A Neurocomputational Perspective: The Nature of Mind and the Structure of Science* (Cambridge: The MIT Press, 1993), 1.

Inter vs. Intra Level Reduction

Robert McCauley offers some helpful insights that illustrate how the relationship between different levels in the hierarchy of the sciences is very complex and the outright elimination of higher-level descriptions is a rare occurrence.[62] Looking at the history of science, an important distinction can be made between *inter*level and *intra*level reduction in the hierarchy of sciences.[63] The most common type of reduction in science is intralevel reduction, which refers to theory replacement or change that occurs over time in a particular level of a science. As Thomas Kuhn demonstrated, changes in scientific theories often involve conceptual revolutions, where the previous theory was shown to be inadequate and replaced by a new one.[64] This does not involve a smooth reduction between the two theories, but the abandonment of the previous theory in favor of the new one without any strong correspondence between the two theories as indicated in the standard model of reduction.

Interlevel reduction is the reduction of theories or whole sciences between levels and is closer to the idea of eliminative reduction. However, interlevel reduction of whole sciences is extremely rare and McCauley offers several reasons for the continuation of higher levels in the hierarchy of sciences. In many cases, lower-level sciences must appeal to findings from higher-level sciences to support their own conclusions.[65] In the case of the cognitive neurosciences, descriptions of brain activity provided by the neurosciences, which are intended to describe some facet of psychological phenomena, often require behavioral descriptions at a higher level to define exactly what type of phenomenon the neurosciences are trying to describe. For example, the dopamine hypothesis, as an account of the epidemiology of delusions and hallucinations, is dependent upon a higher-level description of the behaviors and mental states that define the psychological disorder known as schizophrenia.[66] Understanding schizophrenia as a mental disorder depends on psychological research and reliance on definitions supplied by the Diagnostic and Statistical Manual (DSM-IV) that categorizes this disorder according to behavioral and cognitive criteria, not neural criteria.[67] Furthermore,

---

[62] Robert N. McCauley, "Reduction: Models of Cross-Scientific Relations and Their Implications for the Psychology-Neuroscience Interface," in *Handbook of the Philosophy of Science: Philosophy of Psychology and Cognitive Science*, ed. Paul Thagard (Amsterdam: Elsevier, 2007).

[63] William Wimsatt, "Reductionism, Levels of Organization, and the Mind-Body Problem," in *Consciousness and the Brain*, ed. A. Globus, G. Maxwell, and I. Savodnik (New York: Plenum Press, 1976).

[64] Kuhn, *Scientific Revolutions*.

[65] McCauley, "Reduction," 122.

[66] Neil R. Carlson, *Physiology of Behavior*, 6th edn. (Boston: Allyn and Bacon, 1998).

[67] American Psychiatric Association, *Diagnostic and Statistical Manual of Mental Disorders*, 4th edn. (Washington: American Psychiatric Association, 2000).

the validity of several fMRI studies on brain activity has been called into question recently because of their *lack* of behavioral and psychological criteria for describing the processes they claim to explain.[68]

Many scientists are not interested in reducing other levels of science; they are looking for whatever help they can find to confirm or disconfirm their own theories by other scientific perspectives.[69] They want to find ways to expand and understand their own findings in other contexts and explore methods to refine their own theories so that they can be a more accurate representation of whatever phenomenon they are trying to study. Scientific progress would be greatly impoverished if any time there was a discrepancy between two different interlevel theories, one theory was simply eliminated in favor of another one. Paul Feyerabend makes a strong case that any scientific theory, regardless of its current state of destitution, may yet yield important results at some unspecified point in the future.[70]

Many cases of reduction that are assumed to be interlevel are simply cases of intralevel reduction co-occurring in separate sciences at the same time through the process of cross-scientific pollination between two different explanatory paradigms.[71] A relevant example is already occurring between cognitive neuroscience, philosophy and theology. Research in the cognitive neurosciences has slowly accumulated a large body of evidence that demonstrates that different functions that used to be attributed to the properties of a nonphysical mind or soul can now be explained according to physiological processes of the brain and body.[72] Thus, the ontology of a human being can be defined as a physical organism, rather than a physical body plus a nonmaterial soul or mind. This did *not* lead to the elimination of theories about the functions of the mind in the philosophy of mind, but fostered different types of conceptual development and refinement that occurred as a result of what was occurring in the cognitive neurosciences.

In philosophy of mind, some form of physicalism or materialism has been a live option for many years.[73] For example, although Richard Rorty was surely influenced by neuroscience in his critique of Cartesian dualism in *Philosophy and the Mirror of Nature*, it is still a work of conceptual analysis in the area of philosophy.[74] In fact, most of the science is out of date and untenable in relation to current theories in the cognitive neurosciences, but the conceptual developments

---

[68] Greg Miller, "Growing Pains for fMRI," *Science* 320 (2008): 1412-1414.

[69] McCauley, "Reduction," 135.

[70] Feyerabend, *Against Method*.

[71] McCauley, "Reduction," 130.

[72] Patricia Churchland, *Brain-Wise: Studies in Neurophilosophy* (Cambridge: MIT Press, 2002); Owen Flanagan, *The Science of the Mind*, 2nd edn. (Cambridge The MIT Press, 1991).

[73] Brian P. McLaughlin, "Philosophy of Mind," in *The Cambridge Dictionary of Philosophy*, ed. Robert Audi (Cambridge: Cambridge University Press, 1999).

[74] Richard Rorty, *Philosophy and the Mirror of Nature* (Princeton: Princeton University Press, 1979).

and philosophical critique are still highly valuable. Thus, physicalism, which is currently the dominant view in philosophy of mind, is an instance of intralevel change in philosophy that has been greatly influenced by intralevel changes in the cognitive neurosciences. Cognitive neuroscience has probably yielded an *increase* in philosophical theories about the mind that are committed to physicalism, yet are trying to understand how human cognition works at a more abstract level.

A similar trend has occurred in the development of theological anthropologies that assume some form of physicalism.[75] However, this has *not* included the reduction or elimination of theological theories about the soul, but rather conceptual development about the nature of the soul. Investigation in Biblical studies has shown that although dualism is often assumed as the default position contained in scripture, there is no real consensus in the bible about the nature of the person.[76] A physicalist account of the person is a better interpretation of the scriptures in several passages of both the Old and New Testaments.[77] Thus, theologians have not come to accept physicalism simply because the cognitive neurosciences allege it to be true, but investigation in the cognitive neurosciences and philosophy of mind raised the issue in theological studies and many theologians came to the conclusion that there are good theological reasons for accepting a physicalist view of the person. This did not involve interlevel reduction, but intralevel conceptual change based on cross-scientific pollination among different levels in the sciences.

Based on the distinction between intralevel and interlevel changes in the hierarchy of science, it seems highly unlikely that the by-product theory or empirical evidence from the cognitive science of religion will lead to the elimination of theology or other higher-level descriptions of religious phenomena. Explanations of different phenomena involve multiple levels in the hierarchy of science; no one level is able to give a complete account. Thus, the existence of supernatural beings is a metaphysical proposition that cannot be answered by any

---

[75] Warren S. Brown, Nancey Murphy, and H. Newton Maloney, eds., *Whatever Happened to the Soul?: Scientific and Theological Portraits of Human Nature* (Minneapolis: Fortress Press, 1998); Joel Green, ed., *What About the Soul?: Neuroscience and Christian Anthropology* (Nashville: Abingdon Press, 2004); Malcolm Jeeves, ed., *From Cells to Souls—and Beyond: Changing Portraits of Human Nature* (Grand Rapids: Wm. B. Eerdmans, 2004); Nancey Murphy, *Bodies and Souls or Spirited Bodies?* (Cambridge: Cambridge University Press, 2006).

[76] Nancey Murphy, "Human Nature: Historical, Scientific, and Religious Issues," in *Whatever Happened to the Soul? Scientific and Theological Portraits of Human Nature*, ed. Warren S. Brown, Nancey Murphy, and H. Newton Maloney (Minneapolis: Fortress Press, 1998).

[77] Joel Green, "Bodies—That Is, Human Lives: A Re-Examination of Human Nature in the Bible," in *Whatever Happened to the Soul? Scientific and Theological Portraits of Human Nature*, ed. Warren S. Brown, Nancey Murphy, and H. Newton Maloney (Minneapolis: Fortress Press, 1998); Joel Green, *Body, Soul, and Human Life: The Nature of Humanity in the Bible*, Studies in Theological Interpretation (Grand Rapids: Baker Academic, 2008).

one level in the hierarchy of science. The by-product theory alone, as an empirical scientific statement, is insufficient as an explanation to warrant the elimination of theology or the existence of supernatural agents. Rather, the by-product theory is sometimes used as empirical evidence as part of the larger tradition of philosophical naturalism.

Differentiating Science from Metaphysics

Two of the popular texts in the cognitive science of religion are Pascal Boyer's *Religion Explained* and Scott Atran's *In Gods We Trust*.[78] Now in one sense, these are works in science and anthropology; they are up-to-date collections of the latest empirical research on religion. However, as philosophy of science has clearly shown us, science does not consist of collections of self-interpreting facts; empirical facts are theory-laden and interpreted according to certain types of metaphysical assumptions within a group of like-minded scientists.[79] Thus, the difficulty is differentiating between the empirical statements in the cognitive science of religion and metaphysical statements, whether explicitly stated or implicitly held.

Many scientists would dispute the idea that they are doing any sort of metaphysics; metaphysical claims are abstract speculations, free from any form of determinative criteria for judging the accuracy of such statements. However, in today's culture, scientists are quickly becoming the new metaphysicians who provide a rational view of reality. Scientists and scientific facts are afforded a special place in many popular debates. However, the line between a scientific fact and a metaphysical proposition is not always clearly delineated. In fact, for the "new atheism" science is ultimately synonymous with metaphysics; the only way to gain a true picture of the world and how it functions is through scientific investigation into the nature of the universe.[80]

The problem for a theologian who is committed to the existence of a nonmaterial being (i.e. God) is that the by-product theory of religion is an empirical statement that is sometimes interpreted according to certain metaphysical implications about the ontological existence of supernatural beings. In fact, Richard Dawkins uses the theory to promote his own version of atheism in order to expose *The God Delusion*.

> ... [R]eligious behavior may be a misfiring, an unfortunate by-product of an underlying psychological propensity which in other circumstances is, or

---

[78] Atran, *In Gods We Trust*; Boyer, *Religion Explained*.
[79] Feyerabend, *Against Method*; Kuhn, *Scientific Revolutions*.
[80] Richard Dawkins, *The God Delusion* (Boston: Houghton Mifflin Harcourt, 2006); Daniel Dennett, *Breaking the Spell: Religion as a Natural Phenomenon* (New York: Viking, 2006).

once was, useful. On this view, the propensity that was naturally selected in our ancestors was not religion per se; it had some other benefit, and it only incidentally manifests itself as religious behavior.[81]

The by-product theory of religion becomes a metaphysical statement when normative judgments are added to the theory in some way or another. For example, when Dawkins refers to religion as "unfortunate" or when Boyer refers to religion as an "airy nothing," these are judgments about the ontological possibility and value of religion, not empirical statements. If religious beliefs were created solely by manipulation of natural evolutionary domains this would obviously be problematic for a theologian who considers religious experiences to be informed by divine action. However, there is nothing immediately objectionable about the realization that human minds and our cognitive evolutionary history play an important role in the formation of religious beliefs.

The extent to which different facets of cognition are the direct result of evolutionary adaptations or by-products of cognitive abilities intended for other purposes is an open scientific question. Stephen Gould refers to these by-products as "spandrels" and includes several different forms of human behavior and cognition such as religion, writing, art, science, commerce, war, and play.[82] However, when the by-product theory incorporates value statements or implies the impossibility of the actual existence of supernatural agents it is being used as a metaphysical statement, not necessarily a scientific one. Metaphysical claims about the existence or non-existence of supernatural beings involve argumentation from multiple levels in the hierarchy of science. Thus, the by-product theory, as an empirical scientific statement, is insufficient on its own to eliminate the possibility of supernatural beings. It requires additional arguments that are typically related to a larger philosophical tradition. In this case those arguments are part of the tradition of philological naturalism and atheism.

Philosophical naturalism can be understood as a particular tradition of rational inquiry that is often contrasted with theism.[83] MacIntyre defines a tradition as an extended argument through history with shared texts and evidence contained in a particular narrative.[84] Several contributors can be identified as part of this tradition including Baron d'Holbach, David Hume, Friedrich Nietzsche, and

---

[81] Dawkins, *The God Delusion*, 174.

[82] Stephen. J. Gould, "Exaptation: A Crucial Tool for Evolutionary Psychology," *Journal of Social Issues* 47 (1991): 43-46.

[83] Nancey Murphy, "Naturalism and Theism as Competing Traditions," in *29th International Wittgenstein Symposium* (Kirchber am Wechel, Austria: Austrian Ludwig Wittgenstein Society, 2006), 1.

[84] Alasdair MacIntyre, *After Virtue: A Study in Moral Theory* (Notre Dame: University of Notre Dame Press, 1981); Alasdair MacIntyre, *Whose Justice? Which Rationality?* (Notre Dame: University of Notre Dame Press, 1988).

Sigmund Freud with more recent contributions from the "new atheists."[85] Thus, the philosophical problem with the by-product theory is the assumption that an empirical statement can simply eliminate contrary theological explanations without needing to rely on a larger body of argumentation. Philosophical naturalism is a viable metaphysical position, but scientific evidence from the cognitive and evolutionary sciences is insufficient to simply eliminate equivalent theological explanations of religious beliefs.

A helpful distinction is the difference between metaphysical (or philosophical) naturalism and methodological naturalism.[86] Methodological naturalism is the practice by which scientists study different types of phenomena by focusing on natural explanations based in physical causation. Methodological naturalism does not necessitate the further metaphysical claim that the only ontological substance that exists in the universe is physical matter. Instead, it is an approach by which the focus of study is on the physical determinants of any particular event while leaving aside any metaphysical implications that may or may not be a consequence of that event.

Thus, scientific claims can be separated from metaphysical claims, each being part of a different domain with different forms of argumentation. In the cognitive science of religion, this can be understood as the acceptance that the objects of study are different forms of natural explanations for religious phenomena. However, this does not necessitate that religious phenomena are exclusively the product of natural causes, just that for this particular type of study the focus is on evolutionary and cognitive explanations rather than theological or religious ones. In the cognitive science of religion, and especially among the new atheists, the distinction between scientific and metaphysical statements has become problematic. Thus, more clearly differentiating between metaphysical and methodological naturalism would be a great asset and help delineate between scientific and metaphysical statements.

Integrating a Theological Worldview

Not all participants in the cognitive science of religion assume that the findings inherently undermine traditional religious belief. Theodore Brelsford argues that even if religious beliefs arise from unconscious cognitive adaptations, it may not

---

[85] Ronald Aronson, "The New Atheists," *The Nation*, June 25 2007; Paul Henry Thiry Baron d'Holbach, *System of Nature, or, the Laws of the Moral and Physical World*, 2 vols. (London: 1797); Sigmund Freud, *The Future of an Illusion* (New York: Norton, 1961); Friedrich Nietzsche, *Genealogy of Morals*, trans. Walter Kaufmann (New York: Random House, 1966).

[86] Michael Ruse, "Methodological Naturalism under Attack," in *Intelligent Design Creationism and Its Critics: Philosophical, Theological, and Scientific Perspectives*, ed. Robert T. Pennock (Cambridge: The MIT Press, 2001).

be the case that these adaptations determine all aspects of religious belief.[87] Certain intuitions afforded by cognitive adaptations may be modifiable according to more explicit or conscious cognitive processes. Justin Barrett argues that certain aspects of cognitive adaptations may make certain theologies better equipped for transmission and comprehension than others.[88] Children very easily acquire concepts of God very similar to those from monotheistic traditions (Judaism, Christianity, and Muslim) based on mental tools such as theory of mind. It seems that the cognitive science of religion merits a theological engagement that is both critical of certain propositions, but open to learning from its empirical findings like any other science.[89]

A theological outlook can offer a competing perspective for philosophical naturalism as a basis for metaphysical claims about the reality of supernatural entities based on evidence from the cognitive sciences. Arthur Peacocke argues that theology should be considered another level in the hierarchy of science using reasonableness as a criterion for judging the different types of truth claims in theology.

> For theology, like science, also attempts to make inferences to the best explanation—or rather, it should be attempting to do so. In order to do this it should use the criteria of reasonableness already mentioned, for these are criteria, which at least have the potentiality of leading to an inter-subjective consensus.[90]

For Peacocke, theology should be considered the science at the top of the hierarchy of sciences because it integrates all of the other levels of explanation into a transcendent reality that is able to go beyond the history of the universe itself. It also attempts to describe the relationship between God and the universe, which would arguably be the most complex type of interaction and a basis for the ultimate meaning and significance of the corresponding levels.[91]

Metaphysical assumptions contained within a particular theological worldview describe an overall picture of the purpose and goal of the universe. Ian Barbour argues that no one level in the hierarchy of science can give a complete description of any phenomenon; thus, any full explanation must appeal to multiple levels.[92] McCauley and Bechtel define this as explanatory pluralism.

---

[87] Theodore Brelsford, "Lessons for Religious Education from Cognitive Science of Religion," *Religious Education* 100, no. 2 (2005): 174-191.

[88] Justin L. Barrett, *Why Would Anyone Believe in God?* (Walnut Creek: AltaMira Press, 2004).

[89] Lluis Oviedo, "Is a Complete Biocognitive Account of Religion Feasible?" *Zygon* 43, no. 1 (2008): 103-126.

[90] Arthur Peacocke, *Theology for a Scientific Age: Being and Becoming—Natural and Divine* (Oxford: Basil Blackwell, 1990; reprint, Minneapolis: Fortress Press, 1993), 17.

[91] Ibid., 23.

[92] Ian Barbour, *Religion and Science: Historical and Contemporary Issues* (San Franciso: Harper San Francisco, 1997).

Connections between sciences at different levels of analysis offer scientists working at each level resources (theoretical, practical, evidential) that would be unavailable otherwise.[93]

If the connections between sciences are important for scientific explanation, it would seem to follow that larger theological claims would also involve several different levels in the sciences. Metaphysical assumptions contained in broader conceptions of ultimate reality play a crucial role in a more comprehensive explanation of phenomena. These types of explanations are not merely scientific, but also advocate for certain metaphysical pictures of the world.

Nancey Murphy and George Ellis argue that some type of metaphysical framework is necessary to answer questions that the individual levels in the hierarchy of science cannot answer.

> ... some metaphysical or theological account of the nature of ultimate reality is needed to top-off the hierarchy of the sciences. ... the sciences at the top of the hierarchy call for a concept of ultimate reality in order to answer questions that cannot be answered from within those sciences themselves.[94]

These questions are usually referred to as "boundary questions," which are situations in which one level of explanation must rely on entities or theories from another level to explain certain types of phenomena.[95] Although another level of science can provide answers to some of these questions, it if often the case that appeals must be made to some sort of metaphysical understanding of ultimate reality to properly answer the question at hand.

The cognitive science of religion can answer certain types of questions about the natural foundations of religious beliefs and concepts, but it cannot answer metaphysical or ultimate questions about the truth claims contained within those religious beliefs. Those questions can only be answered by appealing to other levels, specifically the metaphysical framework (i.e. theism, atheism, etc.) used to define ultimate meaning and purpose. Theologians, scholars of religion, and cognitive scientists can study the cognitive and evolutionary foundations of religion as a particular science while leaving the metaphysical debate for a different context. Scientific statements are often a component of larger metaphysical arguments but the two are not inherently synonymous because of the larger role that the

---

[93] Robert N. McCauley and William Bechtel, "Explanatory Pluralism and the Heuristic Identity Theory," *Theory and Psychology* 11 (2001): 742.

[94] Nancey Murphy and George F. R. Ellis, *On the Moral Nature of the Universe: Theology, Cosmology, and Ethics* (Minneapolis: Fortress Press, 1996), 21.

[95] Bernd-Olaf Küppers, "Understanding Complexity," in *Chaos and Complexity: Scientific Perspectives on Divine Action*, ed. Robert John Russell, Nancey Murphy, and Arthur Peacocke (Berkeley and Vatican City State: The Center for Theology and the Natural Sciences and Vatican Observatory Publications, 1995).

top-level metaphysical framework plays in defending metaphysical claims. Identical scientific claims may be a part of competing metaphysical arguments. Thus, agreement may be found on the accuracy of scientific statements while disagreement abounds in regard to their metaphysical implications.

Conclusion

Although aspects of religious beliefs and rituals may be by-products of cognitive adaptations, two problems were identified in the standard model in regard to scientific explanations of religion. The first was related to the issue of causal reductionism, which describes causation as primarily a bottom-up process from part to whole. The concept of emergence is able to explain certain causal processes at work in the formation and function of religious beliefs that are not reducible to cognitive adaptations. The second problem was related to the philosophical problem of differentiating between scientific and metaphysical statements. The by-product theory is often assumed to lead to some form of philosophical naturalism. However, the empirical evidence from the by-product theory (and cognitive and evolutionary science in general) is insufficient to simply eliminate a theological explanation for religious belief. A theological perspective can offer a competing metaphysical framework for interpreting this research.

Certainly, reduction, especially methodological reduction, is an important aspect of science; reducing composite wholes to their component parts is helpful in explaining different types of natural phenomena, and religion is no exception in this regard. However, many components of religion are not a by-product of cognitive adaptive modules; they are an *emergent* property of the human representational systems that develops through the formation of neural representations and top-down cognitive and environmental constraints imposed by personal experiences and religious communities. Religious beliefs are representations that develop in the causal nexus of emergent processes, top-down constraints, and the symbolic mind. The incorporation of emergent complex systems and top-down constraints into an explanation of causation in the hierarchy of the sciences provides a better account of the multiple causal factors involved in the development of religious concepts. Chapter two begins to describe the different emergent processes involved in human cognition and provides a different model of how religious cognition works in contrast to the standard model.

Chapter 2
Counterintuitive Religious Concepts and Emergent Cognition

Two important components of the standard model in the cognitive science of religion are the counterintuitive hypothesis and cultural epidemiology. In the counterintuitive hypothesis, religious beliefs and concepts are based on the cognitive categorization of naturally occurring phenomena (i.e. person, tool, animal) while also violating theses categories in predictable ways. Counterintuitive religious beliefs are transmitted through the process of cultural epidemiology, which argues that religious concepts are analogous to a pathogen that spreads according to its ability to exploit certain features of cognitive inference systems. Although the counterintuitive hypothesis provides a partial explanation for the formation of religious concepts, emergent processes explain other aspects of cognitive representational formation not contained in the standard model. The standard model makes too strong a distinction between internal cognitive constraints and external cultural variables. Human cognition is dependent upon and actively incorporates external information in the formation of representations, which makes the distinction between internal and external highly problematic.

Understanding the emergent properties of conceptual formation overcomes the internal vs. external distinction and provides a more accurate picture of human cognition. There are three key aspects of emergence that help to illuminate the development of different aspects of cognition: initial conditions, feedback, and pattern formation. Cognitive representational ability develops through the emergence of patterns of neural activation. These patterns are not just a by-product of cognitive adaptations, but emerge through the cooperative action of neural systems embedded in particular environments. Several theories in the cognitive neurosciences such as protracted neural development, neural constructivism, and neural Darwinism demonstrate the active role of environmental feedback in the development of cognitive representations based on neural patterns. Thus, conceptual representations emerge through the complex interplay of patterns of neural activation in cooperation with feedback from the natural and social environments in which persons are embedded.

Counterintuitive Religious Concepts

According to the counterintuitive hypothesis, human cognition has evolved to pay particular attention to certain aspects of the environment and process them in a unique way based on specialized inference systems that interpret and conceptualize information.[1] Most of these systems operate below the level of conscious awareness, which makes them much more salient and effective in constructing aspects of religious cognition. Religious concepts differ from other concepts because they have a particular etiology developed through the inference systems of the human mind. Religious concepts are based on an intuitive ontology of the physical world; this ontology is the result of the unconscious inference systems that are a basic part of human cognition. A concept is religious or supernatural according to its counterintuitive properties, which violate aspects of natural categorization in cognitive inference systems in predictable ways.[2] However, the counterintuitive properties are never so extreme that they violate all aspects of the intuitive ontology.

Counterintuitive concepts are based on templates, which specify certain attributes in the formation of a concept. Each template corresponds to a particular category that was an important factor in the evolution of human cognition such as a person, artifact, or animal.[3] For example, the concept of a *giraffe* is based on the animal template, which provides broader categorical inferences based on general properties of animals in comparison to either persons or tools. The animal template is a cognitive mechanism that arranges different important properties of an animal according to memorable features such as its name, where it lives, what it eats, how it reproduces, and its body design.

As relevant information and experience with the animal increases, the concept of a giraffe will become much more sophisticated. Boyer provides a helpful illustration:

> A child is shown a new animal, say, a walrus, and told the name of the species. What the child does—unconsciously of course—is add a new entry to her mental "encyclopedia," an entry marked "walrus" that probably includes a description of a shape. ... we also know that the child spontaneously adds some information to that entry, whether we tell her or not. For instance, if she sees a walrus give birth to live cubs, she will conclude that this is the way all walruses have babies. You do not need to tell her that "all walruses reproduce that way."[4]

Templates are important because they allow persons to learn concepts quickly and unconsciously using only fragmentary information. Templates function as

---

[1] Pascal Boyer and Clark Barrett, "Evolved Intuitive Ontology: Integrating Neural, Behavioral and Developmental Aspects of Domain Specificity " in *Handbook of Evolutionary Psychology*, ed. David Buss (Hoboken: John Wiley & Sons, Inc., 2005).

[2] Pascal Boyer, "Religious Thought and Behavior as By-Products of Brain Function," *Trends in Cognitive Sciences* 7, no. 3 (2003): 119-124.

[3] Pascal Boyer, *Religion Explained: The Evolutionary Origins of Religious Thought* (New York: Basic Books, 2001), 42-45.

[4] Ibid., 42.

a type of "mental recipe" for producing new concepts that fall into a particular category.[5]

Templates provide stable ontological categories for processing important information from the environment. Each time a template processes information; the human mind assumes a default inference, concluding that the general properties stipulated by the template must apply to the formation of each new concept. For example, the tool template helps in the formation of concepts such as *axe* by assuming that this concept includes properties such as manmade, shape fits function, and inanimate.[6] Thus, whenever a person learns about a new tool, there are certain expectations about what can be done with the tool or its structural composition. These templates strongly constrain conceptual development and human imagination. They provide mini-theories about navigating our environment and prime human cognition to recognize certain types of objects in the world in particular ways.

Religious concepts are formed just like any other ordinary concept, but with an important variation. Religious concepts *violate* certain aspects of intuitive expectations about a template category while retaining others.[7] Religious concepts use the same templates, but add a special feature that violates the general properties of the category. Here are some examples of counterintuitive religious concepts:

Omniscient God = [PERSON] + special cognitive powers

Visiting ghosts = [PERSON] + no material body

Reincarnation = [PERSON] + no death + extra body available

Listening statue = [TOOL] + cognitive functions

Guardian River = [NATURAL OBJECT] + incest abhorrence[8]

The counterintuitive nature of religious concepts appears to be a cross-cultural phenomenon. Boyer and Charles Ramble conducted experiments in diverse cultures such as France, Gabon, and Nepal and found that across cultures, concepts violating certain natural phenomena were much more memorable, while familiar natural concepts were not retained for any significant amount of time.[9]

---

[5] Ibid., 54.
[6] Ibid., 59.
[7] Ibid., 62.
[8] Ibid., 64.
[9] Pascal Boyer and Charles Ramble, "Cognitive Templates for Religious Concepts: Cross-Cultural Evidence for Recall of Counter-Intuitive Representations," *Cognitive Science* 25 (2001): 535-564.

Consider the example of a ghost. When persons listen to stories about ghosts, there are certain properties that violate the concept of person: walking through walls, being a spirit, being dead, or having special powers. Yet, there would also be certain properties that a person would unconsciously assume because the concept of *ghost* is part of the person template. You would assume general sensory abilities such as sight and hearing, plus cognitive functions such as memory and the existence of some sort of mind.[10] So despite the fact that this was a completely unnatural experience, much of it would still be processed relying on templates designed by natural evolutionary processes.

Cultural Epidemiology

According to Boyer, one of the primary factors involved in the spread of counterintuitive religious beliefs in tribes and society is cultural epidemiology.[11] Cultural epidemiology builds on the theory of memes to describe the transmission of cultural information. The theory of memes was originally articulated by Richard Dawkins in his book *The Selfish Gene* and has been expanded by Susan Blackmore and Daniel Dennett.[12] The theory of memes describes cultural transmission in terms analogous to genetic transmission.

> When you imitate someone else, something is passed on. This "something" can then be passed on again, and again, and so take on a life of its own. We might call this thing an idea, an instruction, a behaviour, a piece of information … but if we are going to study it we shall need to give it a name. Fortunately, there is a name. It is the "meme."[13]

Cultural transmission occurs through individual minds processing certain types of memes in similar ways. Any concept that is stable or well defined in a certain culture only has that property to the extent that it contains a particular advantage in human minds.

According to cultural epidemiology, religious concepts spread in a predictable way, similar to a pathogen or virus, from person to person. Certain types of religious ideas are more contagious in particular populations. Epidemiological models attempt to explain macro-level cultural processes through micro-level cognitive processes in individuals.

---

[10] Boyer, *Religion Explained*, 73-74.

[11] Dan Sperber, *Explaining Culture: A Naturalistic Approach* (Oxford: Blackwell Publishers, 1996).

[12] Susan Blackmore, *The Meme Machine* (Oxford: Oxford University Press, 1999); Richard Dawkins, *The Selfish Gene* (Oxford: Oxford University Press, 1976); Daniel Dennett, *Darwin's Dangerous Idea: Evolution and the Meanings of Life* (New York: Simon and Schuster: A Touchstone Book, 1995).

[13] Blackmore, *The Meme Machine*, 4.

All epidemiological models, whatever their differences, have in common the fact that they explain population-scale macro-phenomena, such as epidemics, as the cumulative effect of micro-processes that bring about individual events, such as catching a disease. In this, epidemiological models contrast starkly with "holistic" explanations, in which macro-phenomena are explained in terms of other macro-phenomena—for instance, religion in terms of economic structure (or conversely).[14]

Cultural transmission of religious concepts is reduced to the ability for certain concepts to spread easily in cultures according to their exploitation of the default properties of cognitive inference systems. Thus, the cause of cultural transmission of religious beliefs is bottom-up from individual cognitive functions to macro-level cultural information. Macro-level cultural explanations are abstractions or summarizations of individual implicit cognitive adaptations that process relevant cultural information

> One problem is that, were culture to constrain people's thoughts, it should have a causal influence on them, and this is only possible if culture is something physical. ... It is, in fact, more natural to consider that culture is not a physical state or event at all, but a metaphorical name for a precipitate of mental and public representations. Thus, it cannot be used as a causal explanation of anything.[15]

Thus, according to this theory, the only plausible way to understand culture is to look at the cognitive processes that constrain the types of information transmitted between persons.

Causal reductionism becomes an issue in cultural epidemics to the extent that religious thoughts and traditions are reduced to micro-processes in individual minds. Jesper Sørensen provides two criticisms of the epidemiological approach.

> My two objections can be summarized in (a) a rejection of the notion that culture is only a statistical phenomena without any causal efficacy, and (b) a rejection of the epiphenomenalism involved in the argument that all aspects of culture and religion can be explained by reference to cognitive processes of individuals.[16]

Cultural epidemiology is helpful to the extent that it helps us recognize the features of religious concepts that may be easily transmitted, but it is unhelpful to the extent that this is the only way in which cultural transmission occurs. The reduction of culture to a statistical variable or an epiphenomenon misses the causal complexity

---

[14] Sperber, *Explaining Culture*, 2.

[15] Ilkka Pyysiäinen, *How Religion Works: Toward a New Cognitive Science of Religion* (Leiden: Brill 2003), 30.

[16] Jesper Sørensen, "Religion, Evolution, and an Immunology of Cultural Systems," *Evolution and Cognition* 10, no. 1 (2004): 62.

of culture and the ways in which culture acts as a top-down constraint on our thoughts and beliefs. Human beings are a highly social species, which imitates other persons and shares information through language in the development of individual cognition and behavior. The plasticity of the human mind allows for many transformations throughout the life cycle in both thought and mood. Cultural epidemiology only describes part of the story of human religious cognition and provides a misguided picture of the emergent nature of cognition.

Critique of the Counterintuitive Hypothesis

There is good empirical evidence to support the counterintuitive thesis in regard to the types of cognitive processes involved in the formation of religious beliefs and concepts. To claim that religious symbolism, imagination, and imagery are partially constituted by the representational content of natural phenomena in everyday environments of human culture is a common assumption of many interpretations of religion. Religious beliefs are highly intertwined with general aspects of the natural world as demonstrated by the anthropomorphisim present in many Christian interpretations of God or the animism present in many indigenous religions. However, the acceptance of this theory as a working hypothesis on the formation of religious beliefs does not necessitate the adoption of the by-product theory as the primary explanation for the existence of religious beliefs and the corresponding problems in causal and eliminative reductionism as discussed in Chapter 1.

One problem of explanations of religion based primarily on counterintuitive properties and cultural epidemiology is the sharp distinction between internal properties of human cognition and the external world of events, objects, and culture that may be internally represented. The distinction between the internal world of the perceiver and the external world of that which is perceived is partially a consequence of radical dualism, the thesis in philosophy of mind that contrasted mental events (*res cogitans*) from the body (*res extensa*) developed by Rene Descartes at the beginning of the Modern era in philosophy.[17] For Descartes, the mind and its cognitive functions were separate from physical reality and, thus, not constrained by physical law, while the body was a type of machine, separate from the mind but still under its control. This fostered the idea of "Cartesian materialism" in that there was an internal space (usually located in the brain) where cognitive functions were executed.[18]

The internal/external divide is dependent on additional factors in the history of philosophy and theology besides the work of Descartes. This idea goes back to

---

[17] Rene Descartes, "Meditations (1641)," in *The Essential Descartes*, ed. Margaret D. Wilson (New York: Meridian, 1969); Rene Descartes, "Discourse (1637) " in *Discourse on Method and Related Writings* ed. Desmond M. Clarke (London: Penguin Books, 1999).

[18] Daniel Dennett, *Consciousness Explained* (Boston: Little, Brown and Company, 1991), 107.

the thought of St. Augustine, who conceptualized aspects of Christian spirituality in terms of inwardness and separation from the body.[19] In the development of his theology, St. Augustine incorporated aspects of Neo-Platonic metaphysical categories to explain the relationship of God to the universe. Influenced by the writings of Plotinus, St. Augustine helped to develop the concept of an inner self as the primary channel of communication with God. Thus, the true essence of humanity and individual identity resided in the properties and functions of the soul, which was internal and separate from the body and the natural world.

Although most scientists have endorsed some form of physicalism, aspects of the internal/external divide still seem to linger. Most definitions of physicalism in philosophy of mind assume that cognitive functions can be explained as processes of the brain and body not a separable, immaterial soul. However, forms of dualism still permeate many explanations of cognition and behavior. This leads to unfortunate assumptions regarding the nature of cognition as somehow internal to and separable from the body and the external cultural context despite the fact that brains are as natural a phenomena as the body and the environment.

The by-product theory as described in the standard model falls prey to this problematic dichotomy by assuming an easy disconnect between the internal properties of human cognition and the external properties of the physical environment and culture. There are certainly aspects of religious beliefs that are explainable as by-products of certain features of human cognition, but this cannot stand as a complete explanation of religion because not all aspects of human cognition are separable from the development of religious beliefs, values, and behaviors in particular cultures and environments. Human cognition does not function independently, nor separately from the environment and human culture; it is an extension of those properties and emerges naturally through cooperative engagement of cognitive and cultural variables.

Cartesian materialism seems to be an unspoken factor in the cultural epidemiological approach to the spread of religious beliefs and concepts as depicted by the strong distinction between mental representations and public representations. Mental representations are only present in individual cognitive structures while public representations are separate and largely independent of them.[20] A transfer process is necessary to change mental representations into public ones and *vice versa*.

> Most of these representations are found in only one individual. Some, however, get communicated: that is, first transformed by the communicator into public representations, and then re-transformed by the audience into mental representations.[21]

---

[19] Phillip Cary, *Augustine's Invention of the Inner Self: The Legacy of a Christian Platonist* (Oxford: Oxford University Press, 2000).
[20] Sperber, *Explaining Culture*, 81.
[21] Ibid., 25.

This distinction between mental and public assumes that internal cognition is distinct from the external world rather than dynamically linked. The transformation and re-transformation language suggests that there is a larger discontinuity between inner perceptions and the external environment.

Part of the problem in cultural epidemiology may be explained by paying special attention to the work of Ludwig Wittgenstein. One of the primary targets of critique in Wittgenstein's philosophy was the apparent distinction between internal and public thought. In *Philosophical Investigations*, Wittgenstein identifies the concept of an inner self in the work of St. Augustine as a problematic aspect of Western philosophy, which promoted the idea that thoughts occur inside the head.[22] Wittgenstein argued that thoughts are not locked inside the mind, but are in a real sense public and part of the social fabric of interactional processes between persons.

> The simile of inside or outside the mind is pernicious. It is derived from in the head when we think of ourselves as looking out from our heads and of thinking as something going on in our head. But then we forget the picture and go on using language derived from it.[23]

The standard model of cognition and cultural epidemiology is susceptible to a Cartesian way of viewing the world through a sharp distinction between internal cognitive states and external forms of cultural and environmental information. The notion that cognitive science can better describe religious beliefs assumes that thought is a hidden process which it is the aim of the scientist to penetrate, but according to Wittgenstein there is no more direct way of reading thought than through language. "Thought is not something hidden; it lies open to us."[24]

Counterintuitive properties may constrain aspects of religious beliefs and concepts, but emergent processes still play an important role in their formation and comprehension. Counterintuitive properties describe aspects of categorization and memory that emphasize internal cognitive processes, but cognitive development is not an isolated, individual, activity disconnected from environmental, social and cultural variables. Instead religious beliefs, values, concepts, and behaviors develop through dynamic internal and external variables from a variety of sources. Religious beliefs cannot be reduced to counterintuitive properties because cognition is not primarily in the head but emergent, embodied, and dynamically constructed. The theory of emergence describes several important factors that more accurately describe human cognition than the standard model currently used in the cognitive science of religion. To understand the emergent properties of human cognition, it is important to first develop a working definition of the concept of emergence.

---

[22] Ludwig Wittgenstein, *Philosophical Investigations*, trans. G. E. M. Anscombe, 3rd edn. (New York: Macmillan, 1958).

[23] Desmond Lee, ed., *Wittgenstein's Lectures Cambridge 1930-1932* (Oxford: Blackwell, 1980), 25.

[24] Ibid., 26.

Defining Emergence

The concept of emergence was present during the ancient period of philosophy in the work of Galen, writing in the second century.[25] He made the distinction between properties of a composite entity and properties that were the result of the interactions of the parts. Victor Caston notes this distinction offered by Galen:

> For anything constituted out of many things will be the same sort of things the constituents happen to be, should they continue to be such throughout; it will not acquire any novel characteristic from outside, one that did not also belong to the constituents. But if the constituents were altered, transformed, and changed in the manifold ways, something of a different type could belong to the composite that did not belong to its first elements.[26]

Galen demonstrates an early version of emergence theory; a composite object made of constituent parts can exhibit properties not inherent in the constituent parts. Rather, the whole may contain properties not exhibited in the parts, which emerge from the interaction among the constituents.

During the mid to late nineteenth century, John Stuart Mill and George Henry Lewes developed concepts of emergence, which were the starting point for later reflection in the twentieth century. Mill was looking for a term to describe the effects of intersecting causal laws, which formed properties that were not indicative of the laws themselves.[27] Lewes expressed a definition similar to Galen in his use of the term to describe properties of a whole that cannot be deduced from their constituent parts.[28] Their work contributed to later discussions of conceptualizing the process of evolution without using terms such as vital forces, souls, or radial energies as nonmaterial principles or entities that had a causal effect on matter.[29]

Samuel Alexander, C. Lloyd Morgan, and C. D. Broad were British emergentists who took up this challenge by looking for an alternative to vitalism that would better capture the character of emergent properties, but could not be accounted for

---

[25] R. James Hankinson, "Galen," in *The Cambridge Dictionary of Philosophy*, ed. Robert Audi (Cambridge: Cambridge University Press, 1999).

[26] Victor Caston, "Epiphenomenalism, Ancient and Modern," *Philosophical Review* 106 (1997): 310.

[27] John Stuart Mill, *A System of Logic*, 8th edn. (London: Longmans, Green, Reader, and Dyer, 1943).

[28] George Henry Lewes, *Problems of Life and Mind*, vol. 2 (London: Kegan, Paul, Trench, Turbner & Co., 1872).

[29] Francisco J. Ayala, "Introduction," in *Studies in the Philosophy of Biology: Reduction and Related Problems*, ed. Francisco J. Ayala and Theodosius Dobzhansky (Berkeley and Los Angeles: University of California Press, 1974), viii.

in reductionistic terms.[30] A similar movement was occurring in America in the work of Roy Wood Sellars, A. O. Lovejoy, and Stephen Pepper. Emergence theorists attempted to articulate a different way of understanding the role of complex systems and their effect on constituent parts. Yet many philosophers perceived this as an insertion of a metaphysical view that was inconsistent with the relative success of reductionism in the sciences. With the acceptance of reductionistic views, such as logical positivism in philosophy, emergence was largely ignored by mainstream philosophy.[31]

A notable debate occurred between Roger Sperry, John Eccles, and Karl Popper. Eccles and Popper were dualists,[32] while Sperry was a monist. Both Eccles and Sperry attempted to argue against materialism and reductionism, but each developed a different explanation to counter the problems observed in these two concepts. Sperry articulated two major premises for his argument:

> 1. First, it contends that mind and consciousness are dynamic, emergent (pattern or configurational) properties of the living brain in action.
>
> 2. Second, the argument goes one critical step further and insists that these emergent properties in the brain have causal potency—just as they do elsewhere in the universe.[33]

Sperry argued against Morgan and others who postulated an epiphenomenal view of the relation between the mental and physical. He wanted to show that consciousness could be "… put in the driver's seat, as it were, they give the order, and they push and haul around the physiological and the physical and chemical processes as much as, or more than the latter processes direct them."[34] Sperry attempted to accomplish two difficult tasks: (1) to be consistent with neuroscientific research that showed the brain as the location of cognitive activity, and (2) to avoid the reduction of cognition and behavior to a deterministic neuroscience.

Another important psychological theory Sperry was attempting to refute was the behaviorism of B. F. Skinner. Skinner attempted to define all of psychology in terms of behavior to the exclusion of the involvement of internal cognition.[35] So, by subscribing to a mentalist program, Sperry was not attempting to describe

---

[30] Jaegwon Kim, "Being Realistic About Emergence," in *The Re-Emergence of Emergence: The Emergentist Hypothesis from Science to Religion*, ed. Philip Clayton and Paul Davies (Oxford: Oxford University Press, 2006).

[31] Ibid., 190.

[32] Karl Popper and John Eccles, *The Self and Its Brain* (New York: Springer-Verlag, 1977).

[33] Roger W. Sperry, *Science and Moral Priority: Merging Mind, Brain, and Human Values* (New York: Columbia University Press, 1983), 32.

[34] Ibid., 31.

[35] B. F. Skinner, *Beyond Freedom and Dignity* (New York: Knopf, 1971).

a new immaterial force that pushed and hauled the physiology inside the cranium. Instead, he was refuting Skinner and arguing that cognition had an active role to play in behavior. The options open for Sperry were not very appealing. He could subscribe to an epiphenomenal view where consciousness has no causal role, subscribe to a form of dualism with the problem of interaction between the immaterial mind and the brain, or subscribe to reductionism and reduce consciousness to laws at the physiological level of neural activity.

Introducing his own perspective, Sperry understood consciousness not as a force or a contradiction to the laws of nature, but the systemic influence of configurational regularities.

> The difference I envisage here is not in respect to events at the neuronal level but in more systemic, organizational, relational, configurational aspects and design features of the cerebral integration.[36]

These organizational, systemic, and configurational aspects included parts of human cognition that have an impact on behavior, which include "the stored memories of a lifetime, value systems, both innate and acquired, plus all the various mental powers of cognition, reasoning, intuition, etc."[37] With the beginning of revival in cognitive psychology, Sperry attempted to argue against behaviorism and show that aspects of cognition (memory and reasoning) could have an effect on behavior.

It is important to note that Sperry is not an *anti*-reductionist. In fact, he was firmly committed to the methodology of reductionism for understanding human nature, but he was able to articulate the limitations of a reductive research program.

> It is only the reductionist reasoning that therefore things can be reduced to "nothing but" their parts that is rejected, or that all science can be reduced, in theory, to a basic unity in one fundamental discipline, or that the "essence" of anything is to be sought in its components.[38]

This is really at the heart of emergence theory; not an attempt to remove reduction from scientific research, but an acknowledgment of its limitations and a move towards looking at systemic and configurational factors involved in different types of cognition.

---

[36] Sperry, *Moral Priority*, 95.
[37] Ibid., 90.
[38] Ibid., 97.

Emergent Cognition

Emergence plays an important role in explaining certain facets of cognition. In this section, I shall argue that three key aspects of emergence help to illuminate particular aspects of cognitive functioning: initial conditions, feedback, and pattern formation. The first aspect shows how component parts following simple rules are able to form emergent patterns that enable the execution of complex processes. The second key aspect shows the role of feedback in the modification of emergent patterns, enabling the pattern to interact with the environment. Distinguishing between direct and indirect emergence provides a helpful qualification in discussing the role of feedback in emergence. Cognition is particularly dependent upon environmental input in the development of cognitive processes. Finally, the third key aspect incorporates the first two aspects with the addition of the formation of patterns of neural activation, which are the basis for cognitive representations. Cognitive representations are defined as information stored in particular neural patterns that affect futures states of the overall system.

Initial Conditions

The first key aspect of an emergent view of cognition is initial conditions. The term *initial condition* is a theoretical component of chaotic systems theory and primarily refers to the beginning or starting state of a system.[39] Initial conditions are starting state properties of a particular system, which constrain the possible outcomes or futures states of that system. However, initial conditions do not fully determine the eventual outcome of a process nor can they be used to predict every possible future state, especially in chaotic systems. Initial conditions bias or constrain futures outcomes while still allowing for a certain amount of flexibility in the development of subsequent states of the system. Initial conditions, by providing constraints on the development of the system, actually enable the emergence of novel processes and flexibility in systems.

Several different factors could be defined as initial conditions, which are necessary for human cognitive abilities. Proper functioning of neural and chemical communication in the brain is obviously foundational, as well as the role of different brain systems, which enable different forms of perception and attention. Localization of function shows the relative contribution of brain systems such as the occipital lobe in vision and the primary motor cortex in movement.[40] Damage to particular areas of the brain leads to deficits in cognitive functioning. For example, damage to the hippocampus causes problems in explicit or conscious

---

[39] Kathleen T. Alligood, Tim Sauer, and James A. Yorke, *Chaos: An Introduction to Dynamical Systems* (New York: Springer-Verlag, 1996).

[40] Neil R. Carlson, *Physiology of Behavior*, 6th edn. (Boston: Allyn and Bacon, 1998), 82-83.

forms of long-term memory.[41] Thus, the structure and function of the human brain provides an initial constraint on the emergence of human cognition and subsequent development of conceptual representations. However, it is not just the human brain that acts as an initial condition in human cognition because human cognition is an embodied rather than disembodied process. Cognitive science has taken a significant turn in the direction of affirming the role of bodily experience in human cognition.[42] To a significant degree, the formation of a representational concept is dependent upon bodily experience to specify certain dimensions of that concept. Thus, the human body also serves as an initial condition in human cognition.

A third type of initial constraint is the social or cultural world in which a person in embedded. Humans are highly social animals and the selection pressures brought on by living in groups played a primary role in the evolution of human cognition.[43] As embodied views of cognition have brought down the barriers between cognition and bodily experience, the rejection of Cartesian dualism has also reignited the imagination in terms of the role of the environment (both physical and social) in the formation of concepts. Human cognition is very "leaky" in that it is difficult to draw a hard distinction between internal vs. external factors in the formation of human cognition.[44] To a certain extent, this is a chicken and egg type of question because both internal and external processes are necessary conditions for conceptual formation.

The primary research focus in the standard model of the cognitive science of religion is on the properties of human cognition that act as initial conditions and constrain the formation of religious concepts in predictable ways. These types of constraints work independently of cultural or environmental input. These properties are universal across the human species and, thus, helpful for describing how religious concepts are formed regardless of their cultural origin. This is also where an important difficulty arises in the standard model in terms of the extent to which there are *universal* properties of human cognition and how much it actually constrains religious phenomena. This is a difficult question to answer and reinvigorates the debate in the nature vs. nurture controversy. However, research in evolutionary psychology clearly indicates that the mind is not a blank slate.[45] But, evolutionary psychology may define too many cognitive functions internally and not pay enough attention to the embodied and emergent aspects of human cognition.

---

[41] Ibid., 453.

[42] Raymond W. Gibbs, *Embodiment and Cognitive Science* (Cambridge: Cambridge University Press, 2005).

[43] R. I. M. Dunbar, "The Social Brain Hypothesis," *Evolutionary Anthropology* 6 (1998): 178-190.

[44] Andy Clark, *Being There: Putting Brain, Body, and World Together Again* (Cambridge: The MIT Press, 1997).

[45] Leda Cosmides and John Tooby, "Introduction to Evolutionary Psychology," in *The Cognitive Neurosciences*, ed. Michael Gazzaniga (Cambridge The MIT Press, 1995).

The extent to which universal aspects of human cognition constrain religious concepts is an empirical question and continued research is necessary to ascertain the extent and role of the initial conditions. However, regardless of the role of cognitive constraints, the inherent flexibility of human cognition indicates that there is still an important role for emergent processes and the investigation of these processes is important for a correct account of the causal processes involved in the formation of religious phenomena. Even if an intuitive ontology acts as an initial condition in formation of religious concepts, there is still considerable room for novelty and variety in religious concepts and an emergent view of cognition shows the important role of other types of variables in the formation of religious beliefs.

Feedback

Feedback refers to the way in which emergent systems are structured by the environments in which they are embedded. The role of feedback in cognition demonstrates that the categories of inside and outside the mind are much more fluid than commonly assumed. To define feedback, Andy Clark makes a helpful distinction between direct and indirect emergence. Direct emergence is new types of phenomena that arise from the collective activity of the interactional properties of the individual component pieces with environmental conditions playing a background role.[46] Clark uses the example of convection rolls that appear when cooking oil is heated in a pan.[47]

Heat from the bottom of the pan heats the oil, causing it to rise. The cooler oil at the top begins to fall until it rises, causing convection rolls within the oil. This emergent pattern is not independent of external causes, but explanatory focus in on the interactional properties that occur based on the changing temperature of the oil and the pattern that emerges as the oil is heated and then cools. In contrast, indirect emergence is based on the interactional relationship between component parts, which is mediated by complex feedback from the environment. Environmental factors shape and modify the behavior of component parts through simple feedback loops. Indirect emergence "turns on the idea of functionally valuable side effects brought about by the interaction of heterogeneous behavior systems and local environmental structure."[48]

A simple computational program in a walking robot illustrates the combination of initial conditions and external feedback in accomplishing a simple task.[49] Rather than creating a program for the robot to follow a specific trajectory, two simple rules can be used.

---

[46] Clark, *Being There*, 73.
[47] Ibid., 107.
[48] Ibid., 109.
[49] J. C. T. Hallam and M. Malcolm, "Behaviour: Perception, Action and Intelligence—the View from Situated Robots," *Philosophical Transactions: Physical Sciences and Engineering* 349, no. 1689 (1994): 29-42.

You build into the robot a bias to veer to the right, and locate on its right side a sensor which is activated by contact and which causes the device to turn a little to the left. Such a robot will, on encountering a wall on the right, first move away (thanks to the sensor) and then quickly veer back to reencounter the wall (thanks to the bias). The cycle will repeat, and the robot will follow the wall by, in effect, repeatedly bouncing off of it.[50]

The desired behavior emerges from using two opposing directives; initial conditions form a bias that is exploited through feedback mechanisms to accomplish the desired goal of walking across a room. The best part of this type of solution is that it can be used in any type of environment that has walls regardless of the particular configuration of the room. Initial conditions plus environmental feedback can be used to develop adaptive behaviors.

Terrence Deacon describes three levels of emergence that help to illustrate the role of feedback in the formation of emergent properties.[51] The lowest level of emergence is first-order or supervenient emergence. This type of emergence is about the relationship between higher-order properties of a whole and its component parts. This is very similar to Clark's definition of direct emergence where the environment plays a background role as a causal factor. Deacon uses the example of water molecules to describe this phenomenon.[52] The temperature of the air is a background effect on the potential states of water (i.e. ice, liquid, or vapor). This state supervenes on the particular state of the water molecules at that time. When water is a vapor there is a particular relational configuration among the molecules that is different from when the water is ice. Although an exhaustive reductive description can be given to describe these different states of water, the state itself can be said to be a supervenient property as a physical particular of the current state of water.

First-level emergent properties are highly predictable. Thus, it is relatively easy to know the potential supervenient state of water by looking at the particular configuration of molecules at that time. Second-order emergence processes add an additional feature, the presence of autopoietic or chaotic processes. Autopoietic systems are biological systems that self-assemble and self-organize based on initial conditions, which are modified by environmental factors primarily in the form of feedback.[53] These systems require a detailed history of their development to understand their current configurational state; first-order emergent properties typically do not require a historical description. Chaotic and autopoietic systems

---

[50] Clark, *Being There*, 111.

[51] Terrence Deacon, "Three Levels of Emergent Phenomena," in *Evolution & Emergence: Systems, Organisms, Persons*, ed. Nancey Murphy and William R. Stoeger, SJ (Oxford: Oxford University Press, 2007).

[52] Ibid., 97.

[53] Alicia Juarrero, *Dynamics in Action: Intentional Behavior as a Complex System* (Cambridge: The MIT Press, 1999), 112.

are inherently unpredictable and can only be partially constrained according to initial conditions.

Deacon uses the example of a snowflake to illustrate second-order emergence. Snowflakes develop through three interactional factors: micro-configurations of crystal growth, heat dissipation, and the unique history of a particular snowflake as it falls through the air encountering different temperatures. Water molecules constrain the growth of the crystals in a way that biases crystal growth towards a hexagonal shape. In addition, the temperature and history of the growth of the crystal act as macro influences that also shape its development. These macro and micro influences constitute a circle of causality that both influences and constrains one another.

> These feed-forward circles of cause and effect linking events at different levels of scale are the defining features distinguishing second-order emergence from first. This is "second order" because supervenient emergent properties have become self-modifying, resulting in supervenient emergence of new supervenient emergent phenomena.[54]

For snow crystals, the component pieces are the same, so the configurational dynamics tend to be more symmetrical. Autopoetic systems add a further complicating factor by recognizing the role of asymmetrical component structures.[55] When a structure is composed of different kinds of component pieces, the recursive relationships between the structures and the environment becomes much more complex. The interaction on the micro level is highly complicated, but when macro-state influences are added the circularity of causality is distributed across several different configurations, each more complex than the last one. Deacon describes this as a "tangled hierarchy":

> A kind of tangled hierarchy of causality where micro-configurational particularities can be amplified to determine macro-configurational regularities, and where these in turn further constrain and/or amplify subsequent micro-configurational regularities.[56]

Human neural representations can be understood as autopoietic or chaotic patterns that self-organize according to internal and external constraints. They are chaotic in regard to their flexibility as representations and autopoietic in their ability to self-organize or self-assemble into networks that embody information. The human brain, which involves a complexity that is several factors beyond that of a snowflake, develops in an asymmetrical manner, making its development much more susceptible to external influences and ultimately dependent upon them for proper development. Neural networks are emergent systems that develop their

---

[54] Deacon, *Three Levels*, 103.
[55] Ibid.
[56] Ibid., 104-105.

particular configurations through interactions with environmental variables, which set different parameters for the emergence of patterns of representation. Many factors in proper cognitive development are based on regular interactions with the environment in which an organism is embedded.

Pattern Formation

Human cognition is dependent upon feedback to develop cognitive representational abilities. Rather then primarily relying on initial conditions to construct cognitive representations according to certain parameters, representational development exploits the use of external feedback in the formation of patterns of neural activation. The neurons of the brain, forming the component pieces of cognitive processing, allow higher-level cognitive functioning to emerge based on the properties of neural communication, but these same processes are also dependent upon external information through feedback in order to develop specific functions. This provides a corrective to the emphasis in the standard model on cognitive adaptations and the assertion that religious concepts are a by-product of cognitive adaptations. Religious concepts are a product of the properties of the brain and the social and cultural environments in which a person is embedded.

A cognitive representation is constructed through coordinated neural activity, which is dependent upon initial conditions and feedback from the environment. Thus, *pattern formation* is a helpful analogy for describing the process of assembling cognitive representations. A helpful illustration of this emergent process is the collective activity of an ant colony.[57] In an ant colony, ants accomplish complex social behavior such as assigning roles and providing food for the colony without any type of direct leadership from the ant queen. Ants are only capable of minimal cognitive skills (cognition does not even really apply here) and only communicate through the use of pheromones.

Steven Johnson uses ant colonies to describe emergent behavior:

> We see emergent behavior in systems like ant colonies when the individual agents in the system pay attention to their immediate neighbors rather than wait for orders from above. They think locally and act locally, but their collective action produces global behavior.[58]

The intelligence of an ant colony is produced through individual ants following local rules of interaction with other members. Individual ants would have no way of knowing the size and needs of an entire ant colony, but instead use the encounters with individual ants to modify their behavior. So an ant may start off as

---

[57] Deborah Gordon, *Ants at Work: How an Insect Society Is Organized* (New York: Free Press, 1999).

[58] Steven Johnson, *Emergence: The Connected Lives of Ants, Brains, Cities, and Software* (New York: Scribner, 2001), 74.

a forager, but if it encounters a certain number of ants performing a different task, it can switch to a different job and modify its behavior accordingly. Obviously, ants would not always accurately choose to fulfill the correct function, but when this rule is distributed across hundreds or thousands of ants, on the average, enough ants would perform the correct function to produce effective behavior.

For an ant colony to accomplish its goals it takes a certain type of critical mass to produce the necessary behaviors. One or two ants in isolation or even ten ants are not able to accomplish these goals. But take two thousand ants and you suddenly have enough ants to minimize errors, correctly identify food sources, and pass the information to others.[59] It is at this critical mass level that a distinction can be made between microbehavior and macrobehavior. The macrobehavior exhibited by a sufficiently large number of ants acting as a colony produces specific results that the microbehavior of individual ants could not produce.

Interestingly, the ignorance of the ants to the overall goals of the ant colony actually contributes to the efficiency of task completion. If the ants were in some way smarter, they would not be able to exhibit the same complex emergent behavior as they can through ignorance. In these types of emergent systems, the simple elements allow for the complex behavior to "trickle up" rather than each component part being able to assess the current configurations and problems of the entire system.[60] Emergent systems encourage random meetings. When ants explore new terrain without specific directives, they are able to find new food sources and provide new information to the colony. Random encounters produce subtle shifts and small adjustments in the behavior of the colony as small bits of information are transmitted between different ants. The overall global effect of small informational exchanges produces emergent behavior of the colony as a system.

Ants rely on patterns in the semiochemicals secreted by other ants, which is a certain type of pheromone that leads them toward a particular food source or may switch them to a different work assignment. Pattern detection allows "metainformation to circulate through the colony mind: signs about signs."[61] Thus, the overall behavior of the entire colony is directed by the simple detection of different pheromones. By gaining simple information from the behavior and pheromones of other ants, each ant is able to make a shift in its behavior that contributes to the global behavior of the ant colony. "The persistence of the whole over time—the global behavior that outlasts any of its component parts—is one of the defining characteristics of complex systems."[62]

Johnson's definition of emergence provides many helpful insights into the emergence of human cognitive functioning, which are consistent with computational

---

[59] Gordon, *Ants at Work*.
[60] Johnson, *Emergence*, 78.
[61] Ibid., 79.
[62] Ibid., 82.

theories of cognition. Alan Turing developed the first computational theories in the early 1930s, which sought to explain how the brain represents knowledge.[63] The computational hypothesis contains two important assumptions:

1. The physical states of the brain represent the external world, the body, and other parts of the nervous system.
2. Transitions between these physical states constitute computations or transformations on these representations.[64]

The physical brain is able to represent aspects of the environment that can be modified both by other cognitive systems in the brain and by future experiences in the environment. The brain acts as a type of hardware and different cognitive programs run as software. This distinction is far from exact. The physiology of the brain provides certain types of constraints to representational information. Evolution has biased human cognitive processing in certain ways; yet the plasticity of the human brain allows for the emergence of representations that do not come pre-wired in the brain.

The basic unit of cognitive function in the brain is the neuron. In a sense, our neurons act as the "worker ants" of our cognitive systems. In isolation, neurons are unable to deliver the robust capabilities of human cognition, but when linked together the component parts are able to achieve emergent global patterns. The brain is composed of hundreds of billions of interconnected neurons, which receive and transmit information to each other.[65] The number of neurons within the brain is easily much larger than the number of ants in a colony. It has achieved a level of complexity allowing it to accomplish larger goals that could not be accomplished by individual neurons alone. It is the macro behavior of the neurons working in larger systemic configurations that allows for the types of cognitive abilities that the micro behavior of the neurons would be unable to achieve in isolation.

A neuron varies its firing rate at various levels to influence the release of neurotransmitters across the synapse, which in turn influences the firing of a target neuron.[66] As in the example of the ants, individual neurons are ignorant of their overall functional role, but this is ultimately the power of the neural system, in that certain forms of cognition are able to trickle up based on the properties of neural communication. The process of pattern formation in neural networks is much

---

[63] Alan Turing, "On Computable Numbers, with an Application to the Entscheidungsproblem," in *Proceedings of the London Mathematical Society* (London: 1937); Alan Turing, "Computing Machinery and Intelligence," *Mind* 49, no. 236 (1950): 433-460.

[64] P. Read Montague and Steven Quartz, "Computational Approaches to Neural Reward and Development," *Mental Retardation and Developmental Disabilities Research Reviews* 5 (1999): 86-87.

[65] Carlson, *Physiology of Behavior*, 28-29.

[66] Ibid., 39-41.

more complex than the simple semiochemicals secreted by ants, yet the principle is the same in that a group of neurons working as a system are able to represent the meta-information contained in the overall pattern. By paying attention to the neighbors, in this case neurons, an overall emergent pattern of activation begins to develop. A single neuron is one node in a highly complex network of potential connections and information transmission. The overall activation of millions of neurons working together is able to represent different aspects of the environment and perform computations on those patterns.

Emergent properties are reliant upon feedback from the environment, which change based on the complexity of the interaction between the system and the environment. Terrence Deacon argues that feedback in emergent systems produces "relationships of recursive causality in which the feedback is from features of a whole system to the very architecture of its components and how these levels interact."[67] This leads to an "amplification of configurational features" in which we begin to see the possibility of higher-order regularity (forms of informational representation) affecting the component parts at various levels of scale.[68] This type of recursive causality occurs in what Deacon defines as the third level of emergence.

This type of emergence in cognition is demonstrated when a pattern of neural activation acts as a cognitive representation, which is defined as the way in which the informational content of a configurational pattern affects the future states of a system. In this sense, representation is very similar to a type of memory embodied within a system. Third-order emergence is Deacon's most important contribution for understanding emergent cognition. Third-order emergence builds on and embodies all of the earlier levels of emergence, but adds an important element of information held in memory.

> The result is that specific historical moments of higher-order regularity or of unique micro-causal configurations can additionally exert a cumulative influence over the entire causal future of the system. In other words, via memory constraints derived from specific past higher-order states can get repeatedly re-entered into the lower-order dynamics leading to future states, in addition to their effects mediated by second-order processes.[69]

Third-order emergence exhibits a developmental trajectory where macro-level influences are amplified and "remembered" by the system itself and repeatedly re-entered into the system at particular times. So the history of a system can be used to maintain a particular global configuration that is repeatedly entered back into the system. Global configurations are held in memory as a representation of

---

[67] Deacon, *Three Levels*, 96.
[68] Ibid.
[69] Ibid., 105-106.

past states of the system or organism, which suggests an understanding of living organisms in terms of "representation, adaptation, information, and function."[70]

This description of emergence can be understood as a hierarchy of complex causal relationships. This account illustrates the immensely complex task of discovering the cause of particular events, especially human behavior. The brain is a highly complex bundle of overlapping hierarchical cognitive systems, which can be described as a type of emergence machine:

> Brains might be characterized as "emergence machines," increasingly churning out complex high-level virtual functions, virtual environments, and virtual evolutionary linkages to track and adapt to the complexity of the world.[71]

Once a particular pattern becomes instantiated in a neural network, that representation can be used in order to influence current cognitive processing tasks. In this way, the pattern acts as a type of constraint on the possible outcomes in cognitive tasks. Cognitive processing power is increased by categorizing information according to previous tasks that are held in memory as representations. This incorporates aspects of the world that are learned into current cognitive tasks.

An emergent model of cognition provides a different framework for describing the causal factors involved in the formation of religious concepts and beliefs. The standard model characterizes religious cognition from a causally reductive perspective, but the emergent processes of feedback and pattern formation show that cognitive representations of a religious nature are not just a by-product of cognitive adaptations but rely on external variables that provide their own form of constraint. Both internal and external constraints work cooperatively in the formation of cognitive representations of religious concepts. Interestingly, different areas of research in cognitive neuroscience also support an emergent perspective on cognition, in that feedback plays an important role in the formation of different aspects of the neural networks that form the basis of representational content.

Evidence of Emergence from Neuroscience

Several areas of research in the cognitive neurosciences support an emergent view of cognition based on initial conditions, feedback, and pattern formation. In the animal kingdom, the human brain takes the longest time to fully develop, with new neural connections forming late in life. The cortical organization of the brain

---

[70] Ibid., 107.
[71] Ibid., 110.

is highly complex and involves several different types of connecting fibers.[72] The neocortex is unique in mammals, in that it takes up about 60 to 80 percent of the total brain mass.[73] The corpus callosum is composed of 200 to 800 million neural fibers that transmit information between the right and left hemispheres.[74] Many areas of the left hemisphere are connected with identical areas in the right hemisphere. Association fibers connect distant areas within the brain and short u-shaped fibers connect adjacent areas. Projection fibers are ascending and descending fibers that connect areas of the neocortex to areas of the brainstem.[75]

Evolutionary processes would seem to favor organisms that develop adaptive behaviors quickly, thus increasing their chances of survival and reproduction from an early age. Yet there is a protracted length of time for many developmental processes of humans. The human infant is virtually helpless on its own and needs constant support in order to obtain food and security. The human brain takes the longest amount of time to fully develop. While the chimpanzee brain reaches 95 percent of its final mass by age two, it takes the human brain until age five to reach this same level. The frontal lobe itself is still in the process of maturation late into adolescence.[76] As the mammalian species has evolved, the frontal lobe has become larger and more complex as gyri began to mushroom and fissures developed perpendicularly across the cortex.[77]

Rather than a deficit to human cognitive development, the amount of time it takes for the human person to mature may be a helpful component of the emergence of different cognitive functions. The reason this tends to be overlooked is the emphasis placed on intrinsic maturation, which emphasizes the role of internal systems that direct the development of different organs and other physiological structures. Steven Quartz suggests that development is more of an interactive process between organisms and the environments in which they are embedded.[78] The evolutionary innovation in brain development is the use of external information to provide key ingredients to developmental programs. In terms of emergence, protracted neural development highlights the role of feedback as an indispensable process in cognitive development. An emergent view of cognition

---

[72] Bryan Kolb and Ian Q. Whishaw, *Fundamentals of Human Neuropsychology*, 4th edn. (New York: Worth Publishers Incorporated, 1995), 336.

[73] R. Nieuwenhuys, H. J. Donkelaar, and C. Nicholson, *The Central Nervous System of Vertebrates* (New York: Springer, 1997).

[74] Kolb and Whishaw, *Human Neuropsychology*, 336.

[75] Ibid.

[76] J. N. Giedd, "Structural Magnetic Resonance Imaging of the Adolescent Brain," *Annals of the New York Academy of Sciences* 1021 (2004): 105-109.

[77] Joaquín M. Fuster, *Cortex and Mind* (Oxford: Oxford University Press, 2003), 4.

[78] Steven R. Quartz, "Toward a Developmental Evolutionary Psychology: Genes, Development, and the Evolution of the Human Cognitive Architecture," in *Evolutionary Psychology: Alternative Approaches*, ed. Steven J. Scher and Frederick Rauscher (New York: Springer Publishing Co., 2002), 185.

argues for the importance of reciprocal relationships between initial conditions of human cognitive functions and feedback from the environment in which a person is embedded. As an alternative to describing cognitive development primarily through initial conditions, an emergent perspective on human cognition emphasizes the crucial role of the environment in constructing particular neural structures and cognitive systems.

Brain development and neural complexity do not occur equally in all areas of the brain, there is a hierarchical structure to the development of different neural systems. Human brains share certain simple neural systems with other animals, but other systems have been built upon these more basic systems to enable a more complex cognitive architecture.

> As we shall see, at the heart of who you are is a complex blend of new and old regions, a Picasso-like prefrontal cortex ground in the old masters of more ancient brain structures, some of them so old that humans share them with insects.[79]

Developmental neuroscience is an important contributor to understanding the role of feedback in the emergence of neural systems. Sensory systems develop many of their abilities earlier in development, followed by more abstract forms of reasoning.

> The brain appears to process information in a roughly hierarchical manner; that is, brain regions near the sensory windows represent quite basic features of the world and support specific sensory and motor functions. Areas further away encode more abstract or complex features and have a more integrative function in a hierarchy of information.[80]

Each step up in complexity allows for greater flexibility in adapting to the current needs of the present context. Each system allows the organism to modify its behavior according to instinctual drives and goals. With humans, these goals can become more abstract based on complex reasoning, yet these systems are dependent on rudimentary forms of behavioral modification.

> The longer the brain develops, the more opportunities there are for specific contributions from the world to guide the buildup of more and more complex circuits—opportunities that are essential to build a mind capable of navigating the complexities of human existence.[81]

---

[79] Steven R. Quartz and Terrence J. Sejnowski, *Liars, Lovers, and Heroes: What the New Brain Science Reveals About How We Become Who We Are* (New York: William Morrow & Company, 2002), 35.
[80] Ibid., 51.
[81] Ibid.

In the following sections, I will discuss the theories of neural constructivism and neural selectionism. Both of these theories argue that the neural patterns that instantiate basic forms of representations are not directed exclusively by initial conditions, but that there is a cooperative process between initial conditions, environmental feedback and neural patterns of activation.

Neural Constructivism

The theory of neural constructivism highlights several emergent processes in the construction of representations, which emphasizes developmental processes that occur during the formation of neural patterns in different organisms. Representations are built according to the informational content of what is currently being processed.

> The representational features of the cortex are built from the dynamic interaction between neural growth mechanisms and environmentally derived neural activity … . Neural constructivism suggests that the evolutionary emergence of neocortex in mammals is a progression toward more flexible representational structures, in contrast to the popular view of cortical evolution as an increase in innate, specialized circuits.[82]

Human cognition is unique in its inherent flexibility based on the plasticity of neural systems, which develop cognitive strategies according to the current demands of the environment. Neural constructivism attempts to discover the relative contribution of intrinsic factors (initial conditions) in relationship to nonstationary (feedback or developmental) factors.[83]

Quartz and Sejnowski developed a method to test the complexity of neural development over time. If their hypothesis is true, research should demonstrate two things: (1) structural development of neurons enables the development of increases in representational complexity and (2) structural development is dependent upon environmental factors that guide the process.[84] This reflects the view of developmental psychologist Jean Piaget, who considered cognitive development to occur in stages as the child interacts with learning communities and accomplishes cognitive goals.[85] Neural development becomes more complex as robust representational learning strategies develop. Representational complexity is measured according to three categories: synaptic numbers, dendritic arborization,

---

[82] Steven R. Quartz and Terrence J. Sejnowski, "The Neural Basis of Cognitive Development: A Constructivist Manifesto," *Behavioral and Brain Sciences* 20 (1997): 537.

[83] Ibid.

[84] Ibid., 538.

[85] Jean Piaget, *The Psychology of the Child* (Paris Presses Universitaires de France, 1966).

and axonal arborization. The next sections highlight some of the research in neural constructivism as discussed and compiled by Quartz and Sejnowski.

Synaptic Numbers

Synaptic number is a measure of the density or number of synaptic connections within a certain area of a mammalian brain. The synapse is the small space between two neurons where different biochemical reactions either increase or decrease the potential firing of a target neuron.[86] Research in the synaptic connections of the primate cortex is one example of a genetic blueprint model of neural development, which assumes that neurons develop according to a pre-defined plan based in the instructions given by the genes.[87] One experiment measured synaptic density in several areas of the cortex of a rhesus monkey, including the motor, somatosensory, visual, and prefrontal cortex.[88] Synaptic density changed uniformly across all areas of the cortex, peaked between two and four months, than radically declined. Thus, it would seem that an internal genetic blueprint regulates the initial neural growth across the cortex. Yet, a more recent study of the rhesus monkey showed that synaptic density peaked at two months of age, but did not begin to decline until puberty and this decline was gradual up until about 20 years of age.[89] Thus, synaptic connections are not set early on in the lifespan, but take almost 20 years to fully develop. This opens up the possibility of the involvement of external factors in development.

Several studies look at the effect of the environment on the density of synaptic connections. Neural cells in the visual cortex of a mouse (stellate and pyramidal cells) show a decrease in density when the mouse is raised in the dark, but placing those same mice in a normal environment can reverse this condition.[90] Similar results were found in rabbits with visual deprivation.[91] Additionally, research shows that rats raised in complex environments (i.e. equipment to play on, room to move around) increases the density of neural cells in the visual cortex.[92] Several

---

[86] Carlson, *Physiology of Behavior*, 29.

[87] Quartz and Sejnowski, *Liars, Lovers, and Heroes*, 37.

[88] Pasko Rakic and others, "Concurrent Overproduction of Synapses in Diverse Regions of the Primate Cerebral Cortex," *Science* 232 (1986): 232-235.

[89] J. P. Bourgeois, P. S. Goldman-Rakic, and P. Rakic, "Synaptogenesis in the Prefrontal Cortex of Rhesus Monkeys," *Cerebral Cortex* 4 (1994): 78-96.

[90] Facundo Valverde, "Apical Dendritic Spines of the Visual Cortex and Light Deprivation in the Mouse," *Experimental Brain Research* 3 (1967): 337-352; Facundo Valverde, "Rate and Extent of Recovery from Dark Rearing in the Visual Cortex of the Mouse," *Brain Research* 33 (1971): 1-11.

[91] A. Globus and A. B. Scheibel, "The Effect of Visual Deprivation on Cortical Neurons: A Golgi Study," *Experimental Neurology* 19 (1967): 331-345.

[92] A. Globus and others, "Effects of Differential Experience on Dendritic Spine Counts in Rat Cerebral Cortex," *Journal of Comparative and Physiological Psychology* 82 (1973): 175-181.

other studies have shown similar results in areas of the cortex devoted to motor learning, sensitization, and habituation.[93] This supports the idea of emergent cognition in that the patterns formed by synaptic connections among neurons rely on feedback in the formation, organization, and functionality of different sensory areas in mammals.

Axonal and Dendritic Arborization

Another area of neural growth discussed in neural constructivism is axonal and dendritic aborization.[94] This is the increasing growth and complexity of axonal and dendritic connections to other neural cells. A. Antonini and M. P. Stryker emphasize the role of directed neural growth and increases in axonal complexity throughout the developmental process.[95] As was the case with synaptic numbers, the presence or absence of environmental and activity-dependent stimuli produced an effect on axonal arborization in cats and rodents.[96] As one example, a study showed that monocular deprivation in cats stunted the growth of particular neural cells and disrupted normal development of visual capabilities.[97] Several areas of research have shown dendritic expansion in different areas of the mammalian brain based on environmental factors, including the rabbit visual cortex, pyramidal cells of the rat visual cortex, and stellate cells of the rat visual cortex.[98] Dendritic arborization can be seen in the development of human pyramidal cells from the time of infancy through adulthood, which suggests that dendritic connections may be modified throughout early adulthood.[99] In the human cortex, dendritic expansion occurs in the Broca's area, the parahippocampal gyrus, human visual cortex and the sensorimotor cortex.[100] In Broca's area, expansion occurs into the sixth year and in the sensorimotor cortex the dendrites expand from 300 m to a total length of 1600 m in adulthood.[101]

---

[93] Quartz and Sejnowski, *Constructivist Manifesto*, 542.

[94] Ibid.

[95] A. Antonini and M. P. Stryker, "Development of Individual Geniculocortical Arbors in Cat Striate Cortex and Effects of Bionocular Impulse Blockade," *Journal of Neuroscience* 13 (1993): 3549-3573.

[96] Quartz and Sejnowski, *Constructivist Manifesto*, 544.

[97] M. J. Friedlander, K. A. C. Martin, and D. Wassenhove-McCarthy, "Effects of Monocular Visual Deprivation on Geniculocortical Innervation of Area 18 in Cat," *Journal of Neuroscience* 11 (1991): 3268-3288.

[98] Quartz and Sejnowski, *Constructivist Manifesto*, 547.

[99] J. P. Schade and W. B. van Groenigen, "Structural Organization of the Human Cerebral Cortex I: Maturation of the Middle Frontal Gyrus," *Acta Anatomica* 47 (1961): 72-111.

[100] Quartz and Sejnowski, *Constructivist Manifesto*, 546.

[101] T. L. Petit and others, "The Pattern of Dendritic Development in the Cerebral Cortex of the Rat," *Brain Research* 469 (1988): 209-219; R. J. Simonds and A. B. Scheibel,

Based on these studies and the work of Quartz and Sejnowski, cognitive representation can be best described as an emergent process based on initial conditions of neural functioning and complex feedback from the environment. Each of these studies demonstrates that neural patterns emerge based on the cooperative causal effects of neural development working in conjunction with environmental feedback. Thus, the environment acts as a constraint on the formation of neural patterns of cognitive representations. The studies on synaptic, axonal, and dendritic complexification show the highly plastic properties of neurons, which may be modified throughout the lifespan.

Neural Darwinism

Neural constructivism works in parallel with neural Darwinism (also known as neural selectionism), a theory developed by Gerald Edelman.[102] It is based on two aspects of evolution: natural selection and somatic selection. Natural selection refers to the ability for a particular species population to survive and reproduce, while somatic selection refers to selection within an individual human organism.

> When we say somatic selection, we mean what occurs in a single body in time frames ranging from fractions of seconds to years and, obviously, ending with an animal's death. Thus, selection and variation can also occur in the cellular system of animals.[103]

Edelman argues that selection occurs in the human nervous system through competition among synaptic connections. This leads to the selection of particular neural groups according to usage during development.

Selection involves three main tenets: developmental selection, experiential selection, and reentry.[104] During developmental selection, genes and inheritance play a vital role in the initial parameters of neural development. These parameters specify basic structures of the brainstem and cortex and lead to the remarkable similarity in brain structure across the human species. However, from the early embryonic stages, somatic selection plays a primary role in the connectivity of individual synapses.[105] Thus, over time, neurons that fire concurrently with one

---

"The Postnatal Development of the Motor Speech Area: A Preliminary Study," *Brain and Language* 37 (1989): 42-58.

[102] Gerald M. Edelman, *Neural Darwinism: The Theory of Neuronal Group Selection* (New York: Basic Books, 1987); Gerald M. Edelman, *Bright Air, Brilliant Fire* (New York: Basic Books, 1992); Gerald M. Edelman and Giulio Tononi, *A Universe of Consciousness: How Matter Becomes Imagination* (New York: Basic Books, 2000).

[103] Edelman, *Universe of Consciousness*, 82.

[104] Ibid., 83-85.

[105] Ibid.

another become coupled with each other and form particular groups. Neural growth in the early stages of development is pruned over time according the co-activation of neurons.[106] The use of a particular group will be dependent upon both internal and external factors, the external factors mostly showing up through experiential selection. From the earliest stages of human development, feedback provided by experience plays a vital role in the development and strengthening of neural and synaptic connections.[107]

Reentry is the last stage in neural Darwinism and involves the connection of several different neural events.

> The correlation of selective events across the various maps of the brain occurs as a result of the dynamic process of reentry. Reentry allows an animal with a variable and uniquely individual nervous system to partition an unlabeled world into objects and events in the absence of a homunculus or computer program.[108]

This correlation allows different aspects of cognition to be linked with each other such as the coordination of motor movement and sensory input. Reentry is primarily the association of different areas of the cortex with each other allowing for more robust forms of knowledge and representation. These processes are the basis of perception and the development of memory, language, and other cognitive functions.

Conclusion

One of the primary components of the standard model is the counterintuitive hypothesis, which states that religious concepts are formed according to an intuitive ontology that is violated in predictable ways. Religious concepts spread according to the process of cultural epidemiology, which is analogous to the spread of a virus that exploits the universal features of human cognition in terms of the intuitive ontology. The counterintuitive hypothesis demonstrates that religious beliefs and concepts are dependent upon the same sorts of cognitive processes used to process a variety of different types of objects and information. But aspects of the standard model, especially cultural epidemiology, assume a strong distinction between internal cognitive processes and external environmental and cultural information, which may be the result of lingering Cartesian views of internal cognitive states.

Emergence serves as a partial corrective to the standard model by emphasizing the role of feedback and pattern formation based on external constraints that

---

[106] Neil R. Carlson, *Physiology of Behavior*, 6th edn. (Boston: Allyn and Bacon, 1998), 78.
[107] Edelman, *Universe of Consciousness*, 84.
[108] Ibid., 85.

partially constitute the formation of cognitive representations. Human cognition is an emergent process dependent upon a dynamic and fluid relationship between internal cognitive constraints and the contexts in which those representations are formed. An emergent view of cognition can be described according to three primary aspects: initial conditions, feedback, and pattern formation. The cognitive science of religion focuses on the initial conditions, which is an important aspect of cognitive functions. However, the other two properties (feedback and pattern formation) demonstrates aspects of cognitive representations that are not causally reducible to by-products in the standard model as discussed in Chapter 1.

Research on processes such as protracted neural development, neural constructivism, and neural Darwinism provide evidence from the neurosciences that demonstrates the emergent processes involved in the construction of cognitive representations. These processes play a complementary causal role in the formation of neural representations, which are the foundation for the formation of conceptual representations of religious content. Religious concepts cannot simply be reduced to by-products of cognitive adaptations (or initial conditions as I have described them here) because the environment in which they emerge actively constrains the development of religious representational content. Environmental conditions play as important a role in the formation of religious representations as initial conditions. Thus, the causally reductive aspects of the standard model in the cognitive science of religion are not an accurate description of the emergence of religious beliefs and behaviors.

Chapter 3
Theological Incorrectness and the Causal Relevance of Religious Beliefs and Theological Reasoning

Based on assumptions from the standard model, the theological incorrectness hypothesis argues that the professed beliefs of religious members may not be the same types of beliefs used in everyday situations. Unconscious cognitive constraints play a larger role in the formation of religious beliefs than abstract theological doctrines. This raises the issue of the function of religious beliefs in producing subsequent thought and behavior. Although the theologically incorrect hypothesis correctly demonstrates that certain religious beliefs may be epiphenomenal to the everyday actions and beliefs of religious persons, other areas of research in the cognitive neurosciences demonstrate that in certain contexts beliefs are able to have a top-down effect on thought and behavior. Thus, religious concepts act as top-down constraints in the formation of systems of belief and subsequent actions.

Cognitive science typically defines top-down constraints as forms of top-down processing, which is the use of previously learned information for the execution of current cognitive tasks. The neural architecture of the human brain demonstrates the use of top-down and bottom-up processing in the formation of different types of representational content. This architecture also illustrates the possibility of different forms of belief having a role in planning, modulating and implementing particular behaviors. Religious beliefs are not just products of internal representations, but rely on different forms of cognitive scaffolding in terms of the cultural and institutional structures that act as type of external memory. The causal role of religious beliefs in directing behavior can only be ascertained by investigating their function in a larger cultural and social context. Religious beliefs are partially constituted according to external cognitive scaffolding and provide a top-down structuring constraint on the behaviors of religious members of a community.

Top-down constraints are based on the idea of top-down causation, which is a form of causation prevalent in emergent systems and works in concert with efficient forms of causation. Top-down constraints can be demonstrated in computational models of cognitive functions such as facial and emotional processing. Recurrent neural networks illustrate how previously learned information can have an effect on current processing tasks through the use of attractors and pattern completion. These types of processes are analogous to certain aspects of theological reasoning, where a wide range of sources (experience, tradition, history, context) are organized into a coherent whole that provides a theological picture of the world.

Theologically Correct or Incorrect?

The theological correctness hypothesis states that persons have different representations of God on a continuum of relative complexity.[1] Increasing the cognitive demands of a task (i.e. time constraints or amount of information) makes it more difficult to process abstract theological concepts. When cognitive demands are decreased and time is allotted for reflection, persons will typically answer in theologically correct ways; providing answers that cohere with the explicit theological doctrines of their faith. In experimental settings with time constraints, questionnaire answers tend to be more concrete and simple, often attributing human characteristics to God (i.e. limited knowledge; specific spatial location, etc.). In these situations, persons have to process information quickly without time for reflection; thus, they will rely on explanations based on intuitive ontological categories.

In a study conducted with persons of several different faith traditions, subjects were asked to remember stories about different gods in a particular narrative.[2] Here is one example:

> A boy was swimming alone in a swift and rocky river. The boy got his left leg caught between two large, gray rocks and couldn't get out. Branches of trees kept bumping into him as they hurried past. He thought he was going to drown and so he began to struggle and pray. Though God was answering another prayer in another part of the world when the boy started praying, before long God responded by pushing one of the rocks so the boy could get his leg out. The boy struggled to the river bank and fell over exhausted.[3]

Researchers attempted to ascertain what mental representation of God was being used to process this story. The mental representation of God was considered anthropomorphic according to the way different aspects of the story are reported by the participants. One example would be reporting that God finished answering one prayer and then started to answer another, which would violate the theological doctrine of omnipresence.

> The results of the narrative comprehension task suggested that, when processing stories, adults tend to use a concept of God having few abstract, "god-like" properties. Rather, participants quite readily attributed to God properties such

---

[1] Justin L. Barrett, "Theological Correctness: Cognitive Constraint and the Study of Religion," *Method and Theory in the Study of Religion* 11 (1999): 325-339; D. Jason Slone, *Theological Incorrectness: Why Religious People Believe What They Shouldn't* (Oxford: Oxford University Press, 2004).

[2] Justin L. Barrett and Frank C. Keil, "Conceptualizing a Non-Natural Entity: Anthropomorphism in God Concepts," *Cognitive Psychology* 31 (1996): 219-247.

[3] Ibid., 224.

as having a limited focus of attention, having fallible perceptual systems, not knowing everything, and having a single location in space and time.[4]

The participants were given a questionnaire without time constraints that allowed more time for theological reflection. For each question, the participant could answer yes or no to abstract theological questions such as: God can read minds; God can do multiple mental activities simultaneously; God is spatial (in a particular place or places) or non-spatial (God is everywhere). Without time constraints, participants would answer questions about the character of God in theologically correct ways: God is omnipotent, all knowing, infallible, etc. But the same participants who answered in theologically correct ways on the questionnaire would answer in theologically incorrect ways on the narrative comprehension test. This suggests that perhaps religious persons have more than one concept of God that is used in different situations.

D. Jason Slone argues that this phenomenon should be understood as *theological incorrectness* in that everyday religious beliefs are often inconsistent with the abstract doctrines of a particular religious system.[5] This explains why there is a difference between specific religious creeds and how religion is experienced in everyday life. Highly theological accounts are thought to be "maximally counterintuitive" in that they violate several properties of intuitive ontological categories.[6] These maximally counterintuitive concepts are very hard to remember and use in everyday life because they violate too many default inferences in an intuitive ontology as discussed in regard to the standard model in Chapter 1.

Take for example this description of the Judeo-Christian God and his attributes.

> God is an omnipresent, omnipotent, omniscient essence with multiple forms derived from the same substance that has no creation or cessation point.[7]

There are too many violations of intuitive ontological categories for this type of knowledge to be used in everyday religious reasoning. Thus, religious adherents will develop conceptual models based on ontological categories that are easier for them to process and understand. This suggests a difference in the beliefs religious persons say they have and those they actually use in everyday contexts. To this extent, Slone argues that abstract theological doctrines may not be an accurate description of the cognitive content of everyday religious beliefs.

> Humans can know one thing in one context but represent it differently (even contradict their deeply held "beliefs") in another context, if the context demands generating rapid, easy-to-recall or infer representations. ... Even when humans

---

[4] Ibid., 327.
[5] Slone, *Theological Incorrectness*, 10.
[6] Ibid., 63.
[7] Ibid., 65.

employ religious concepts, the religious concepts they generate might be more consistent with folk knowledge than with official theology. Sorry, clergy, but theological ideas simply do not determine, per se, how or what people think.[8]

According to Slone, one failure of a maximally counterintuitive theology was the early Puritans' attempt to adhere to a Calvinist theology.[9] Slone argues that according to this theology the eternal destiny of each person is already known and determined by God. Yet this contradicts the intuitive ontological category that specifies some form of human agency. Although the theologically correct doctrine would dictate a type of divine determinism, in everyday usage, most religious members will tend to develop concepts that reflect their intuitive knowledge. As a result, laws were developed to restrain the tendency for human agency (even though their behavior was already predetermined). Puritans also consulted non-theological sources such as the Farmer's Almanac and astrology to decipher and predict the future.

More importantly, in mainline Christianity, Calvinism was eventually replaced with Arminianism, which placed an emphasis on free will and human agency. During the Great Awakening of the eighteenth century, street preachers, tent revivals, and camp meetings stirred religious fervor in many Americans. The fiery preachers of this era used highly emotional imagery and fear to persuade people to "make a decision for Christ." This type of conversion required action on the part of the believer as well as God and called for a concept of free will. Slone argues that the best explanation for the success of Arminianism is the particular fit between cognitive inferences about self-agency and the Arminian emphasis on believers "reaching out to God."[10]

Slone provides helpful insight into the way that everyday religious beliefs do not always match the abstract theological doctrines taught from the pulpit. It also seems highly plausible that persons have several different concepts of God, some of which may be inconsistent with one another. Pastors and theologians have often recognized the disconnection between abstract theological doctrines and everyday beliefs.[11] But, does this amount to theological incorrectness? Many disciplines contain highly abstract theories that students and teachers often simplify to make understandable. Should anthropological and even theological theories about the Great Awakening be reduced to by-products of the functions of adaptive cognitive modules?

Slone illustrates the same type of reductionism evident in the standard model in the cognitive science of religion. Explicit abstract theological concepts are not an accurate description of the beliefs of religious persons. These explicit

---

[8] Ibid., 66.
[9] Ibid., 94.
[10] Ibid., 96.
[11] James Wm. McClendon, Jr. and James M. Smith, *Convictions: Defusing Religious Relativism* (Valley Forge: Trinity Press International, 1994).

concepts can be reduced to the implicit concepts that are a product of the intuitive ontology provided by cognitive adaptations. The implicit concepts do the real causal work below the level of consciousness in determining the everyday beliefs of religious persons. Explanations for the Great Awakening are not attributed to social or political factors, let alone the activity of God in the world. Instead these explanations are reduced to the cognitive fit of certain religious concepts to the inference systems of cognitive adaptations. Those religious concepts that match the parameters imposed by the intuitive ontology are transmitted and remembered more often than others. Although I would agree that certain cognitive factors play an important role in religious concepts, cognitive and evolutionary science provides an insufficient explanation for religious belief. Religion cannot be reduced to cognitive and evolutionary science. The standard model cannot provide a complete picture of the multiple causal factors involved in the formation of religious belief. Theological incorrectness correctly addresses a very common problem in theology; abstract beliefs do not always match the beliefs that are used in everyday situations and these two may be in conflict. Yet, the cognitive neurosciences can also help to explain the situations in which religious beliefs act as a top-down constraint on thought and behavior. Understanding the role of top-down processing in human cognition sets the stage for the possibility of top-down constraints.

Understanding Bottom-up and Top-down Processing

Bottom-up vs. top-down processing is a common distinction in cognitive science. Margaret Matlin defines top-down processing as the use of higher-level cognitive processes such as "concepts, expectations, and memory" in the processing of information.[12] Top-down processing works in tandem with bottom-up processing in order to facilitate normal cognitive functioning.

> Bottom-up processes are driven by sensory information from the physical world. Top-down processes actively seek and extract sensory information and are driven by our knowledge, beliefs, expectations, and goals. Almost every act of perception involves both bottom-up and top-down processing.[13]

Thus, representations of current experience are influenced by the representations of past experience. These representations are often higher-level, abstract representational networks that act as top-down constraints on the processing of incoming information.

The word superiority effect illustrates the top-down functions in everyday human cognition. This effect is demonstrated when a phrase is quickly identified

---

[12] Margaret W. Matlin, *Cognition*, 6th edn. (Hoboken: John Wiley & Sons, 2005), 26.

[13] Edward Smith and Stephen Kosslyn, *Cognitive Psychology: Mind and Brain* (Upper Saddle River: Pearson Prentice Hall, 2007), 55.

according to the context of the sentence.[14] For example, in the phrase *the cat* in Figure 3.1, the H and A are actually identical, but most persons easily identify the phrase correctly using the context of the sentence to process the information.[15]

TAE CAT

Figure 3.1   The cat—word superiority effect

This same effect can be demonstrated in speech perception as in the case of phoneme restoration. In one study by R. M. Warren and R. P. Warren, a coughing sound was inserted in the middle of a sentence, so that the participants only heard the sound *eel.[16]

It was found that the *eel was on the axle
It was found that the *eel was on the shoe.
It was found that the *eel was on the orange.
It was found that the *eel was on the table.[17]

The participants were able to successfully identify the correct word in the sentence based on the contextual words that occurred later. Bottom-up and top-down processes are ubiquitous in many different cognitive functions. Neuroscientific evidence explains some of the basic features of the hierarchical architecture of neural networks and the role of bottom-up and top-down processes in the formation of cognitive representations in the brain. Typically, bottom-up processing forms the basic properties of representations based on sensory information, while top-down processing uses memories, concepts, and other information from the past to process the incoming sensory data.

---

[14] Ibid., 89.

[15] O. Selfridge, "Pattern Recognition and Modern Computers," in *Proceedings of the Western Joint Computer Conference* (Los Angeles, CA: Institute of Electrical and Electronics Engineers, 1955).

[16] R. M. Warren and R. P. Warren, "Auditory Illusions and Confusions," *Scientific American* 223, no. 6 (1970): 30-36.

[17] Matlin, *Cognition*, 60.

Neuroscience of Hierarchical Networks

Several neural systems play a role in the formation of cognitive representations based on bottom-up and top-down processes. Joaquín Fuster defines the basic units of cognitive representation as cognits, which are aspects of information based on perception and action that have been "associated with one another by learning or past experience" and composed of neural connections in the brain.[18] Cognits are formed according to the constraints of basic features of the primary sensory modalities and feedback from the environment. Cognits develop based on the Hebbian principle of association through the co-activation of neurons, which is a two-step process.[19]

First, a neuron is repeatedly temporally linked with another neuron such that the first neuron begins to facilitate activation in the second neuron. Secondly, some type of neural growth or cellular change occurs such that the firing of the first neuron is more likely to cause the firing of the second neuron. "Any two cells or systems of cells that are repeatedly active at the same time will tend to become "associated," so that activity in one facilitates activity in the other."[20] This association of neurons forms representations based on the experiences of the person, which develop and expand over time. Representations may be perceptual, motor, or other facets of cognition. Cognits are the mechanism behind the emergence of basic representations and ultimately demonstrate how rudimentary forms of representations combine to form more complex and abstract ones. Each cognit is part of a larger hierarchy of memory representation, which starts from rudimentary aspects of perception and motor activity and link together to form more complex representations.[21]

As networks of representations expand beyond the primary sensory areas there is more input from top-down constraints and complex, abstract representations.[22] Consequently, there is a cooperative process between bottom-up processes in the primary sensory modalities and the top-down environmental constraints instantiated through feedback. These processes work together with the top-down cognitive constraints of abstract forms of categorization in the form of representations. Much of this process is unconscious in that persons do not consciously direct the categorization of this type of information, yet the process is top-down in that the constraints of the network formed from earlier experiences of the person bind incoming information into existing categories.

Cognitive representations are arranged hierarchically and heterarchically according to the level of abstraction of the representation and are divided between

---

[18] Joaquín M. Fuster, *Cortex and Mind* (Oxford: Oxford University Press, 2003), 14.
[19] Donald O. Hebb, *The Organization of Behavior* (New York: Wiley, 1949).
[20] Ibid., 70.
[21] Fuster, *Cortex and Mind*, 60.
[22] Ibid., 51.

executive and perceptual categories.[23] Executive memory is the top-most level of representations associated with the motor hierarchy, located mainly in the frontal lobe. Executive memories include concepts, plans, and programs for action that provide top-down constraints on the enactment of motor actions.[24] Perceptual memory is the top-most level of representations associated with the sensory hierarchy located in the parietal lobe close to the division between the parietal and temporal lobes in Brodmann's area 39. Conceptual, semantic, and episodic representations provide top-down constraint on the lower-level sensory representations.

There is a two-way circular loop of connectivity between these two hierarchies that includes both top-down and bottom-up constraints. The prefrontal cortex and Brodman's area 39 are most likely the areas where the most complex and abstract information is processed, but the memories themselves are distributed throughout the cortex activating different areas depending on the context. An object may activate a representation at any level in the hierarchy.

> An object is represented at several hierarchical levels, from the sensory to the symbolic. The perception can activate its representation at any one of those levels. Under most circumstances, it will activate a heterarchical cognitive network that represents sensory as well as symbolic—that is, semantic—aspects of the object.[25]

Each cognit may be part of several different memories and may play different functional roles depending on the particular activated memory. Our past experiences and memories play a vital role in our current perceptions of the world, which are always "anchored in past experience."[26] So new perceptions rely on information processed and conceptualized in the past in order to classify and categorize current information. This neural architecture is the primary structure that enables the formation of beliefs. Religious beliefs are more abstract and theoretical than other basic forms of perception, but they rely on the same neural networks. These networks also serve as the basis of more advanced forms of cognition in terms of pursing goals and directing action.

Top-down Processing and Behavior Modulation

The coordinated activities of the executive and perceptual hierarchies function as networks of neural activation that enable the development of new representations and the initiation of action in the pursuit of particular goals. Different neural networks perform different functions for the organism; some networks, such as

---

[23] Ibid., 128.
[24] Ibid., 74.
[25] Ibid., 106.
[26] Ibid., 84.

those in the frontal lobe, are able to exert top-down control over other systems in the hierarchy. As Quartz argues, throughout human development there is an increase in both the usage and connection between frontal lobe structures and other areas of the brain, which forms a type of control structure.

> The hierarchical organization of the control structures that constitute the human cognitive architecture is apparent developmentally, with human cognition and behavior becoming increasingly mediated by frontal structures. ... Thus, behavior and cognition increasingly comes under the mediation of frontal structures from subcortical structures across development, a process sometimes referred to as frontalization of behavior.[27]

Fuster defines this as the "perception-action cycle" with both the perceptual and executive hierarchies playing an important role in the pursuit of a goal.

> Goal-directed behavior depends on the continuous operation of the cycle at several cortical levels simultaneously. ... More complex and novel behaviors will bring in the cortical areas of association. In the progression toward a goal, posterior and frontal cortices will engage with each other in the continuous and circular processing of mutually dependent signals and acts.[28]

Thus, goal-directed behavior not only involves the control structures of the frontal cortex, but also the perceptual and conceptual categories of the association cortex. Both work in tandem in processing cognitive representations of different goals in the modulation and execution of behavior.

An example of the control structures of the frontal cortex is provided by the work of Etinene Koechlin, Chrystele Ody, and Frederique Kouneiher who developed a model of cognitive control based on a hierarchical model of the frontal lobe.[29] Cognitive control, in this model, is defined as the connection between internal cognitive representations of conceptual goals and their influence on subsequent behavior. Cognitive control is accomplished through a cascade of processes in the frontal lobe that coordinate different aspects of control, including sensory, contextual, and episodic. By varying the demands of different tasks in an experiment, Koechlin and her colleagues were able to differentiate the different

---

[27] Steven R. Quartz, "Toward a Developmental Evolutionary Psychology: Genes, Development, and the Evolution of the Human Cognitive Architecture," in *Evolutionary Psychology: Alternative Approaches*, ed. Steven J. Scher and Frederick Rauscher (New York: Springer Publishing Co., 2002), 198.

[28] Fuster, *Cortex and Mind*, 108.

[29] Etienne Koechlin, Chrystele Ody, and Frederique Kouneiher, "The Architecture of Cognitive Control in the Human Prefrontal Cortex," *Science* 302, no. 5648 (2003): 1181-1185.

types of control that were active and the corresponding areas of the cortex.[30] Sensory control was involved in selecting actions that were directly related to the visual stimulus. Contextual control selected actions based on the current visual stimuli present in addition to the initial visual stimulus. Finally, episodic control selected actions based on past experiences in similar contexts and goals related to the initial visual stimulus.

An fMRI analysis of cortical activation indicated that different areas of the brain were active depending on what type of control was currently being used. Sensory control was correlated with higher activations in the lateral premotor cortex; contextual control was correlated with higher activations in the posterior section of the lateral prefrontal cortex; and episodic control was correlated with higher activations in the anterior section of the lateral prefrontal cortex. As Fuster argued, representations are hierarchically arranged according to the level of abstraction and it appears that control structures are organized in a similar fashion. The more complex representations involved in contextual and episodic control were able to have a top-down influence on the activation of different behaviors.

> We concluded that caudal LPFC regions select premotor representations associating stimulus and motor responses and mediating the selection of motor responses with respect to stimuli. In the task experiment, the effects of context and episode observed in premotor regions simply reflected the top-down control that caudal LPFC regions exert on premotor regions.[31]

Contextual control involves feedback in the identification of relevant aspects of the current scene, and episodic control is based on specific memories of the current scene and the processing of particular behavioral outputs. This research demonstrates that the frontal cortex contains structures used for different types of cognitive control based on the context. This research also suggests the possibility of defining these structures as a means of evaluation for determining potential actions for a person.

Donald McKay, in his book *Behind the Eye*, developed a theory of how persons interact in the world by using different means of evaluation.

> If you ask what we are, what it is about us that distinguishes us most from sticks and stones and other objects, and contemplate the various aspects of our conscious experience, I think that the core of the answer is that we have the capacity—indeed the necessity—to evaluate.[32]

McKay defined this ability as a "conditional readiness to reckon," which is the means by which we evaluate different potential goals, beliefs, and behaviors and

---

[30] Ibid., 1182.

[31] Ibid.

[32] Donald M. MacKay, *Behind the Eye*, ed. Valerie MacKay (Oxford: Blackwell, 1991), 143.

their consequences for implementation in the environment.[33] What differentiates human cognitive ability from other animals is the complexity by which humans are able to evaluate potential plans of action and the ability to use prior experience and learning in forming future behaviors. These are the types of cognitive and neural processes where beliefs could have a real effect on behavior.

Murphy and Brown argue that the structures studied by Koechlin and her colleagues are the neural systems humans use to reckon in the environment, which McKay defined as supervisory systems.[34] Agents modulate their behavior according to feedback loops between internal representations of plans for action and behavioral outputs. These structures are control hierarchies nested in supervisory systems, which modulate behavior based on complex and abstract forms of representations and goals.

> MacKay does not speculate as to what might be the various forms of comparisons and evaluations in the higher-level loops, but it is reasonable to presume that they would involve more complex memories, information distributed over longer epochs of time, and (at least in humans) more abstract forms of representations involving symbolic systems.[35]

This model suggests that the functional organization of cognition is structured according to these nested hierarchies. Cognitive systems designed for the basics of stimuli detection are nested within larger supervisory systems that are able to process information in terms of more abstract concepts and goals, which act as a top-down constraint on the processing of information.

The research conducted by Koechlin and colleagues supports this view that different forms of top-down control enable the processing of current contextual concerns in a particular situation as well as the relevant previous events and current goals. This shows the plausibility of contextual and episodic controls that are religious in nature and act as top-down constraints on the processing of a particular experience. Thus, a religious concept can act as a causal variable in certain situations that call upon past religious experiences and goals in the selection of particular representations relevant for acting in a religious way. Murphy and Brown suggested that supervisory systems are embedded in a nested control hierarchy. It is reasonable to argue that at least some of these control hierarchies may contain abstract religious concepts and beliefs that influence the interpretation of current events and provide plans for action based on religious concerns. However, an additional element is needed to understand the ways in which religious beliefs can affect goals and behavior. Human cognition

---

[33] Ibid, 112.
[34] Nancey Murphy and Warren S. Brown, *Did My Neurons Make Me Do It? Philosophical and Neurobiological Perspectives on Moral Responsibility and Free Will* (Oxford: Oxford University Press, 2007), 128.
[35] Ibid., 130.

is also highly dependent upon external resources that scaffold and extend the representational functions of an individual. One of the primary advancements in human cognition is the nesting of individual minds in larger cultural and social systems of information.

Cognition and External Scaffolding

Advanced forms of human cognition are dependent upon external structures for memory storage and our ability to dissipate reasoning tasks across several different types of cultural resources.

> The idea, in short, is that advanced cognition depends crucially on our abilities to dissipate reasoning: to diffuse achieved knowledge and practical wisdom through complex structures, and to reduce the loads on individual brains by locating those brains in complex webs of linguistic, social, political, and institutional constraints.[36]

Religious beliefs, as a form of cognition, are highly influenced by cultural structures such as churches, temples, mosques and the overall society in which persons are dynamically related to each other. Thus, religious beliefs are the product of the interactional properties of persons reasoning within a certain culture with a particular language that informs how events are conceptualized in their life and the actions they take because of that understanding.

Many cognitive tasks (both difficult and simple) rely on external resources in order to perform important operations. External institutions and social processes act as a type of *scaffold* that structures and provides external resources for more advanced forms of representation and reasoning.[37] The amazing part of human cognition is our use of external resources in order to simplify the amount of work our cognitive systems must perform. Consider the computational task of dividing 1235 by 43; most of us would need a piece of paper to work this problem out using long division. The paper functions as an external representation of the problem so that all of the numbers and calculations do not need to be remembered. The paper acts as a type of external memory in which certain aspects of the problem are stored and processed. Our internal computation relies on different semantic information about how to perform long division, certain basic properties of addition and subtraction ($7 + 5 = 12$, $12 - 6 = 6$, etc.), and on procedural memories for writing out the answer. We learn the relevant information (memorizing addition tables), and then learn the techniques for externalizing that information in order to perform the mathematical task.

---

[36] Andy Clark, *Being There: Putting Brain, Body, and World Together Again* (Cambridge: The MIT Press, 1997), 180.

[37] Ibid., 187.

An even better example is a calculator. Once it was recognized that there were certain regularities in mathematical computation, it was possible to construct a device that could perform those operations quickly and correctly. Many types of advanced mathematics rely on some type of calculator or more advanced computational technology. Cognitive abilities rely on external information and structures to decrease the cognitive load on individual minds and increase the possibilities for different forms of cognition.

> The basic form of individual reason (fast pattern completion in multiple neural systems) is common throughout nature and that where we human beings really score is in our amazing capacities to create and maintain a variety of special external structures (symbolic and social-institutional). These external structures function so as to complement our individual cognitive profiles and to diffuse human reason across wider and wider social and physical networks whose collective computation exhibit their own special dynamics and properties.[38]

Persons are not solitary particles that perform cognitive tasks as individual rational deliberators; instead persons are embedded in a rich social fabric of systemic relations among persons, cultures, and external information.[39]

In order to perform several different cognitive acts, there are several types of external prompts that reduce the load on individual minds, including books, computers, and especially other persons.

> Context-sensitive constraints established by positive feedback weave both the environment and history into the agent's cognitive and conative states, thereby achieving the embeddedness in space and time that characterizes those complex systems.[40]

Religious beliefs are not just a product of isolated individual minds, but actively incorporate aspects of the environment to perform cognitive tasks. Thus, religious beliefs are not simply internal cognitive representations; aspects of religious belief are part of the external networks of religious cultural information. Religious beliefs are partially determined by the cognitive scaffolding provided by religious institutions and communities. This allows persons to go beyond the representations in their own minds and exploit all the information that lies outside it, which would include religious doctrines, cooperative patterns within a religious community, and specific rituals performed by the community. The environment is an extension of individual cognition; it is very difficult to draw

---

[38] Ibid., 179.

[39] Alicia Juarrero, *Dynamics in Action: Intentional Behavior as a Complex System* (Cambridge: The MIT Press, 1999), 197.

[40] Ibid.

a definitive boundary between individual minds and the environments in which they are embedded.

Recall the theological incorrectness hypothesis, discussed earlier, which states that persons do not use abstract theological doctrines in their everyday processing of religious information.

> Even when humans employ religious concepts, the religious concepts they generate might be more consistent with folk knowledge than with official theology. Sorry, clergy, but theological ideas simply do not determine, per se, how or what people think.[41]

According to the theory of cognitive scaffolding, this would indeed be true, since many aspects of cognition may not be inside the person, but rather contained in the scaffolding. However, everyday processing may not use abstract theology, yet still be theologically *correct*. For example, in the everyday use of statistics, most researchers are not able to give abstract mathematical proofs for the usage of a specific statistic in a research project. In fact, most researchers use SPSS or some other type of computer program to perform statistical calculations. This involves simply inputting the numbers and using a mouse to click on the specified statistic (i.e. ANOVA, t-test, etc.).This obviously does not make this cognition *statistically* incorrect, but simply shows that in everyday cognition we rely on simpler cognitive behavioral outputs to achieve the ends specified by more abstract mathematical proofs.

Similarly, in everyday cognition, religious believers do not use abstract theological treatises to direct their behavior, but rely on simpler cognitive behavioral outputs to achieve the directives of a particular doctrine. So the "outpouring of God's everlasting love through the atoning sacrifice of Jesus Christ's death upon the cross ushering in the *parousia* of God's kingdom on Earth" is highly abstract and doctrinal, but living out this doctrine through selfless acts of love like feeding the poor is cognitively simpler, yet theologically correct. The theological incorrectness hypothesis is helpful in that it shows that religious believers do not simply download abstract religious doctrines through preaching for use in life. On the other hand, the two poles of the thesis (intuitive constraints vs. religious doctrines) leaves out a considerable amount of cognitive and behavioral processes involved in the formation of religious beliefs and the role of those beliefs in different behaviors.

Beliefs as Causes

Humans and most other organisms are uniquely interdependent on their environments, which plays an important role in the development of different

---

[41] Slone, *Theological Incorrectness*, 66.

cognitive strategies to perceive and act in the world. For human cognitive systems, there is no need to keep detailed, complete, representational maps of the world because that amount of information would simply overload human cognition unnecessarily.

> The idea is that we reduce the information-processing load by sensitizing the system to particular aspects of the world—aspects that have special significance because of the environmental niche the system inhabits.[42]

Several studies suggest that humans are blind to different changes that occur in the perceptual environment.[43] Change blindness studies investigate human perceptual awareness of different aspects of the environment, especially when the environment changes. One experiment investigated the amount of perceptual information that was retained while giving directions to a stranger. As an experimenter was giving directions to a participant, other experimenters would (quite rudely) walk between the stranger and the person giving directions and the stranger would be replaced with a *different* person. Sometimes the person would be different, other times the person would be dressed different, as in changing from a construction worker to a businessman.

The interesting part of this study was how often persons did not notice the change, they would simply continue giving directions to an entirely new person. During normal perception, many of the details of the environment are not encoded in detail.[44] Thus, perception is a temporally distributed property involving active perceptual feedback from the environment, which enables the processing of different events.

> One way to put this point is that *what we see* is not the value of a function over isolated fixations; it is, rather, the result of a temporally extended process of *looking*.[45]

This is ultimately the way in which we must understand how beliefs function as causes, not as a property of the brain or isolated fixations of brain processes, but as a temporally extended process of using past information for making decisions about current actions in the world.

Nancey Murphy and Warren Brown define mental events as "contextualized brain events" in that the representational properties of a particular neural state

---

[42] Clark, *Being There*, 24.

[43] For a detailed review see H. Intraub, "The representation of visual scenes" (*Trends in Cognitive Sciences*, 1(6), 1997), 217–221; D. J. Simons and D. T. Levin, "Change Blindness" (*Trends in Cognitive Sciences*, 1(7), 1997), 261–267.

[44] Alva Noë, Luiz Pessoa, and Evan Thompson, "Beyond the Grand Illusion: What Change Blindness Really Teaches Us About Vision" (*Visual Cognition*, 2000, 7), 93–106.

[45] Ibid., 102.

can only be determined by identifying the relevant contextual or environmental factors that constitute its role in directing behavior.[46]

> Mental events can best be understood in terms of their relations to states of affairs in the environment (or the organism itself) that are relevant for redirecting the organism's behavior. Mental events are not reducible to brain events, because mental events are largely constituted by relations to action in the environment.[47]

Understanding the role of a belief can only be determined by understanding the cultural and environmental context in which it is embedded. Beliefs do not determine actions in the moment, which is usually accomplished by lower-level neural systems trained to automatically react to different situations, but beliefs link persons to a larger cultural context and narrative that explains the relevance of different actions and behaviors.

A simple thermostat serves as a helpful analogy. Thermostats regulate the heat in a room by monitoring the current temperature based on the contraction or expansion of an internal metal coil. Based on molecular properties of the metal coil, the temperature in the room causes its changes in state, which will trigger the heater when the temperature gets below a certain threshold. However, the thermostats informational or representational properties (i.e. "too cold") can only be ascertained based on its participation in a larger informational context.[48] Physics can describe why the coil contracts or expands, but the functional properties of the thermostat can only be understood based on its role in heating a room for some purpose. Thus, the properties of design, function, or purpose can only be understood by a higher-level explanation of the thermostat's role in reaching some goal. This type of explanation is not in opposition to the explanation from physics, but serves a different role in providing an account of the other functional properties of a thermostat.

Applying this analogy to religious beliefs, neuroscience and cognitive science provide explanations for different aspects of religious beliefs. Neuroscience explains different aspects of neural and brain processes involved in the formation of religious beliefs. Cognitive science identifies basic properties of human cognitive functioning that may constrain aspects of religious beliefs and identifies some of the functional properties as well. Yet, there are also aspects of religious beliefs that must be understood in relation to the role they play in a larger cultural context as a causal factor in modulating behavior. At the very least, the only way a belief can be identified as "religious" is according to its participation in a larger informational and narrative context that cannot be described by neuroscience or cognitive science.

Beliefs are a higher-level description of cognitive and neural events, which involve a host of additional causal and contextual factors. Beliefs are not simply occurrences of internal cognitive activity, but are intrinsically connected to the

---

[46] Murphy and Brown, *Did My Neurons*, 195.
[47] Ibid., 209.
[48] Ibid., 196.

contexts in which they are utilized. Following the work of Fred Dretske, beliefs can be defined as *structuring* rather than *triggering* causes. Using the analogy of a bomb maker and the detonation of a bomb, Dretske illustrates the distinction between these two types of causes.

> A terrorist plants a bomb in a general's car. The bomb sits there for days until the general gets in his car and turns the key. ... The bomb is detonated (triggered) by turning the key in the ignition and the general is killed.[49]

Turning the key is the triggering mechanism that kills the general, but the bomb maker is ultimately responsible for creating the structure or condition under which this particular series of events will lead to the death of the general. Thus, beliefs are the structuring causes that facilitate the conditions under which particular cognitive and neural states will realize some religious goal or value.

Religious beliefs are not always a structuring cause in behavior. Many times persons believe they are acting for one reason, but another reason may be operating, often times unconsciously, under the surface. Sometimes persons are unaware of conflicting reasons or actively ignore or repress other motivations for actions. However, this does not negate the role of all religious beliefs in forming behavior and actions and structuring causes provide us a helpful definition of how those beliefs may function as a cause.

Consequently, religious beliefs are extended across brain, environment, culture, and time; religious beliefs are connected to larger systems of meaning and narrative; our cultural institutions, language systems, and norms actually structure and situate our beliefs enabling the possibility of religiously motivated actions. However, understanding religious beliefs as a top-down constraint requires additional resources. Top-down constraints and the idea of top-down causation is a hotly debated philosophical topic, yet it is possible to bring together philosophical and scientific evidence to clarify the role of top-down constraints in theological reasoning.

Philosophical Issues

Top-down or downward causation is a type of causation by which a pattern or systemic configuration constrains component parts. According to Deacon, this is one of the defining characteristics of emergence.

> The existence and relative autonomy of higher-order ensemble properties of systems and of a kind of top-down influence over the properties and dynamics

---

[49] Fred Dretske, "Mental Events as Structuring Causes of Behavior," in *Mental Causation*, ed. John Heil and Alfred Mele (Oxford: Clarendon Press, 1995), 122-123.

of system constituents remains both the key defining character and the most criticized claim of arguments for emergence.[50]

An emergent explanation gives an account of how higher-order properties may "drag along" constituent parts by their participation in systemic configurations.[51] Thus, the particular pattern of configuration exhibits a causal effect on the behavior of the system as a whole. In this section, I shall discuss some of the pertinent philosophical issues involved in understanding top-down constraints, followed by a description of top-down processes involved in human cognition and theological reasoning.

It is important to avoid certain forms of dualism in defining top-down constraints; these constraints do not indicate the effort of a separate entity or substance at work in the causal functions of a cognitive system. Rather, top-down constraint is a term used to specify properties of the cognitive system that limit aspects of human perception. This occurs through *selection* rather than *alteration* of the underlying physical laws and properties of the brain. Top-down constraint is a helpful amendment to the modern understanding of causation that emphasized efficient causes at the expense of systemic and configurational constraints. Recurrent neural networks are a key innovation in computational modeling that emulates cognitive functions. These types of systemic and configurational constraints act as attractor states and constrain the overall organization of neural patterns of information.

Historical Factors

The problem of defining top-down causation is partially based on assumptions about the general nature of causation developed during modernity. In ancient philosophy, Aristotle categorized causation according to four different types: material, formal, efficient, and final.[52] However, the rise of modern science was primarily based on the Newtonian view of a mechanistic universe. This view limited causal explanation to efficient causation and discounted the role material, formal, and final causation.[53] Scientific explanations defined causation as a chain of actions and reactions, A causes B causes C and so on. In 1932, Roy Wood Sellars argued that this conception of causation was similar to describing the components of the universe as "microscopic billiard balls" colliding with one

---

[50] Terrence Deacon, "Three Levels of Emergent Phenomena," in *Evolution & Emergence: Systems, Organisms, Persons*, ed. Nancey Murphy and William R. Stoeger, SJ (Oxford: Oxford University Press, 2007), 94.

[51] Murphy and Brown, *Did My Neurons?*, 80.

[52] Michael V. Wedin, "Aristotle," in *The Cambridge Dictionary of Philosophy*, ed. Robert Audi (Cambridge: Cambridge University Press, 1999).

[53] Juarrero, *Dynamics in Action*, 21.

another and causing each other to move.[54] Yet billiard balls are independent of one another and only move by bumping into each other. This view conceptualizes natural systems as composed of independent parts, rather than reflecting the many layers of interdependency and mutuality that occur in natural phenomena.

This definition of causation reinforces a causally reductionistic framework in that the actual cause of a particular phenomenon must be found by looking for cause A in a linear procession of causes, not how A, B and C interact. By neglecting Aristotle's notion of a formal cause, in terms of the pattern or structure of the whole (macrostructure) that constrains the functions of component parts (microstructure), an important element of causal explanation has been lost. This is complicated by the relationship between Aristotle's classification of causation and the hylomorphic view of matter and form. The form or essence of something was correctly rejected on metaphysical grounds because forms as something that is a separate substance from matter makes little sense in the contemporary scientific worldview. Yet, is it possible to postulate the existence of a type of cause similar to a formal cause without the corresponding ontological baggage?

Alicia Juarrero argues that a new understanding of causation must be developed to account for the recursive relationship among organisms, their environment, and the past "to account for the way organisms simultaneously participate in and shape the contextual niche in which they are situated, and to which their dispositions are attuned and respond.[55]" Thus, proponents of top-down causation argue in favor of modifying the existing understanding of causation with the addition of top-down constraints. It is a different type of causation than efficient causation but necessary to accurately explain different types of events, especially those involved in cognitive processes. This type of causation looks at the systemic interactions of several components and how their structure affects the eventual probability of particular actions.

Based on systems theory and nonequilibrium theromodynamics, Juarrero argues that our understanding of causation needs to include an account of "interlevel causality" where a whole acts as a constraint upon its constituent parts.[56] This type of causation works by limiting the degrees of freedom of the constituent parts. Once a system has self-organized into a particular configuration the possibility of the constituent parts operating in a way that is inconsistent with the overall configuration becomes highly unlikely.

> Top-down constraints that wholes exert on their components are inhibiting, selectionist constraints. ... The constraints that wholes impose on their parts are

---

[54] Roy Wood Sellars, *Philosophy of Physical Realism* (New York: Macmillian, 1932), 5.
[55] Juarrero, *Dynamics in Action*, 75.
[56] Ibid., 128.

restrictive insofar as they reduce the number of ways in which the parts can be arranged, and conservative in the sense that they are in the service of the whole.[57]

The degrees of freedom for the operation of the constituent parts is now limited based on the overall configuration. This is the way in which top-down causation works, as a constraint.

Michael Silberstein and John McGeever argue that causal properties are an important part of a definition of emergence, which was discussed in Chapter 2. An ontological definition of emergence is based on the causal properties of the whole.

> By this we mean features of systems or wholes that possess causal capacities not reducible to any of the intrinsic causal capacities of the parts, nor to any of the (reducible) relations between the parts. Emergent properties are properties of the system taken as a whole which exert a causal influence on the parts of the system consistent with, but distinct from, the causal capacities of the parts themselves.[58]

This is not to indicate a new type of ontological entity, but simply to state that different systems or levels of complexity within an entity contain new types of causal powers that exert an influence different from the influence that the constituent parts are able to exert in isolation, a different level of causal complexity in the same entity.

These systems are able to exert a causal influence on the overall cognitive system through affecting the likely activation of constituent parts.

> Such patterns can affect which causal powers of their constituents are activated or likely to be activated. A given physical constituent may have many causal powers, but only some subset of them will be active in a given situation. The larger context (i.e. the pattern) of which it is a part may affect which of its causal powers get activated. ... Thus the whole is not any simple function of its parts, since the whole at least partially determines what contributions are made by its parts.[59]

In this sense, the higher-order pattern, which is active during top-down causation, does not violate the lower-level laws of neural or brain functioning at work, but *selects* the particular attributes of a constituent part and confines its use within a pattern established at a higher-level of complexity.[60]

---

[57] Ibid., 144.

[58] Michael Silberstein and John McGeever, "The Search for Ontological Emergence," *Philosophical Quarterly* 49 (1999): 182.

[59] Robert Van Gulick, "Who's in Charge Here? And Who's Doing All the Work?," in *Mental Causation*, ed. John Heil and Alfred Mele (Oxford: Clarendon, 1995), 251.

[60] Ibid., 252.

Computational Modeling and Top-down Processing

One of the major breakthroughs in understanding cognition is the use of computer modeling to replicate cognitive functions. Artificial computer simulations emulate neurons and neural networks to test the similarity of computational systems to human cognition.

Computational modeling illustrates the three aspects of emergence covered in Chapter 2: initial conditions, feedback, and pattern formation. A closer look at artificial neural networks also demonstrates some of the important properties of top-down constraints. In these networks the basic units are computational processing units that try to emulate neurons. A simple model contains units that are either on or off depending on the input. A more complex model may contain units that fire as neurons do with varying output frequencies, on a range from one to ten, with one being the lowest or least activated and ten being the highest or most activated. Each of the basic units obey simple rules, so the real work of the net occurs through the coordinated activation of several units working together, which creates a pattern of activation.

A network contains three layers of processing units. The first layer is the input layer, which receives the initial training according to the original input. In the second layer, a pattern of activation emerges in the hidden units of the system that embodies the training according to the informational input. The third layer is the output units, which encode the overall response of the system according to a particular vector.[61] The feedback or input from the environment changes and modifies the overall pattern contained within the neural network. Once the network has been trained, the pattern acts as a type of representation that can be used to identify inputs that match the original information that was learned by the network. Facial information processing and emotion information processing show the way in which a particular pattern can emerge in a computational network.

Facial Information Processing

Computational modeling has been able to simulate certain aspects of cognition using artificial neural networks. One interesting program is called Facenet, which encodes different face pictures and discriminates or categorizes those same faces through artificial computation.[62] For Facenet, the input of the face is through a 64 x 64 pixel grid, which can differentiate between 256 shades of brightness. This

---

[61] Paul M. Churchland, *The Engine of Reason, the Seat of the Soul: A Philosophical Journey into the Brain* (Cambridge: The MIT Press, 1996), 55.

[62] See Patricia Churchland, *Brain-Wise: Studies in Neurophilosophy* (Cambridge: MIT Press, 2002); G. W. Cottrell, "Extracting Features from Faces Using Compression Networks: Face, Identity, Emotions, and Gender Recognition Using Holons," in *Connectionists Models: Proceedings of the 1990 Summer School*, ed. D. Touretzky et al. (San Mateo: Morgan Kauffman, 1991).

is a very simple model of visual perception. The human eye uses several different types of cells within the retina that encode several different aspects of the visual world: light/dark, color, movement etc. The grid was presented with 64 different black and white photographs of 11 people as well as 13 photos of non-face objects.

In this type of network, the process of representing faces uses vector coding, which "depends on the idea that features are represented in specific patterns of activity in a population of units."[63] Thus, a vector represents a pattern of activation in a four-dimensional computational space. For each picture, the pixel grid identifies different levels of light per pixel and places that particular pattern of activation in a vector space that represents that face. Each pixel has a particular level of activation, which represents the amount of lightness or darkness that a particular pixel was able to detect. The pattern is the particular activation of the network according to the input of a face. The vector space is considered layer two of the network and represents the particular activation for that face in comparison to the activation of other faces and non-faces.

> Each input unit projects a radiating set of "axonal" end branches to each and every one of the 80 units in the second layer, and this layer maps an abstract space of 80 dimensions (a dimension for each unit) in which the input faces are explicitly coded. (A two- or three- dimensional space is readily understood; now just think of adding axes.)[64]

So the face is represented in an abstract space according to different dimensions along several different axes. Back propagation, a training algorithm, is able to repeatedly adjust the configuration according to errors to match the correct one.

After training, the network will then transform these particular inputs into output vectors that identify the faces, genders, and names of the pictures. The program was able to identify faces according to these criteria 100 percent of the time after it was trained. It was also able to identify the same faces when they were turned to the side 98 percent of the time or partially blocked by a black bar. Even more impressive, it was also able to discriminate between faces and non-faces and specific genders of novel pictures that were presented to the network. So not only was it able to categorize certain visual inputs, but it was also able to generalize that information to other domains. It appears that the network was able to discriminate between faces by developing a "holon" or general face that represented the common aspects of faces in general.[65] Each face was then placed in a vector space according to how much it differed from the holon face along various dimensions.

---

[63] Churchland, *Brain-wise*, 290.
[64] Ibid., 295.
[65] Ibid., 298.

Emotional Information Processing

Mathew Dailey, Garrison Cottrell, Curtis Padgett, and Ralph Adolphs developed a program called EMPATH to discriminate between different types of facial expressions of emotion.[66] The program was similar to Facenet in that the program used "holons" to help categorize different facial expressions, yet contained four layers (input, perceptual, gestalt, and category) rather than three. After training, the network was able to discriminate facial expressions at a similar accuracy level to that of humans. Humans tend to have little difficulty identifying happy faces, but more problems identifying fearful faces. The network also reflected this same difficulty with fearful faces and it was postulated that this is because fearful faces are more difficult to discriminate because they are similar to other facial expressions. What is interesting about these models is that the processing outcome is not pre-specified by initial conditions of the network prior to training. Rather, the network builds up and self-organizes over time and learns by having a few initial parameters and then allowing the network to build connection strengths through training.

The neural networks such as EMPATH and Facenet show how a particular cognitive function may emerge. These models demonstrate an important innovation in computational models, the concept of parallel distributed processing (PDP).[67] This type of processing suggests that several different computational nodes process information in parallel with one another. Information travels at a much faster rate distributed across several different nodes in a pattern of activation. Earlier models of cognition were based on serial processing, where the information travels from one process to another in a step-wise fashion. PDP processing shows how cognition functions in terms of several components working in parallel with each other. The important difference between serial and PDP processing is that more than one channel is communicating information; the information is distributed among many channels which encode the message. This closely mirrors the vast networks of neural wiring in the brain and the various brain systems involved in processing information.

Once the network is able to embody a pattern, either faces or emotional expressions, the particular configuration can be stored as a representation for identifying future inputs. This same information can be generalized to other domains to identify novel types of stimuli. Interestingly, in the case of EMPATH, the network is able to identify emotions almost as well as humans do. These feedforward networks are highly functional and show that pre-programmed responses are not necessary for the emergence of highly effective abilities

---

[66] M. N. Dailey and others, "Empath: A Neural Network That Categorizes Facial Expressions," *Journal of Cognitive Neuroscience* 14, no. 8 (2002): 1158-1173.

[67] D. E. Rumelhart, J. L. McClelland, and PDP Research Group, *Parallel Distributed Processing: Explorations in the Microstructure of Cognition*, 2 vols. (Cambridge: The MIT Press, 1986).

similar to human cognition. Feedforward networks illustrate the way in which a neural network may embody information in a type of representation, but what really differentiates human cognition is its ability to take previously processed information and feed it back into the original inputs of the network. These systems are called recurrent networks and they help to illustrate the possibility of top-down constraints in cognitive networks.

Recurrent Neural Networks

The neural network models discussed previously were feedforward models. Although they were able to embody informational patterns, they still lacked certain features of human neural networks necessary to describe cognition. Human neural networks not only contain feedforward connections, but also recurrent connections. These connections take informational patterns that have already been processed and send it to earlier stages of the network, forming a type of short-term memory. Consequently, these models use recently processed information to influence current processing, which forms feedback loops in the architecture of the computational structure. The computational models discussed earlier (EMPATH and Facenet) were feedforward models, but the human brain is much more complex and interconnected than these models.

In the human brain, most feedforward systems are complemented by recurrent connections. Both ascending and descending connections are located throughout the brain, reciprocally linking various areas of the brain with each other. In recurrent networks the information embodied in a particular pattern is sent to earlier stages of the network providing a feedback loop within the network itself.

> Since a recurrent axon originates in a cell farther along in the pipeline, a descending or recurrent pathway therefore makes information about the network's past activity available for current processing, specifically, at the layer of neurons where the descending pathway touches down for a landing.[68]

One of the primary design features of the human brain is the interconnectivity of different areas of the brain. The recurrent features of the human brain enable the autopoietic character of neural systems, which self-organize according to feedback loops in the environment and recurrent loops within the network itself. The information contained in these emergent patterns is dynamic and sensitive to the contextual constraints external to the pattern of activation and in the pattern itself.

---

[68] Churchland, *Engine of Reason*, 100.

Attractors and Pattern Completion

The human brain is a massively interconnected information processor with millions upon millions of recurrent connections. As the network is trained through the interplay of genetic instructions, experience, cultural information, and other mental representations, recurrent connections enable the autopoietic character of the patterns of neural activations to emerge. Alicia Juarrero argues that when a network begins to develop it is far from equilibrium, but through the dynamic interplay of neural activation and updates from within and outside the system, it settles into attractor states.

> The output of recurrent networks, on the other hand, is dynamic: these networks create attractors—they settle gradually into a characteristic pattern. ... because they embody constrained pathways within the state space, attractors provide evidence of self-organized subregions of that space. ... feedback takes the network far from equilibrium. In response, the connection weights in a recurrent network's hidden layer can recalibrate and self-organize.[69]

These states act as a recurring pattern, which constrains the future states of the overall system.

> Finding oneself within a basin of attraction means that one's future behavior will be constrained by that attractor—that is, directed and channeled by the contour of its valley (by its dynamics) thereby increasing the likelihood of being drawn in one direction rather than another.[70]

The simplest example of an attractor is a pendulum. The pendulum swings back and forth, but the attractor (the work of gravity) will consistently bring the pendulum to a stop.[71] An external force is required to dislodge the pendulum from its attractor state. Other types of attractors are able to embody and sustain greater fluctuations. These types of attractors are known as chaotic or strange attractors because they are complex and allow a considerable amount of disorder so that an overall picture of organization is difficult to discern. Although the different states of these systems are allowed to fluctuate, the particular basins of attraction still constrain possible alternatives. The fluctuation in possible attractor states suggests that attractor states may be multiply realizable. Thus, similar global states may be achieved by different overall arrangements within the system.

One of the interesting properties of recurrent networks and attractors is vector or pattern completion, which occurs when an input is partial or incomplete. The network is able to generalize to a best guess based on what

---

[69] Juarrero, *Dynamics in Action*, 166.
[70] Ibid., 153.
[71] Ibid., 152.

was previously learned. The recurrent connections identify the partial data and relate it to other attractor states instantiated in neural patterns of information that have already been configured. In terms of cognition, there are many examples of ambiguous figures that are identified according to different patterns of perceptual interpretation. Figure 3.2 is an example:

Figure 3.2   Old/young woman

Is this a picture of a young or old woman? The picture actually allows for two different interpretations, either a young woman seen from the side or an old woman hunched over with a large nose. The visual processing of the different elements of the picture (i.e. lines, shapes, blackness, empty space) is the same, but it is how the whole picture is organized according to an overall pattern that enables the multiple perceptions of the same picture. One pattern of activation can act as an attractor state that forms the elements into a picture of an old woman, while another attractor state may arrange the elements in a different way. Depending on which features are linked with a particular attractor state, the ambiguous picture can be identified in two ways. Often the picture will jump back and forth between the two interpretations. Recurrent connections allow higher levels of visual abstraction or categories to identify the two possible interpretations. The raw sensory data of the picture is constrained by more abstract forms of categorization, which could be visual or even semantic. Thus, different types of cognitive information constrain the possible interpretations of perceptual content. This type of constraint is top-down and not dependent upon the visual scene itself, but the use of higher levels of abstract categories of object recognition in order to bring the ambiguous figure into focus.

Another example of this phenomenon is the ability to perceive form from motion.[72] Gunnar Johannson dressed up actors in black clothing and attached lights to several points on their bodies: elbows, knees, hands, etc. He then made movies of them doing various actions such as running, jumping, and kicking in a dark room so that only the attached lights could be seen. Even though the test subjects could only see the lights in the films, they could readily identify the actions the actors were performing. Consequently, the persons were able to identify the form of a particular human action through the motion of nonhuman identifiers, which in this case were lights. E. D. Grossman and R. Blake used this study to find a specific region in the brain (posterior temporal sulcus) that was activated during this process.[73] When subjects were shown a random association of lights, this brain region was not activated.

This study and the ambiguous pictures suggest that cognition is dependent upon higher-level complex conceptual representations to interpret incoming stimuli in meaningful ways. Conceptual representations act as attractor states that constrain the interpretation of visual information. In this case, a conception of human action is used to understand an arrangement of lights. This conception was developed through many experiences of watching persons perform actions in the environment and developing a concept of kicking to understand this particular motion. Top-down cognitive constraints use larger conceptual systems, contained in emergent neural patterns, to categorize incoming stimuli. These patterns act as attractor states to provide structure and organization to our interpretation of the world. We do not simply interpret incoming stimuli as it is, but through our own grid of experiences, beliefs, and conceptions.

---

[72] Gunnar Johansson, "Visual Perception of Biological Motion and a Model for Its Analysis," *Perception and Psychophysics* 14 (1973): 201-211.

[73] E. D. Grossman and R. Blake, "Brain Activity Evoked by Inverted and Imagined Biological Motion," *Vision Research* 41 (2001): 1475-1482; E. D. Grossman and others, "Brain Areas Involved in Perception of Biological Motion," *Journal of Cognitive Neuroscience* 12 (2000): 711-720.

Theology as Pattern Completion

Recurrent neural networks and pattern completion make it possible to develop different perceptions of an ambiguous figure. The same types of cognitive principles can also be applied to scientific reasoning and theological reasoning. Paul Churchland uses the example of different theories of planetary movement to describe the application of pattern completion to general reasoning abilities.[74] Throughout history, different philosophers and scientists interpreted astrological and planetary data in various ways depending on current scientific theories, historical context, philosophical analysis, and religious belief. Aristotle conceived of planetary motion in terms of a giant rotating sphere, while Reńe Descartes used the idea of a vortex to explain how the planets move.

Newton's theory used the concept of gravity to conceive of planetary motion in terms of falling objects; while Einstein developed an entirely different concept based on geodesic paths and considered the force of gravity an illusion. For each theory, particular inputs are manipulated recurrently until a coherent perception can be found that unites the information into a meaningful whole. There are obviously certain inputs that may not fully cohere in the whole, but the overall pattern completion attempts to organize the larger body of information. Recurrent networks feed different types of information back into the original inputs in order to organize a group of ambiguous inputs.

Theology functions in a similar way. Like a scientific theory, theological and religious theories attempt to organize a vast number of events, experiences, and narratives into a meaningful whole. Theological theories draw upon the history of a religious tradition, sacred scriptures, and religious experiences to provide an overall interpretation or picture of an uncertain world. These theories are developed through the process of pattern completion, similar to the perception of ambiguous figures, but drawing on a significantly larger body of data. Theology emerges in response to experience, cultural information and a vast array of mental representations.

Theology contains an important theoretical component, which is evident in the history of different perspectives in systematic theology. The theology and doctrines of the Christian church have changed throughout the centuries, which is similar to the way in which cosmological theories have developed and changed from Aristotle to Einstein. Nancey Murphy argues that theology is similar to a scientific theory, which uses data (religious experience, work of the Holy Spirit) interpreted by doctrines and judged as either progressive or degenerate according to a Lakatosian framework.[75] Stanley J. Grenz argues that there are three sources or norms for theology:

---

[74] Churchland, *Engine of Reason*, 114-121.

[75] Nancey Murphy, *Theology in the Age of Scientific Reasoning* (Ithaca: Cornell University Press, 1990).

The three sources or norms for theology are the biblical message, the theological heritage of the church, and the thought forms of the historical cultural context in which the contemporary people of God seek to speak, live, and act.[76]

The connections among these three sources are not self-evident. Theology requires certain types of theories to make connections between church history, biblical message, and individual experiences to bring these different types of information together. Biblical study alone has gone through several methods and interpretive frameworks, including the historical-critical method and, more recently, narrative methods.[77]

Theological reasoning is dependent upon the same cognitive structures used in everyday reasoning; no special areas of the brain are activated. Different types of theological activity will be dependent upon the theological imagination of the theologian and his or her community. Certainly, different types of theological activity (religious experience, doctrinal theories, bible study) will look different depending on the specific task. This reflects the different areas of the brain and the various ways in which information is processed. Thus, there are several different types of cognitive processes that interpret information and unfold through experience.

> Suppose also that the internal character of each of these representational spaces is not fixed by some prior decree, either divine or genetic, but is rather shaped by the extended experience of the developing animal, to reflect the peculiar empirical environment and practical needs that it encounters, and the peculiar learning procedures embodied in the brain's ongoing business of synaptic modification. These internal spaces may be plastic in varying degrees, and may hold out the promise of an enormous range of conceptual and perceptual possibilities.[78]

Theological reasoning is emergent to the extent that it develops over time through learning and experience. Although certain aspects of the structure of human cognition constrain aspects of theology, much of it is still an open process dependent upon individual reasoning and the constraints of culture for its development.

---

[76] Stanley J. Grenz, *Theology for the Community of God* (Grand Rapids and Vancouver: Wm. B. Eerdmans and Regent College, 2000), 16.

[77] Janice C. Anderson and Stephen D. Moore, eds., *Mark and Method: New Approaches in Biblical Studies* (Minneapolis: Fortress Press, 2008); Edgar Krentz, *The Historical-Critical Method* (Eugene: Wipf and Stock, 2002).

[78] Paul M. Churchland, *Neurophilosophy at Work* (New York: Cambridge University Press, 2007), xii.

Conclusion

The theological incorrectness hypothesis suggests that the professed beliefs of religious believers are not the actual beliefs that determine most of their daily thoughts and actions. Although this hypothesis is correct to the extent that persons do not always accurately comprehend the causes of their behavior, other areas of research in cognitive neuroscience provide a plausible model for how beliefs can have an effect on planning, goals, and behavior. Top-down processing demonstrates the role of larger abstract and conceptual constraints in the processing of incoming information. The architecture of the neural systems that embody different types of beliefs relies on different types of top-down constraints, which may be either perceptual or contextual. Through the processes of feedback and active exploration of the environment, supervisory systems position human persons to reckon with their environment according to different types of belief systems. Beliefs are partially constituted by the external forms of memory contained in the cognitive scaffolding provided by cultures, institutions, and other mediums. Beliefs can only be identified as causes according to their role in a larger context, which can provide a structuring top-down constraint on different forms of behavior.

In addition to religious beliefs, top-down constraints also play a role in general forms of theological reasoning. Top-down constraints expand the definition of causation to include the role of systemic structures in certain types of cognitive functions. Computational modeling demonstrates how top-down constraints, in the form of recurrent connections, can affect current cognitive processing of relevant material. Over time, cognitive networks can settle into attractor states, which constrain the representational possibilities within the network. When an object of perception has several different types of possible interpretations, abstract conceptual information is used to interpret the ambiguous object. Theology functions in a similar way, by organizing a large set of multiple forms of information (i.e. experiences, history, scripture, tradition) into a meaningful whole.

Chapter 4
Evolutionary Psychology and the Emergence of the Symbolic Mind

One of the primary components of the standard model in the cognitive science of religion is evolutionary psychology. As a relatively new field in cognitive science, evolutionary psychology has greatly contributed to our understanding of human nature including sexuality, morality, and cooperation. Evolutionary psychology draws from the rich amount of knowledge on evolutionary anthropology to describe different features of contemporary human psychology. However, the cognitive modules identified by this field are not the only important evolutionary changes that have occurred in the formation of human cognition. Symbolic processing plays an important role in the development of human cognition and is the result of several co-evolutionary changes in both the human brain and culture. The nature of symbolic representation is an important aspect of religious cognition and understanding its evolutionary roots in human cognition will greatly contribute to our depiction of religious beliefs.

As discussed in earlier chapters, several factors involved in the formation of cognitive representations are based on emergent and top-down processes. The feedback mechanisms and top-down behavioral modulation suggest an emergent view of cognition in the formation of religious concepts. Aspects of the standard model in the cognitive science of religion presume that cognition functions primarily in a causally reductive fashion from cognitive adaptations to religious concepts. As an alternative, I argue that several emergent and top-down factors are involved in the evolution of human cognition, in particular, the emergence of the *symbolic* mind. The emergence of symbolic representation is a co-evolutionary process involving changes in the structures of the brain as well as changes in the cultural transmission of information. Thus, the evolution of different structures in the brain has significantly altered the way that humans process information. These structural changes have co-evolved with the top-down constraints of different modes of cultural transmission of information.

Top-down constraints describe environmental selection pressures that played an important role in the evolution of cognition. The problem in the standard model in the cognitive science of religion is that the selection pressures are often limited to those described by evolutionary psychology and cultural epidemiology. Evolutionary psychology focuses on environmental factors of our ancient Pleistocene ancestors, often described as the EEA, the environment of evolutionary adaptation.[1] Humans inherited a "stone age" mind that is dependent upon a multitude of adaptations in the form of cognitive modules. Cultural epidemiology suggests that the present day cultural environment is a by-product of the pathenogenic spread of certain ideas based on their ability to exploit features of the cognitive architecture developed on the ancient Savannah. Thus, environmental top-down constraints are limited to what occurred millions of years ago.

However, the environment of our ancient relatives is not the only environment that has affected the evolution of human cognition. Rather, co-evolutionary processes in the emergence of human cognition involved changes in the nature of culture as well as cognition. The social transmission of information in culture has evolved from primitive forms of imitation and shared intentions to the present symbolic form of today. Additionally, the neural structures of the human brain have evolved to take advantage of these changes, which enabled the easy acquisition of symbolic forms of cognition. Thus, rather than a bottom-up approach to the evolution of cognition from cognitive adaptations to culture, a co-evolutionary approach argues that there are both bottom-up and top-down changes both in the structure of environmental cultural constraints as well as top-down constraints of the structure of cognitive representations.

There are three important changes in the cultural transmission of information and resultant changes in neural structures that are important to the evolution of symbolic thought. First, the evolution of imitative behaviors from early primates to humans and the discovery of mirror neurons play an important role in the processing of cultural information. Secondly, the evolution of a theory of mind produces the ability to share and read the intentions of others. Although some evolutionary psychologists suggest that a theory of mind is a particular cognitive module, this ability is an emergent process based on feedback processes and the top-down constraints of relational dynamics. The last important change occurred in human language and the evolution of the symbolic mind. Imitation and shared intentions were important steps in the evolution of the most complex form of cultural communication, language. Language and the brain have co-evolved in the formation of the symbolic mind, which included changes in the connections of the prefrontal cortex to the rest of the brain and the evolution of languages that are intuitively easy to learn.

Evolutionary Psychology

Evolutionary psychology is the investigation of human psychological phenomena (i.e. sexuality, sociality, emotion, cognition, etc.) based on the adaptations that occurred during the evolution of the human species. Every type of organism that

---

[1] John Tooby and Leda Cosmides, "The Past Explains the Present: Emotional Adaptations and the Structure of Ancestral Environments," *Ethology and Sociobiology* 11 (1990): 375-424.

exists today must have adapted to various environmental conditions in terms of survival and reproduction. Genetic variation produced various phenotypes with differential survival and reproductive value; genotypes that produced phenotypes with higher adaptive value are passed on to successive generations and perpetuated the survival of the species. The biological sciences study various organisms based on species-typical behavior, which are the manifestations of various adaptations that occurred in the history of the species. Thus, human adaptations based on genetic transmission must also produce species-typical behavior in humans in regard to mate selection, motivation, social relationships, and other areas of human psychology.

When Charles Darwin originally developed the theory of evolution in the *Origin of the Species*, he imagined that the theory would have far-reaching consequences including a new understanding of human behavior and psychology.[2] William James was one of the few psychologists who attempted to incorporate the ideas of Charles Darwin into the study of human behavior, cognition, and emotion.[3] Evolutionary psychology was built on the foundational sciences of comparative psychology (the study of animal behavior to better understand human psychology) and ethology (the study of specific traits and behaviors of an animal).[4] Based on the successes of these sciences throughout the early and mid 1900s, Edward O. Wilson attempted to integrate these two sciences into a general orientation toward the study of animal behavior (including humans) called sociobiology.[5]

Based in part on ideas from sociobiology, in the 1980s John Tooby and Leda Cosmides began to first develop some of the basic premises of evolutionary psychology. They linked together cognitive science, with its focus on cognitive programs, and the burgeoning science of human origins in evolution. Evolutionary psychology proposes that the mind is composed of adaptations contained in cognitive modules that developed through evolutionary processes that solved certain adaptive problems faced by our ancient Pleistocene ancestors. Current research in evolutionary psychology is attempting to understand several aspects of human behavior, including mate selection, sexual attractiveness, and parenthood.[6]

According to Tooby and Cosmides, evolution has constructed a specific and universal cognitive architecture.[7] This perspective claims that the human brain has specific adaptations, similar to other human organs like the heart, lung, or

---

[2] Charles Darwin, *The Origin of the Species* (London: John Murray, 1859), 458.

[3] William James, *Principles of Psychology* (New York: Henry Holt, 1890).

[4] John Cartwright, *Evolution and Human Behavior: Darwinian Perspectives on Human Nature* (Cambridge: The MIT Press, 2008).

[5] Edward O. Wilson, *Sociobiology: The New Synthesis* (Cambridge: Harvard University Press, 1975).

[6] David Buss, ed., *The Handbook of Evolutionary Psychology* (New Jersey: John Wiley & Sons, Inc., 2005).

[7] Leda Cosmides and John Tooby, "Evolutionary Psychology: A Primer," www.psych.ucsb.edu/research/cep/-primer.html (accessed August 2004).

liver, but these adaptations took the form of cognitive programs, which solved certain problems of hunter-gatherer societies and are passed on genetically. So while phylogenetic similarities across species may provide psychologists a better understanding of the gross anatomical and neurological structures in the animal kingdom, cognitive adaptations have structured a brain with specific modules that solve problems relevant to survival and reproduction.[8]

From this perspective, the human mind is like a Swiss army knife, with different tools used for different problems that arise in the environment.[9] Barrett classifies these tools into three different functions: categorizers, describers, and facilitators.[10] Categorizers are specialized for detecting agency or categorizing different facial features, describers are used for understanding the thoughts of others (theory of mind) or describing founds objects or artifacts, and facilitators are used primarily in social relationships to identify status and hierarchal relationships or provide intuitions about the moral domain. Each cognitive tool is specifically calibrated to solve certain types of problems, which may include mate selection, reasoning about social exchange, and detecting cheaters.[11]

The Swiss army knife model of cognition is in direct contrast to the "standard social science model," where the mind is described as a general-purpose learning machine or "blank slate."[12] According to this model, from birth, humans are blank slates and it is primarily the socialization process of enculturation that enables persons to learn and develop cognitive skills. Humans are born with a brain system that contains general all-purpose cognitive processing applications, but culture and learning are what truly drive cognitive development. In contrast to the blank slate model of cognition, Tooby and Cosmides claim that humans actually have a conceptually rich, universal cognitive architecture, which was constructed according to the cognitive adaptations necessary to thrive in the EEA, which was the environment of our Pleistocene hunter-gatherer ancestors.[13]

To understand these cognitive modules it is necessary to investigate cognition through a type of reverse engineering.[14] The adaptive problems faced by early

---

[8] Leda Cosmides and John Tooby, "Introduction to Evolutionary Psychology," in *The Cognitive Neurosciences*, ed. Michael Gazzaniga (Cambridge The MIT Press, 1995).

[9] Ibid.

[10] Justin L. Barrett, *Why Would Anyone Believe in God?* (Walnut Creek: AltaMira Press, 2004), 5.

[11] David Buss, "The Evolution of Human Mating," *Acta Psychologica Sinica* 39 (2007): 502-512; Leda Cosmides and John Tooby, "Neurocognitive Adaptations Designed for Social Exchange," in *Evolutionary Psychology Handbook*, ed. David Buss (New York: Wiley, 2005).

[12] Cosmides and Tooby, *Evolutionary Psychology: A Primer*.

[13] John Tooby and Leda Cosmides, "Mapping the Evolved Functional Organization of the Mind and Brain," in *The Cognitive Neurosciences*, ed. Michael Gazzaniga (Cambridge: The MIT Press, 1995), 1187.

[14] Steven Pinker, *How the Mind Works* (New York: W. W. Norton & Co., 1997), 21.

humans need to be identified in order to investigate the cognitive programs that would have evolved to solve those problems. In that case, it is not the intellectual capabilities and tasks of modern humans that should be studied, but rather the tasks and problems of our ancient ancestors such as "foraging, kin selection, engaging in social exchange, avoiding incest, choosing mates, caring for children, recognizing emotion, and interpreting threats."[15]

Thus, modern human cognitive abilities are by-products of a "Stone Age" mind.[16]

> Although our architectures may be capable of other kinds of functionality or activities (e.g. weaving, playing pianos), these are incidental by-products of selection for our Pleistocene competencies—just as a machine built to be a hair dryer can, incidentally, dehydrate fruit or electrocute.[17]

Tooby and Cosmides suggest three complementary levels of explanation in evolutionary psychology: adaptive problem, cognitive problem, and neurological basis. These levels of explanation are based on the work of David Marr and his three levels of explanation in cognitive science.[18] The adaptive problem is the problem that a particular cognitive adaptation was designed to solve; the cognitive problem is the specifics of the cognitive solution to that problem, and the neurophysiological basis is the chemical, cellular, and neural systems of the physical brain.

Humans are born with crib sheets that provide cues for the types of environmental stimuli to seek out and intuitive ways to process that information. For example, when a baby is born, he or she will immediately be drawn to stimuli that resemble faces rather than other types of stimuli.[19] At two and a half months, an infant will assume that objects are bounded and cohesive and will be quite surprised by any object that seems to magically go through another one.[20] There are hundreds if not thousands of different cognitive modules that process environmental information and provide solutions to relevant problems. These cognitive modules are domain-specific and only become activated when the relevant adaptation problem is encountered in the environment. For evolutionary psychology, behavioral flexibility is dependent upon acquiring more and more adaptations to solve relevant problems.

---

[15] Tooby and Cosmides, *Mapping Functional Organization*, 1189.

[16] Cosmides and Tooby, *Evolutionary Psychology: A Primer*.

[17] Tooby and Cosmides, *Mapping Functional Organization*, 1189.

[18] David Marr, *Vision: A Computational Investigation into the Human Representation and Processing of Visual Information* (San Francisco: Freeman, 1982), 25.

[19] Mark H. Johnson and John Morton, *Biology and Cognitive Development: The Case of Face Recognition* (Oxford: Blackwell, 1991).

[20] R. Bailergeon, "Representing the Existence and Location of Hidden Objects: Object Permanence in Six and Eight Month Old Infants," *Cognition* 23 (1986): 21-41; Elizabeth Spelke, "Principles of Object Perception," *Cognitive Science* 14 (1990): 29-56.

Hypotheses

Evolutionary psychology has developed several hypotheses that investigate a wide range of behaviors and cognitive phenomena in human psychology. Mate selection has been a primary target of explanation for evolutionary psychology focusing on strategies for both selecting and attracting a potential mate and the differences in strategies based on gender. The hip-to-waist ratio (WHR) specifies a male sexual preference for women with a particular body shape comprised of a ratio of the waist of a woman to her hip size.[21] Men showed a preference for a WHR between .67 and .80. The psychological adaptation may have been a result of discriminating between potential sexual partners and their reproductive potential. Thus, males would be able to distinguish between a younger girl who was not sexually mature enough to be able to conceive a child and an older woman who could conceive. Recent research has also shown that lower-body fat in women may have a positive effect on the supply of fatty acids that play an essential role in the neural development of offspring.[22] Women with lower WHR scores and their children score higher on tests for cognitive ability when other factors are controlled. Thus, the WHR may not just indicate sexual maturity but also health and genetic fitness.

Besides WHR, several different psychological adaptations have contributed to male sexual psychology and what men indicate as attractive. Many of these have to do with indicators of youth such as clear and smooth skin, muscle tone, and energy level.[23] Both males and females favor facial symmetry in a potential long-term mate when compared to faces with less symmetry using computer-generated faces (although symmetry affected male preference to a greater degree).[24] Women often prefer mates who have a higher perceived status based on their likelihood of success in a career, education and degrees, level of maturity, and ambition.[25] Some research suggests that women have an evolved adaptation that is able to raise or lower their standards for a potential mate based on their own mate value.[26]

---

[21] Devendra Singh, "Adaptive Significance of Female Physical Attractiveness: Role of Waist-to-Hip Ratio," *Journal of Personality and Social Psychology* 65, no. 2 (1993): 293-307.

[22] William D. Lassek and Steven J. C. Gaulin, "Waist-Hip Ratio and Cognitive Ability: Is Gluteofemoral Fat a Privileged Store of Neurodevelopmental Resources?," *Evolution and Human Behavior* 29 (2008): 26-34.

[23] David Buss, *The Evolution of Desire*, Revised ed. (New York: Basic Books, 2003).

[24] Randy Thornhill and Steven W. Gangestad, "Facial Attractiveness," *Trends in Cognitive Sciences* 3, no. 12 (1999): 452-460.

[25] Buss, *Evolution of Desire,* 25; 28-31.

[26] David Buss and Todd K. Shackelford, "Attractive Women Want It All: Good Genes, Economic Investment, Parenting Proclivities, and Emotional Commitment," *Evolutionary Psychology* 6, no. 1 (2008): 134-146.

In addition to mate selection, several hypotheses have also explored the cognitive adaptations necessary for social exchange in groups. The theories of kin selection and reciprocal altruism help to explain why cooperation would have evolved in the human species.[27] Kin selection suggests that it is in the best genetic interests of an individual to help someone who has a similar genotype because it increases the chances of genetic transmission over time. Thus, it is hypothesized that cognitive mechanisms evolved to detect others as possible relatives, which estimates genetic relatedness between self and other based on two cues: close association between the offspring and the biological mother after birth and the amount of time cohabitation occurs between siblings.[28]

Reciprocal altruism refers to the process by which humans decide whether to help someone else based on the probability that the help will be returned at a future time. Consequently, it is advantageous to help someone who is a part of the tribe because it is likely that the help will be returned in the future based on the proximity of interactions that will occur over time, while strangers may prove less trustworthy. However, there is always the problem of a free rider or cheater, someone who benefits from the help of the tribe but does not contribute anything in return. As a result, an important cognitive adaptation is the detection of cheaters, identifying other persons that fail to properly reciprocate during economic, social, or occupational exchanges.[29] When comparing two similar tasks based on simple rules of logic, participants performed significantly better when the content of the task involved social rules and regulations (such as policing under age drinking) in comparison to abstract tasks involving propositional logical statements (i.e. *if p, then q*).[30]

Research in evolutionary psychology proposes several other possible cognitive mechanisms that monitor different aspects of social exchange. Newcomers to a group may activate motivational and classification systems, which estimate the tenure of the person and activate a negative bias towards persons new to the group.[31] This may be part of a cognitive adaptation that

---

[27] W. D. Hamilton, "The Genetical Evolution of Social Behaviour," *Journal of Theoretical Biology* 7 (1964): 1-16; Robert L. Trivers, "The Evolution of Reciprocal Altruism," *Quarterly Review of Biology* 46 (1971): 35-57.

[28] Debra Lieberman, John Tooby, and Leda Cosmides, "The Architecture of Human Kin Detection," *Nature* 445 (2007): 727-731.

[29] Leda Cosmides and John Tooby, "Neurocognitive Adaptations Designed for Social Exchange," in *Evolutionary Psychology Handbook*, ed. David Buss (New York: Wiley, 2005).

[30] John Tooby and Leda Cosmides, "The Psychological Foundations of Culture," in *The Adapted Mind: Evolutionary Psychology and the Generation of Culture*, ed. Jerome H. Barkow, Leda Cosmides, and John Tooby (New York: Oxford University Press, 1992).

[31] Aldo Cimino and Andrew W. Delton, "On the Perception of Newcomers: Toward an Evolved Psychology of Intergenerational Coalitions," *Human Nature* 21 (2010): 186-202.

evaluates coalitional alliances based on a number of possible factors including clothing, facial features, posture, gender, mood, or ethnic identity, any of which may be a potential identifier for a particular coalitional relationship.[32] None of these factors is inherently coalitional; the important part of the cognitive program is to identify what cues are associated with cooperative behavior and the corresponding allegiances. In fact, these cognitive mechanisms seem to be well calibrated to use various nonverbal cues such as eye gaze and touch to make decisions about cooperation.[33] Cooperation and coalition building have obvious connections to human morality; in human populations it may become a moral imperative to exclude or include certain persons and praise or punishment is often used to monitor behavior in groups.

Critiques of Evolutionary Psychology

Evolutionary psychology has received criticism from a number of different sources, some deserved, others undeserved. Although evolutionary psychology makes a compelling case for cognitive adaptations and the corresponding aspects of human behavior, there are potential problems with aspects of evolutionary psychology. First, it is difficult to characterize the primary properties of the environment of evolutionary adaptation because it occurred so long ago and it is highly unlikely that the environment remained consistent throughout the evolution of humans. Secondly, evolutionary psychology posits a universal human nature, but this is already complicated by the fact that there is obviously differences in the basic natures of males vs. females, which evolutionary psychology argues have different mating strategies. Additionally, there are some species that thrive on genetic variation that produces different phenotypes that are all equally adaptive, but for different reasons.[34]

In terms of cognition, the massive modularity hypothesis only partially describes important aspects of human cognition. It is highly difficult to map a massively modular mind onto the neurological structures of the human brain, which is abundantly interconnective and shares resources among many different neurological structures for particular cognitive functions. The assumption of domain specificity in cognitive modules does not reflect the plasticity and cognitive fluidity of so many aspects of human cognition. There is still considerable evidence that many aspects of human cognition should be considered *domain general* rather

---

[32] Robert Kurzban, John Tooby, and Leda Cosmides, "Can Race Be Erased? Coalitional Computation and Social Categorization," *Proceedings of the National Academy of Sciences* 98, no. 26 (2001): 15387-15392.

[33] Robert Kurzban, "The Social Psychophysics of Cooperation: Nonverbal Communication in a Public Goods Game," *Journal of Nonverbal Behavior* 25, no. 4 (2001): 241-259.

[34] David Sloan Wilson, "Adaptive Genetic Variation and Human Evolutionary Psychology," *Ethology and Sociobiology* 15 (1994): 219-235.

than *domain specific*. Evolutionary psychology has focused primarily on cognitive programs, but many areas of cognitive science have adopted an embodied view of cognition, which views perception, conceptualization, memory, and emotion as a product of the body in relation to the brain and mind.[35] Thus, adaptations could not be primarily cognitive in nature, but must be aspects of the whole person: body, brain, and mind.

The evolutionary psychology conceived by Steven Pinker, Cosmides, Tooby, and others has been criticized for being too narrow in its understanding of cognitive and neurological processes. Steven Quartz defines this "narrow evolutionary psychology" as a combination of the modern synthesis in biology and nativist cognitive psychology.

> Specifically, narrow evolutionary psychology brings together the modern synthesis of evolutionary biology, which views evolutionary change primarily in terms of changes in gene frequency, with a nativist cognitive psychology, which views the mind as a collection of relatively autonomous specialized processors, or modules.[36]

Narrow evolutionary psychology is highly non-developmental and neglects the role of the environment and maturation in the acquisition of specific cognitive functions. By rendering developmental and environmental perspectives unimportant for understanding cognitive features, evolutionary psychology ignores an important aspect of human cognition.

Quartz and Terrence Sejnowski argue that the view of cognition suggested by evolutionary psychology is a type of "genetic blueprint."[37] From this perspective, different cognitive functions are the product of a specified genetic plan in the cortex that internally directs cognitive development. However, research in the cognitive neurosciences shows that the cortex does not develop through a specific internal plan, but actively incorporates experiential variables in addition to the genetic directives.

> From the late 1980s onward, brain researchers found more and more evidence that cortical development was far from a "precisely programmed" genetic plan.
> ... This is a fundamental issue, because if a cortical area can take on different

---

[35] Raymond W. Gibbs, *Embodiment and Cognitive Science* (Cambridge: Cambridge University Press, 2005).

[36] Steven R. Quartz, "Toward a Developmental Evolutionary Psychology: Genes, Development, and the Evolution of the Human Cognitive Architecture," in *Evolutionary Psychology: Alternative Approaches*, ed. Steven J. Scher and Frederick Rauscher (New York: Springer Publishing Co., 2002), 185.

[37] Steven R. Quartz and Terrence J. Sejnowski, *Liars, Lovers, and Heroes: What the New Brain Science Reveals About How We Become Who We Are* (New York: William Morrow & Company, 2002), 37.

functions, something other than a built-in plan must be instructing it what to become.[38]

Several areas of research point to a different view of the development of human cognition, one that is based on environmental factors and developmental changes in the human cortex.

Current debates in cognitive neuroscience involve the extent to which important basic level features of cognition are innate or develop over time. The missing factor in current evolutionary psychology is an understanding of how environmental feedback can alter the development of representational ability in the cortex as described in Chapter 2. In fact, rather than genes playing the central role in development, new research is indicating that over time the brain has learned to exploit external factors in the environment.

> The process of progressive externalization, mediated in part by heterochronic changes in neural development, whereby the development of cognitive structures became increasingly dependent on prolonged environmental interaction, may thus have been the route to designing a cognitive architecture capable of the highly flexible and context-sensitive behavior necessary for participation in a complex culture.[39]

David Buller argues that the human brain has evolved to become more flexible in response to changing environmental conditions, rather than adding more and more domain-specific cognitive programs.

> Our brains hit on a different, domain-general solution: a plasticity that allows particular environmental demands to participate heavily in tailoring the cortical circuits that process information about those demands. …We evolved a plastic system capable of forming specialized brain circuits in response to the demands of its local environment.[40]

So our cognitive system was not designed to contain hundreds of specific cognitive adaptations, but to be generally adaptable and flexible according to local conditions. Several cognitive functions such as memory, language, and visual processing allow us to survive and reproduce in the environment. Yet certain adaptations, such as language, are neither part of a language module nor genetically determined, but rather are the result of changes in the human cortex and culture that have co-evolved to make learning language easier. This theory of

---

[38] Ibid., 38.

[39] Quartz, *Developmental Evolutionary Psychology*, 205.

[40] David J. Buller, *Adopting Minds: Evolutionary Psychology and the Persistent Quest for Human Nature* (Cambridge: The MIT Press, 2005), 140.

the acquisition of language skills suggests a co-evolutionary process of language acquisition with both cognitive changes and changes in language contributing to its development.

Imitation and Mirror Neurons

Merlin Donald argues that the evolution of human cognition depends on three stages or transitions that include changes in both culture and the architecture of human cognition.[41] These three stages are mimetic culture, mythic culture, and external symbolic storage. During evolution, humans inherited episodic culture, which is a common element of both human and primate cognition. Episodic means that early primates were bound to the immediate or current time frame.[42] The episodic form of memory constrains the cognitive possibilities for representations of current concrete episodes. Through evolution, apes were able to achieve more complex representations than their earlier ancestors, but they were unable "to reflect upon them individually or collectively."[43]

The first major change in the evolution of human cognition was the change from episodic to mimetic culture. This generated the emergence of imitation as a different type of representational and cultural exchange and served as a precursor to symbolic storage. Imitation is slightly different from mimicry; the imitation of behavior involves changes and modifications brought about by the observer.

> Mimicry is literal, an attempt to render as exact a duplicate as possible. Imitation is not so literal as mimicry; the offspring copying its parent's behavior imitates, but does not mimic, the parent's ways of doing things.[44]

Imitation provides a means by which different aspects of cultural information, such as social roles and behaviors, can be transmitted. Some forms of early tool use in chimpanzees, such as using sticks to scoop out termites, involve mimicry while more advanced human tool construction involves innovations in the use and assembly of tools dependent upon imitation. Donald notes that imitation was involved in several cultural transitions in the evolution of cognition, including tool making, coordinated hunting, adaptation to differing climates, social systems, and primitive rituals.[45]

Aspects of imitation appear to be innate to humans, which are often observed in newborn infants. Andrew Meltzoff and M. Keith Moore preformed a study on twelve 21-day-old infants to assess their ability to imitate certain facial expressions,

---

[41] Merlin Donald, *Origins of the Modern Mind: Three Stages in the Evolution of Culture and Cognition* (Cambridge: Harvard University Press, 1991), 16.
[42] Ibid., 149.
[43] Ibid., 160.
[44] Ibid., 169.
[45] Ibid., 198.

including sticking out the tongue and opening the mouth.[46] The infants were able to imitate accurately the facial expressions of the researchers. A larger sample of 80 newborns was later tested and produced similar findings to the original study.[47] The oldest newborn in this study was 72 hours old and the youngest was 42 minutes. These studies indicate that facial imitation is present at a very early age and is seemingly innate. This innate ability may be closer to mimicry rather than imitation, in contrast to the types of imitation that humans use in terms of innovation and representation of action. More complex forms of human imitation are part of an emergent process of feedback, reciprocal interaction, and complex representational systems in the human brain.

An important discovery in the research on imitation is the existence of mirror neurons found in area F5 of the premotor cortex of the macaque monkey.[48] These neurons become active both in observing an action and performing a similar action.

> The novelty of this finding is the fact that, for the first time, a neural mechanism that allows a direct matching between the visual description of an action and its execution has been identified. Such a matching system constitutes a parsimonious solution to the problem of translating the results of the visual analysis of an observed action ... into an account that the individual is able to understand.[49]

Mirror neurons in nonhuman primates may be an evolutionary precursor to mirroring systems in the human brain. Brain imaging studies suggest a human neurological mirror system that includes the superior temporal sulcus, the inferior parietal lobe, and the ventral premotor cortex, including Broca's area.[50] The inclusion of Broca's area raises interesting questions in regard to a language module. Broca's area is often associated with speech production, but the research

---

[46] Andrew N. Meltzoff and M. Keith Moore, "Imitation of Facial and Manual Gestures by Human Neonates," *Science* 198 (1977): 75-78.

[47] Andrew N. Meltzoff and M. Keith Moore, "Newborn Infants Imitate Adult Facial Gestures," *Child Development* 54 (1983): 702-709; Andrew N. Meltzoff and M. Keith Moore, "Imitation in Newborn Infants: Exploring the Range of Gestures Imitated and the Underlying Mechanisms," *Developmental Psychology* 25 (1989): 954-962.

[48] G. di Pellegrino and others, "Understanding Motor Events: A Neurophysiological Study," *Experimental Brain Research* 91, no. 1 (1992): 176-180; G. Rizzolatti and others, "Premotor Cortex and the Recognition of Motor Actions," *Cognitive Brain Research* 3 (1996): 131-141.

[49] G. Rizzolatti, L. Fogassi, and V. Gallese, "Neurophsyiological Mechanisms Underlying the Understanding and Imitation of Action," *Nature Reviews Neuroscience* 2, no. 9 (2001): 663.

[50] Giacomo Rizzolatti, "The Mirror Neuron System and Imitation," in *Perspectives on Imitation: From Neuroscience to Social Science*, ed. Susan Hurley and Nick Chater (Cambridge: The MIT Press, 2005).

would seem to indicate an overlap in function and an important role for imitation in language.[51]

Drawing from the work of Donald, imitation can be understood as a sociocultural process that acts as a top-down constraint on the evolution of cognition and the eventual emergence of symbolic representation and language.[52] This was a co-evolutionary process in which changes in the modes of culture occurred in parallel with changes in the neurological structures of the brain. The evolution of mirror neurons in the monkey and the eventual evolution of mirror systems in the human brain reflect the neurological changes that occurred, but, in addition, changes in the social transmission of information also had an important impact.

> The achievements of early hominids revolved around a new kind of cognitive capacity, mimetic skill, which was an extension of conscious control into the domain of action. It enabled playacting, body language, precise imitation, and gesture. It also acted as a mode of cultural expression and solidified a group mentality, creating a cultural style that we can still recognize as typically human.[53]

Imitation or mimesis is dependent upon several other evolved social behaviors, including "empathy, sympathy, social identification, role-playing, imagination[,] … gesture, and mind-reading."[54] The next section looks at cultural changes that enabled the evolution of mind reading or reading the intentions of another. Bottom-up accounts of cognitive adaptations are ultimately insufficient to describe how this ability evolved. The ability to read the intentions of another is an emergent process based on top-down and bottom-up factors.

Shared Intentions

Michael Tomasello argues that there is not enough time between the break of the hominid lineage from chimpanzees to modern humans to account for the evolution of cognition based solely on genetic variation and natural selection.[55] It required a different mechanism, which was social or cultural in nature, to account for the multitude of cognitive features present in modern human cognition.[56] The special

---

[51] G. Rizzolatti and Michael Arbib, "Language within Our Grasp," *Trends in Neurosciences* 21 (1998): 188-194.

[52] Merlin Donald, "Imitation and Mimesis," in *Perspectives on Imitation: From Neuroscience to Social Science*, ed. Susan L. Hurley and Nick Chater (Cambridge: The MIT Press, 2005), 292.

[53] Donald, *Mind So Rare*, 261.

[54] Donald, "Imitation and Mimesis," 293.

[55] Michael Tomasello, *The Cultural Origins of Human Cognition* (Cambridge: Harvard University Press, 1999), 2.

[56] Ibid., 4.

cultural innovation that occurred is the ability to engage in shared intentional activities together with a common understanding of the intentions of the other.

> In general, shared intentionality is what is necessary for engaging in uniquely human forms of collaborative activity in which a plural subject "we" is involved: joint goals, joint intentions, mutual knowledge, shared beliefs—all in the context of various cooperative motives.[57]

This special mechanism enabled the social transmission of cognitive abilities and the ability to imitate and innovate on the ideas of another. The primary cognitive change was the ability to understand another person as an intentional goal-directed agent.[58] This allows humans to comprehend the current cognitive and behavioral activity of another person from his or her point of view. In this sense, learning is stepping into the mind of another to understand their intentions and goals for a particular activity in order to innovate on the current mode of cognitive reasoning used to solve that particular problem.

An interesting experiment illustrates the ability of children to understand the intentions and goals of others. Andrew Meltzoff took 18-month-old infants and attempted to see how they would re-enact the actions of others.[59] The infants were shown a failed attempt to perform a certain action. For example an adult would try to pull apart a dumbbell-shaped object. Interestingly, infants would imitate trying to pull apart the object whether they watched the adult successfully or unsuccessfully pull it apart. They seemed to understand the intention behind the action and sought to fulfill that goal rather than just mimicking the behavior. In a later study, the infants were given a dumbbell that was glued together so it was impossible to pull apart. When this happened the infants continually struggled to pull it apart and began looking at their parents and making vocalizations. They seemed to be saying, "I'm trying to do what you did, what's wrong here?" When a machine instead of a person performed the same actions, infants imitated the behavior significantly less. From this research, it is clear that there are certain innate predispositions towards understanding the intentions of others, but the work of Tomasello and Donald would suggest that there were also cultural constraints on the evolution of this cognitive ability.

The ability for persons to form representations of the intentions of another is an emergent process partially determined by top-down constraints. The precursory cognitive functions necessary for the ability to comprehend the intentions and

---

[57] Michael Tomasello, *Origins of Human Communication* (Cambridge: The MIT Press, 2008), 6-7.

[58] Michael Tomasello and Malinda Carpenter, "Intention Reading and Imitative Learning," in *Perspectives on Imitation: From Neuroscience to Social Science*, ed. Susan L. Hurley and Nick Chater (Cambridge: The MIT Press, 2005).

[59] Andrew N. Meltzoff, "Understanding the Intentions of Others: Re-Enactment of Intended Acts by 18-Month-Old Children," *Developmental Psychology* 31 (1995): 838-850.

goals of others begins at around nine months of age.[60] This type of cognition expands into the more general ability referred to as theory of mind, which is typically dysfunctional in children with autism.[61] Simon Baron-Cohen suggests that theory of mind is a cognitive module involved in ascribing specific mental states to particular objects, other persons, and the self. Theory of mind evolved as an adaptation to the Pleistocene environment and is dependent on two important factors: (1) humans produce intuitive theories about many different situations, events, and objects in the environment to promote survival; (2) navigating the intricacies of the social world was an important aspect of surviving in the environment.[62]

An alternative to this modular explanation of understanding intention would be to see this ability as an emergent process in that the initial bottom-up constraints of this cognitive program only provides the broadest parameters of its full development. Instead, this cognitive ability is emergent in that it is the interaction of persons in their relational environments that enabled the formation of a theory of mind. At about six months of age, infants begin to interact in reciprocal ways with objects and persons; this interaction includes emotional arousal, taking-turns in reactions, vocalizations, and movements.[63] Evolutionary psychology suggests that the parent-child relationship is a triggering device, which enacts a particular module that processes this information based on internal algorithms and cognitive constraints. As an alternative, the relational interaction itself writes the cognitive program for shared attention and, eventually, for understanding others as intentional agents. Over time, the many interactions that occur between the child and his or her primary caregivers set up a particular network of internal representations that relate the infant to the world and especially to his or her parents.

Certain internal parameters of brain physiology and cognitive wiring set up some of the initial conditions, but the important parts of the program are written by the top-down constraints of the relationship itself, which literally wires the brain to have certain types of expectations about persons and the world. The early stages of the relationship between a parent and a child are essentially a type of reciprocal imitative relationship, a dyadic, emotionally arousing relationship between both partners, which acts as a motivational component driving the interaction.[64] This type of behavior is "interactional synchrony" in which the infant orients its internal

---

[60] Tomasello, *Cultural Origins*, 61.

[61] Simon Baron-Cohen, *Mindblindness: An Essay on Autism and Theory of Mind* (Cambridge: The MIT Press, 1997).

[62] John Tooby and Irven DeVore, "The Reconstruction of Hominid Evolution through Strategic Modeling," in *The Evolution of Human Behavior: Primate Models*, ed. W. G. Kinzey (Albany: SUNY Press, 1987).

[63] Tomasello, *Cultural Origins*, 62.

[64] Marcel Kinsbourne, "Imitation as Entrainment: Brain Mechanisms and Social Consequences," in *Perspectives on Imitation: From Neuroscience to Social Science*, ed. Susan L. Hurley and Nick Chater (Cambridge: The MIT Press, 2005).

rhythms to that of the adult.[65] Marcel Kinsbourne argues that the primary purpose of imitation is affiliation or attachment.

> My argument is that babies love to entrain with adults and that imitation is more about affiliation or attachment than about learning, although it may be about learning too. If so, imitation would be a splinter instance of a much broader, more general behavior, which is entrainment—adopting shared rhythms of behavior.[66]

Rather then merely a splinter of entrainment, imitation and entrainment go hand-in-hand with the development of cognitive functions, including representations of the thoughts of others. In this sense, imitation and entrainment are processes that emerge from several interacting relational, emotive, and cognitive factors and provide the initial parameters of understanding intentions.

Meltzoff developed a hypothesis about understanding the intentions of others called the like me hypothesis, which is a three-step process, involving both intrinsic and experiential factors.

> What we seem to need is a new theory of development, a "starting-state nativism" that includes a rich understanding of people and things but still leaves gaps to be filled in by structured experience.[67]

Step one is the innate aspects of imitation in which observation and execution of actions are coupled together, as shown in the previous example of infant facial imitation. Step two involves the experiential linking of bodily actions with mental representations such as a representation of *sadness* coupled with a corresponding facial expression of *sadness*. Step three is the projection of corresponding mental and bodily states to others. Facial expressions or bodily actions that are similar to mine will have corresponding mental states like mine; thus the like me hypothesis.

It is the reciprocal interaction of infants and others through imitation, which begins to teach the infant about objects, mental states, goals, and intentions.

> Infants use other people to learn about and expand their own actions. The imitation of novelty suggests a bidirectional flow of information—a "like you" as well as "like me" pathway ... If infants can recognize when an entity is acting "like me," this would allow them to make a distinction between people and all other entities in the world.[68]

---

[65] Ibid., 167.

[66] Ibid.

[67] Andrew N. Meltzoff, "Imitation and Other Minds: The 'Like Me' Hypothesis," in *Perspectives on Imitation: From Neuroscience to Social Science*, ed. Susan L. Hurley and Nick Chater (Cambridge: The MIT Press, 2005), 74.

[68] Ibid., 60.

The representation of the intentions of others is an emergent process based on feedback mechanisms between the infant and parent. Thus, the relationship itself acts as a top-down constraint on the formation of these representations, in addition to the bottom-up innate features of both reading intentions and imitation. "Nature designed a baby with an imitative brain; culture immerses the child in social play with psychological agents perceived to be 'like me.'"[69] The evolutionary development of these representations involved changes in culture in terms of mimesis and shared intention, yet the formation of these representations is ultimately an emergent process. Both mimesis and shared intention are precursors for symbolic representation and language. Co-evolutionary changes that occurred in language and the brain promoted the evolution of the symbolic mind.

Co-Evolution of the Symbolic Mind

The evolution of language use in humans is a highly debated topic, with several different competing theories. Following the work of Terrence Deacon, I argue that the development of language is a co-evolutionary process whereby changes have occurred in both the structure of the human brain and the cultural/social transmission of symbolic language.[70] Changes occurred in the neural connections of the prefrontal cortex and in language itself, making it relatively easy for children to learn how to use it.[71] This does not mean that humans are born with a blank slate in which language and culture are simply acquired through a general learning device, but that the symbolic nature of human cognition makes it relatively easy to acquire proficiency in native languages.

The primary assumption in evolutionary psychology is that language developed due to the evolution of a cognitive module that is specialized for processing language. Steven Pinker argues that the language of thought is different from that of spoken languages. Persons do not think in English, Japanese, Spanish, or other languages; these languages are much too complex and complicated to be able to process quickly and efficiently. Language use is based on an internal *mentalese* that is easier to process yet contains elements universal to all human languages.[72] Mentalese is contained in a language module in the brain, which is dedicated to processing language information. In language comprehension, particular sentences are transformed into mentalese and processed in the language module, which is then used either to form new sentences or simply to understand the given input.[73]

---

[69] Ibid., 77.

[70] Terrence Deacon, *The Symbolic Species: The Co-Evolution of Language and the Brain* (New York: W. W. Norton & Co., Inc., 1997), 44.

[71] Ibid.

[72] Steven Pinker, *The Language Instinct: How the Mind Creates Language* (New York: William Morrow, 1994), 72-73.

[73] Ibid., 73.

The language processor contains certain fixed responses to different types of linguistic information. These fixed responses or algorithms are the principles of the underlying universal grammar, which allows a small child to quickly understand his or her native tongue.

Co-evolutionary models offer a different perspective on language development. Deacon offers a novel and highly sophisticated account of language development based on symbolic processing and unique changes to the human frontal cortex. However, it is not only changes in human neurological structures that have enabled the evolution of language abilities; humans have adapted in response to the constraints of language. The evolution of language involves top-down constraints of social and cultural transmission that select the types of neuronal configurations that best enable the acquisition of language. Different forms of cognitive representation progressively evolved to the status of symbolic representation.

Forms of Representation

Deacon uses the work of Charles Sanders Pierce to describe how symbolic representation evolved from iconic and indexical representation. Pierce developed his semiology (theory of signs) based on the different ways in which a representation can be a sign of something else.

> A sign, or a *representamen*, is something which stands to somebody for something in some respect or capacity. It addresses somebody, that is, creates in the mind of that person an equivalent sign, or perhaps a more developed sign. It stands for that object, not in all respects, but in reference to a sort of idea ...[74]

An icon represents according to its intrinsic qualities that resemble something else. Landscape paintings, a photograph, or sculptures are all iconic representations; they bring to mind the object they are representing because they resemble the object.

Two similar objects do not necessarily indicate an iconic representation, but something serves as an icon through an inferential process that recognizes a similarity.[75] Identifying something as iconic does not necessarily exclude the object from also serving as an index or a symbol. Thus, the statue of David is iconic of a man, but it may also be an index or indicator of the work of Michelangelo. Iconic representation may have co-evolved with mimicry and imitation. The purpose of mimicry is to be iconic of the behavior of another by eliciting behaviors that directly match the initial behavior. One example is spontaneously laughing or crying when

---

[74] Charles Sanders Pierce, "Logic as Semiotic: The Theory of Signs," in *Philosophical Writings of Pierce*, ed. Justus Buchler (New York: Dover Publications, Inc., 1955), 99.

[75] Deacon, *Symbolic Species*, 71.

that behavior is observed in others.[76] Imitation involves iconic representations that are manipulated in order to elaborate on the behavior of another.

The second form of representation is an index, which is a sign that causes someone to think of another object without having an intrinsic similarity to the object.

> Indices may be distinguished from other signs, or representations, by three characteristic marks: first, that they have no significant resemblance to their objects; second, that they refer to individuals, single units, single collections of units, or single continua; third, that they direct the attention to their objects by blind compulsion.[77]

An index is an *indicator* of something else; a thermometer indicates the current temperature of a room or a speedometer indicates the current speed of a vehicle. An index represents two icons that have a predictable relationship between each other; one represents the probability of the second one being present.

The alarm call of vervet monkeys serves as an example of indexical communication.[78] Robert Seyfarth, Dorothy Cheney, and Peter Marler identified specific alarm calls that were associated with different kinds of predators, including eagles, leopards, and snakes.[79] Each call indicated a different kind of predator and a different kind of behavioral response. If the eagle call was given, the monkeys would leave the trees, when the leopard call was given the monkeys would climb into the trees, and when the snake call was given the monkeys would rise up and peer into the bushes around them. One general alarm call would not be nearly as helpful as having different types of calls associated with different behaviors depending on the type of predator that was threatening the group.

The final representational category is a symbol, which is a representation that is conventional or operates according to a rule that determines its representational quality:

> A symbol is a Representamen whose Representative character consists precisely in its being a rule that will determine its Interpretant. All words, sentences, books, and other conventional signs are Symbols.[80]

A representation becomes symbolic through a particular social convention, agreement, or code which links two things together. A marriage ring is a symbol

---

[76] Ibid., 429.

[77] Pierce, *Logic as Semiotic*, 108.

[78] Deacon, *Symbolic Species*, 81.

[79] Robert Seyfarth, Dorothy Cheney, and Peter Marler, "Monkey Responses to Three Different Alarm Calls: Evidence of Predator Classification and Semantic Communication," *Science* 210 (1980): 801-803.

[80] Pierce, *Logic as Semiotic*, 112.

for a marital agreement; an "e" represents a particular type of sound used in a word.[81] Symbols represent in virtue of their ability to link together different icons and indices and their relationship to other symbols.[82]

Icons, indices, and symbols are related to each other in a hierarchical manner; indices represent relationships between icons and symbols represent relationships between indices. Symbols emerge from nonsymbolic features of icons and indices to form a higher order pattern of associations that enable symbols to be linked with each other.

> Symbolic reference emerges from a ground of nonsymbolic referential processes only because the indexical relationships between symbols are organized so as to form a logically closed group of mappings from symbol to symbol. This determinate character allows the higher-order system of associations to supplant the individual (indexical) referential support previously invested in each component symbol.[83]

The transition from indexical to symbolic reference is the threshold that humans crossed in the evolution of higher forms of cognition such as understanding abstract concepts, predicting future events, and modifying our behavior according to particular goals.

Symbols and Primate Cognition

Research conducted on chimpanzees illustrates the difficulty involved in teaching chimpanzees symbolic relationships. Sue Savage-Rumbaugh and Roger Lewin devised a computer keyboard, which contained simple abstract shapes that represented lexigram items.[84] Shapes were chosen that had no similarity to the objects they were intended to represent. Originally there were two "verb" lexigrams ("give" for solid foods and "pour" for liquids) and four "noun" lexigrams for foods or drinks. The chimps were trained through many trials to put lexigram pairs together so that lexigram-shape-verb ("give") would be paired with lexigram-shape-food ("banana"), thus "give" + "banana" would yield the result of a chimpanzee getting a banana.

Chimpanzees have difficulty learning important language distinctions such as the difference between types of verbs like "give" and "pour." Savage-Rumbaugh, Duane Rumbaugh, and S. Boysen devised an interesting scenario for the chimpanzees

---

[81] Deacon, *Symbolic Species*, 71.
[82] Ibid., 86.
[83] Ibid., 99.
[84] Sue Savage-Rumbaugh, *Ape Language: From Conditioned Response to Symbol* (New York: Columbia University Press, 1986); Sue Savage-Rumbaugh and Roger Lewin, *Kanzi: The Ape at the Brink of the Human Mind* (New York: Wiley, 1994).

to learn this difference.[85] They first had to teach the chimpanzees all the wrong combination possibilities, such as mistaking the keyboard position as the most important factor, and then extinguishing these behaviors. The only combinations that were rewarded were the correct noun-verb pairings, representative of a simple symbolic language. But could the chimpanzees use these distinctions if novel types of liquids and solids were introduced into the experiment?

The chimpanzees were introduced to new foods and liquids plus their corresponding lexigram. They were able to quickly associate the correct food item with the correct verb. This development was more than just a simple pairing; the chimps were able to understand that there was a particular relationship between the lexigrams. They had developed a level of symbolic insight by recognizing that the relationship a lexigram has to an object is not simply dependent upon its association or correlated appearance (in an indexical manner), but on how that lexigram relates to other lexigrams.[86]

This research suggests how a symbolic system can be learned, but humans seem to acquire symbolic representation so easily. Whereas the chimpanzee must perform a large array of trials to accomplish a minimal amount of symbolic insight, a human child crosses the symbolic threshold with little effort. Although aspects of symbolic representation are learned, the nature of human cognition and language make it much easier for humans to understand symbols. Human cognition processes symbols more rapidly because of two important changes: (1) a re-wiring of the brain to include an overabundance of connections from the prefrontal cortex to the rest of the brain, and (2) changes in the structure of language, which created a user-friendly interface.

The Symbolic Brain

The neural restructuring that occurred in the evolution of symbolic processing required certain physiological and neurological structures necessary for language comprehension and production. The first primary physiological prerequisite for human language ability is the vocal tract; modern humans have a low larynx and a large throat that enables speech production, which is absent from modern apes.[87] From skull reconstructions, Philip Lieberman argues that Neanderthal man was unable to make some of the necessary sounds for modern human language, including "a," "I," and "u."[88] Based on this research, modern language did not exist prior to 100,000 years ago.

---

[85] Sue Savage-Rumbaugh, Duane Rumbaugh, and Sally Boysen, "Symbolization, Language and Chimpanzees: A Theoretical Re-Evaluation Based on Initial Language Acquisition Processes in Four Young Pan Troglodytes," *Brain and Language* 6 (1978): 265.

[86] Deacon, *Symbolic Species*, 86.

[87] Bryan Kolb and Ian Q. Whishaw, *Fundamentals of Human Neuropsychology*, 4th edn. (New York: Worth Publishers Incorporated, 1995), 389.

[88] Phillip Lieberman, *On the Origins of Language: An Introduction to the Evolution of Human Speech* (New York: Macmillan, 1975).

In the human brain, language processing is usually localized in the left hemisphere in two important areas: Broca's and Wernicke's.[89] Broca's area is located in the left inferior frontal lobe and is mainly involved in speech production, while Wernicke's is located in the left superior temporal lobe and is associated with speech comprehension. Most of the research involving the identification of these language areas was discovered through the correlation of aphasias or language deficiencies to brain injuries in these areas. Generally, persons with damage to Broca's area have difficulty articulating words although their comprehension remains intact.[90] Persons with damage to Wernicke's area have difficulty with speech comprehension and produce meaningless speech.[91] This is the classic model of language processing; Broca's and Wernicke's both act as specific language modules, processing language production and comprehension, respectively.

Dividing up language abilities into these two areas glosses over several other areas involved in language processing including the prefrontal cortex, supplementary motor cortex, anterior cingulate gyrus, basal ganglia, and parts of the cerebellum.[92] Deacon argues that the developments of Wernicke's and Broca's area are secondary by-products to the primary structural changes that occurred in the brain during the evolution of symbolic thought.[93] The primary evolutionary change in the human brain is the enlargement of the prefrontal cortex and the structural changes that significantly increased the connections of the prefrontal cortex with the rest of the brain.[94] Over the course of evolution, the prefrontal cortex has become larger and more complex reflected in topography that includes entangled fissures and gyri.[95] The increased size of the prefrontal cortex in comparison to other areas of the cortex allowed more processing power to be devoted to tasks other than sensory representation.

The prefrontal cortex may be subdivided into several areas including the inferior frontal, dorsolateral, and orbital frontal.[96] The dorsolateral area has inputs from the superior temporal sulcus and the posterior parietal areas (this area affords connections to the cingulate cortex, basal ganglia, and superior colliculus). The inferior frontal area connects to the temporal lobe, which includes different regions of auditory, visual, and somastosensory processing.[97] Additionally, the inferior

---

[89] Neil R. Carlson, *Physiology of Behavior*, 6th edn. (Boston: Allyn and Bacon, 1998), 483.
[90] Ibid.
[91] Ibid., 487.
[92] Fuster, *Cortex and Mind*, see Chapter 7.
[93] Deacon, *Symbolic Species*, 316-318.
[94] Ibid., 257.
[95] Joaquín M. Fuster, *The Prefrontal Cortex: Anatomy, Physiology, and Neuropsychology of the Frontal Lobe* (New York: Raven Press, 1997), 4.
[96] Kolb and Whishaw, *Human Neuropsychology*, 306.
[97] Ibid., 307.

frontal area projects subcortically to the amygdala and hypothalamus; these areas play a vital role in managing the functions of the autonomic nervous system.[98]

The influence of the prefrontal cortex on other functions is demonstrated by the connections to different areas involved in vocalization. The prefrontal cortex has connections to the hypoglossal nucleus, nucleus ambiguus, and the facial motor nucleus, which controls the larynx, tongue, and face, as well as connections to the brain stem and upper spinal cord, which control breathing.[99] In other animals, these areas are controlled by links to the midbrain that associate vocalization with states of arousal and emotive behaviors. The re-wiring of the human brain enables these areas to benefit from the more complex processing accomplished by the prefrontal cortex, which allows the suppression of certain instinctive behaviors and enables more sophisticated types of vocalization.[100]

Although vocalization is a key factor in the evolution of language, the true innovation that differentiates human cognitive abilities from other animals is the predominance of the prefrontal cortex in information processing.

> In general terms, human information processing should be biased by an excessive reliance on and guidance by the kinds of manipulations that prefrontal circuits impose upon the information they possess. We humans should, therefore, exhibit a "cognitive style" that sets us apart form other species – a pattern of organizing perceptions, actions and learning that is peculiarly "front heavy," so to speak.[101]

The massive amounts of connections between the prefrontal cortex and other areas allow symbolic processing to dominate higher cognitive functions, and the evolution of the brain has enabled a significant proportion of the cortex to be devoted to this ability.

Nancey Murphy and Warren Brown argue that the structure of the prefrontal cortex enables symbolic language processing according to top-down context-sensitive constraints.[102] Word meanings are embodied in patterns of neuronal activation formed in large associative networks distributed throughout the brain.[103] The structure of the prefrontal cortex enables the use of contextual constraints in processing symbolic language. Chapter 3 reported the research of Koechlin and colleagues demonstrating that the structure of the prefrontal cortex contains a cascade of different sorts of constraints depending on sensory, contextual, or episodic tasks.[104] Murphy and Brown argue that this research shows

---

[98] Ibid.
[99] Deacon, *Symbolic Species*, 247.
[100] Murphy and Brown, *Did my Neurons*, 169.
[101] Deacon, *Symbolic Species*, 257.
[102] Murphy and Brown, *Did my Neurons*, 164.
[103] Ibid., 169.
[104] Koechlin et al., "Cognitive Control," 1181.

a nested control hierarchy of processes that provide top-down constraints.[105] The association networks that constitute symbolic language are dependent upon the contextual cues imposed on the information in order to function as an understandable message.

Language is dependent upon contextual constraints to transmit information; there are many examples of how a letter or phrase alters the probability of the following letter or phrase.

> Some letters or words are more likely or unlikely to occur, not just because of the prior probability distribution of letters in that language, but also depending on the letter or sequence of letters, word or sequence of words that preceded them.[106]

Chapter 3 discussed the role of attractors in processing and constraining information. In language, contextual variables function as attractors that constrain the possible uses of language in a particular context. Murphy and Brown describe language in terms of dynamic systems theory and attractors.

> Syntax (grammar) imposes (or, better, is a set of) context-sensitive constraints. In the language of dynamic systems theory, syntax creates dynamical attractors. Semantics is also a set of context-sensitive constraints. A sentence beginning with "The boy ran to the…" constrains what can follow not only in terms of parts of speech but also in terms of meaning.[107]

In processing symbolic language, contextual variables become embodied in attractors that are formed within the nested control hierarchies, which are readily formed due to the structure of the prefrontal cortex.

This formation is dependent upon neural networks illustrated by computational networks described in Chapter 3. As described by Murphy and Brown, referencing Juarrero, the neural networks form a particular topography of attractor states that is analogous to a landscape of basins and ridges.

> The gradual reorganization of the internal weights is the creation of attractors. Insofar as brains self-organize in similar fashion, it is reasonable to describe language learning as the development of attractors. Or, given the complex relations among multiple attractors, a better description is the development of an ontogenic (probability) landscape of basins (attractors) and ridges (repellers). Semanitics, says Juarrero, is embodied in such a landscape. Categories are basins of attraction for words representing similar items.[108]

---

[105] Murphy and Brown, *Did my Neurons*, 128.
[106] Juarrero, *Dynamics in Action*, 137.
[107] Murphy and Brown, *Did my Neurons*, 165.
[108] Ibid., 174.

This does not mean that the prefrontal cortex is a language or symbolic module; rather it is one particular node in a complex causal process that includes multiple factors. As Deacon describes it, the function and structure of the prefrontal cortex makes humans "lightning calculators of reference."[109] Yet this is not the only important change that initiated the evolution of language in humans. Language has changed to make it easy to learn for humans. What takes chimpanzees a considerable amount of time to learn, humans perform naturally and quickly.

Language Learning Made Easy

The evolution of the prefrontal cortex and its connections throughout the rest of the brain is only part of the story of the symbolic mind; language development is a co-evolutionary process. Both the human brain and language itself have co-evolved together to enable humans to quickly use and understand language. Rather then viewing structures inside the brain as the primary component of the evolution of language, language itself is the missing component of a proper understanding of language origins.

> I think Chomsky and his followers have articulated a central conundrum about language learning, but they offer an answer that inverts cause and effect. They assert that the source of prior support for language acquisition must originate from inside the brain. But there is another alternative: that the extra support for language learning is vested neither in the brain of the child nor in the brains of parents or teachers, but outside brains, in language itself.[110]

Language has become a user-friendly interface; over many generations, it has adapted to be easily understood and passed on to succeeding generations.

Deacon suggests that the evolution of language is analogous to the development of user-friendly computer programs.[111] Early computers were built by engineers, which contained their own languages such as DOS and BIOS that had to be learned from scratch. The breakthrough in computing happened when computers were designed to make usage more intuitive, based on familiar objects and actions. So they developed programs that included a virtual desktop with common icons such as file folders, trashcans, and pointers. All one had to do was move the pointer using a mouse to an icon and then click it to perform certain functions, which would have required a long string of typed commands in a computer language. Language functions in a similar fashion, the basics of language are intuitive and easy to learn.

> The problem faced by a child learning a first language should not be analogous to the problem faced by a computer neophyte trying to learn to use an unforgiving

---

[109] Deacon, *Symbolic Species*, 302.
[110] Ibid., 105.
[111] Ibid., 106.

mechanism. Instead, we should expect that language is a lot more like an intuitive and user-friendly interface. Over countless generations languages should have become better and better adapted to people, so that people need to make minimal adjustments to adapt to them.[112]

The front-heavy cognitive bias afforded by the functions of the prefrontal cortex equips children with simple learning strategies that stack the deck in favor of correct intuitions about language usage.

Human brains take a long time to evolve; thus, languages must have adapted and evolved to be well suited for easy engagement with human learners. Languages that provide the easiest and quickest routes to developing a rudimentary competence will be favored over those that are harder to acquire and pass on. Children are embedded in rich social contexts that allow them to receive constant feedback in the development of their language abilities from multiple sources. They do not learn massive catalogs of words and their meanings, but language has co-evolved with the symbolic mind to contain simple core rules that exploit the guesses made by human children.

The co-evolutionary theory of the origins of symbolic language is partially based on the work of James Mark Baldwin, a psychologist, who introduced a theory on the effect of learning on evolution called the "Baldwin effect."[113] The evolutionary theory of Lamark, which suggested that learned traits could be passed on to offspring, had been discredited in most of contemporary evolutionary theory, but Baldwin and others such as Conwy Lloyd Morgan and H. F. Osborn attempted to describe how learned behaviors could shape evolutionary change.[114] Deacon describes this process as the role of behavioral flexibility in the shaping of environmental variables that modify selection pressures.

> Baldwin suggested that learning and behavioral flexibility can play a role in amplifying and biasing natural selection because these abilities enable individuals to modify the context of natural selection that affects their future kin. Behavioral flexibility enables organisms to move into niches that differ from those their ancestors occupied, with the consequence that succeeding generations will face a new set of selection pressures.[115]

Thus, behavioral flexibility enables humans to modify their environments (e.g., new tools, new locations, or new skills) in such a way that at some point the modified environment becomes a new selective pressure on the process of human evolution.

---

[112] Ibid., 107.

[113] David J. Depew, "Baldwin and His Many Effects," in *Evolution and Learning: The Baldwin Effect Reconsidered*, ed. Bruce H. Weber and David J. Depew (Cambridge: The MIT Press, 2003), 3.

[114] Ibid., 3-5.

[115] Deacon, *Symbolic Species*, 322.

A co-evolutionary account suggests that evolution is not a simply bottom-up process, but also includes different types of top-down constraints. Evolutionary processes cannot be reduced to functional properties that primarily work in a causally reductive fashion. There is a reciprocal relationship between genes, organisms and the environments in which selection takes place with no one essential feature fulfilling the primary causal role. As a classic example, Donald Campbell explains the processes involved in the evolution of the jaw structure of a worker termite.[116] Several processes at the genetic and cellular level work in a bottom-up fashion in the construction of the worker termite jaws. However, there is also a form of top-down causation in that features of the environment constrain what types of adaptations will succeed or fail based on the survival or extinction of different species. Thus, at the genetic level, genes encode for the particular proteins that will eventually construct the jaw, but the environment in which that particular trait is expressed ultimately determines the fitness of the termite according to whether that trait facilitates survival or reproduction.

The laws for constructing DNA and proteins are not the only laws at work. Laws that operate at a higher-level of complexity provide a constraint on which possible jaw structures are optimal to allow the worker termite to survive and reproduce. Thus, the particular protein distribution is selected through the process of a top-down constraint, not the particular configuration of DNA directly. A co-evolutionary account suggests that one environmental variable that has changed through the course of evolution is the cultural transmission of information. Different forms of communication within species have enabled the evolution of different ways of processing information, which has produced a parallel effect on the formation of different cognitive systems that enable the processing of that type of information.

Changes in the environment can affect the expression of different genetic variables. For instance, although most mammals use lactose early in life to break down enzymes in milk, this ability eventually disappears after weaning. However, this changed in humans with the initiation of animal husbandry.[117] This environmental change imposed a selection pressure that acts as a top-down constraint on the evolutionary process, which favored those with higher levels of tolerance to lactose over the life span because milk became a regular part of their diet. A co-evolutionary theory suggests that changes in the organism as well as changes in the environment have modified the evolutionary trajectory of human cognition. Additionally, this theory suggests that the environment has changed as a result of the behavioral flexibility of the organism. The modified environment

---

[116] Donald Campbell, "'Downward Causation' in Hierarchically Organized Biological Systems," in *Studies in the Philosophy of Biology: Reduction and Related Problems*, ed. Francisco J. Ayala and Theodosius Dobzhansky (Berkeley and Los Angeles: University of California Press, 1974).

[117] M. W. Feldman and K. N. Laland, "Gene-Culture Coevolutionary Theory," *Trends in Evolution and Ecology* 11 (1996).

provided different selection pressures that produced new forms of inherited traits. Thus, one of the primary forces of evolutionary change was behavioral flexibility and neural plasticity in addition to the acquisition of cognitive adaptations.

This is different from the description of cognition described by the standard model, because a co-evolutionary account of cognition suggests a greater dependence on neural plasticity and the top-down constraints of culture. According to Deacon, the acquisition of certain cognitive abilities is *learned* based on coordinated activity of social informational transmission and the way the brain is structured to process symbolic information.[118] This theory of co-evolution contradicts some of the original formulations of Baldwin in that the acquisition of certain traits based on changing selection pressures favored *learning* rather than innate dispositions.

> In this regard the process is quite different in consequence from what either Baldwin or Waddington might have predicted. In some ways, the evolutionary dynamic linking language behavior and brain evolution had the opposite effect: the de-differentiation of innate predispositions and an increase in the contribution by a learning mechanism.[119]

Thus, the evolution of human cognition is a result of an increased dependence on top-down cultural constraints and cognitive flexibility as well as the formation of neural structures that make the acquisition of certain types of information relatively easy.

Conclusion

Evolutionary psychology has greatly contributed to our understanding of human nature and demonstrated different aspects of the evolution of cognition. However, humans have not only inherited a Stone Age mind from their evolutionary past, but also a symbolic mind, which enabled the emergence of religious concepts and symbols. The ability to think symbolically and abstractly is a result of the co-evolutionary processes of changes in the way information is transmitted socially/culturally and changes in the structural connections within the brain. In regard to human cognition, imitation was an important advancement in cultural exchange with the corollary effect of the development of mirror systems in humans. Secondly, I discussed the role of shared intentions in our evolutionary history as a new way in which persons were able to communicate. Sharing

---

[118] Terrence Deacon, "Multilevel Selection in a Complex Adaptive System: The Problem of Language Origins," in *Evolution and Learning: The Baldwin Effect Reconsidered*, ed. Bruce H. Weber and David J. Depew (Cambridge: The MIT Press, 2003), 93.

[119] Ibid., 92.

intentions was a precursor for more advanced forms of cognition such as theory of mind. Although evolutionary psychology would suggest that theory of mind is a particular module, I argued that the ability to have a theory of mind is an emergent process that involves complex relational feedback between persons, which works in conjunction with certain innate abilities such as imitation.

Although modular views of language acquisition suggest that language evolved as a result of an innate grammar that enables humans to translate native languages into "mentalese," a co-evolutionary account argues that changes have occurred in both the structure of language and the brain. Human representational ability has evolved through three forms of representation: iconic, indexical, and symbolic. The human brain has evolved in its structure such that most of human cognitive processing is interconnected with the functions of the prefrontal cortex; human cognition has become front-heavy. In parallel, language has become a user-friendly interface in that language is very easy for humans to learn, especially children. Language has evolved to exploit the symbolic character of human cognitive processing, while the top-down constraints imposed by symbolic language have introduced a selection pressure on the structure of the brain to enable symbolic processing.

The evolution of human cognition has involved several changes in cultural exchange and the structure of the brain that have not been covered in this chapter. The difference between a co-evolutionary account and the account offered by the standard model is that the co-evolutionary account of human cognition includes several cultural and social processes that played an important role in the evolution of cognition and, ultimately, religious belief. A co-evolutionary model demonstrates the top-down constraints involved in the evolution of human cognition in addition to the bottom-up constraints that the standard model uses to explain different aspects of religion. A co-evolutionary account takes into consideration the wider nexus of causal processes involved in the evolution of cognition and religious beliefs.

Chapter 5
Evolution, Cognition, and Religion: Toward a Multi-level Perspective on the Emergence of Religious Beliefs

The cognitive science of religion offers several helpful perspectives on the initial conditions involved in the formation of religious beliefs. However, the description of initial conditions provided by the standard model does not adequately represent the multiple types of causal factors involved in the formation of religious beliefs studied at various levels in the hierarchy of science. An explanation for the emergence of religious beliefs requires a multi-level approach with contributions from cognitive science, neuroscience, and evolutionary theory, but also requires contributions from more expansive sciences such as anthropology, sociology, and theology. Religion, as an academic study, cannot be separated from its relationship to politics, history, science, and human nature. But focusing on a particular set of attributes involved in the formation of religious beliefs can illuminate aspects that may be missed in any one discipline and provide avenues for further discovery.

This chapter provides a methodology for relating evidence from the cognitive and evolutionary sciences to our overall understanding of the formation of religious beliefs. This methodology is multi-level in that it starts from general factors of human cognitive processing and neural functioning, then moves on to factors involved in relationships between persons, and then ultimately moves to the level of groups. This is not meant as an exhaustive explanation for religious beliefs, but simply arranges evidence from the cognitive, neural, and evolutionary sciences to give an overall description of the emergence of religious beliefs. This account follows the general pattern outlined in Chapter 2, which described cognitive emergence in terms of initial conditions, feedback, and pattern formation, then expands into the realms of human relationships and group dynamics. In this sense, this is both a cognitive and evolutionary account of the formation of religious beliefs with the conceit that not every factor can or could be included. Thus, my explanation functions as a methodology for relating cognitive neuroscience to other levels in the hierarchy of science with the realization that there are other possible variables and scientific perspectives that may organize an emergent model in a slightly different way.

Counterintuitive Concepts

The counterintuitive hypothesis is the dominant paradigm in regard to religious concepts in the standard model. However, as I discussed in previous chapters, religious concepts are not causally reducible to counterintuitive features or by-products because of the important role of emergent and top-down factors in the formation of religious beliefs. The empirical question that remains to be answered is whether cognition is primarily based on an intuitive ontology that is the product of internal cognitive constraints or by the external features of the world, which become incorporated into cognitive categories based on feedback and pattern formation. Either way, counterintuitive properties are still a helpful way to explain aspects of religion and connect religious beliefs to general aspects of cognitive functions. Religious beliefs are not a product of a specialized area of the brain, but rely on the same types of cognitive and neural systems involved in most areas of thought and behavior.

According to Boyer, religious concepts minimally violate features of natural ontological categories specified by the evolved specialized inference systems of human cognition.[1] Human cognition conceptualizes naturally occurring objects through the elaboration of templates that specify particular ontological categories such as person, artifact, or animal.[2] Each template functions according to specific inferences about the ontological category, which enables quick and easy identification and categorization of an object. Religious concepts are unique in that they *violate* certain aspects of the category while retaining other features, which actually increases the probability of those religious concepts being remembered and transmitted to others in contrast with intuitive concepts alone.[3]

Although counterintuitive properties play an important role in the formation, memorization, and transmission of religious concepts and beliefs, these concepts do not necessarily outnumber other types of concepts used in religious narratives.[4] If counterintuitive properties are the primary component of religious concepts, why would they not replace the use of more general concepts? Most religious texts and stories contain a wealth of mundane and everyday events, behaviors, and thoughts that are not counterintuitive. For example, the Christian bible has a considerable amount of stories focused on simply walking to a new town, fishing, eating, or a number of other commonplace events. In a study by Ara Norenzayan

---

[1] Pascal Boyer, "Religious Thought and Behavior as By-Products of Brain Function," *Trends in Cognitive Sciences* 7, no. 3 (2003): 119-124.

[2] Pascal Boyer, "Natural Epistemology or Evolved Metaphysics?: Developmental Evidence for Early-Developed, Intuitive, Category-Specific, Incomplete, and Stubborn Metaphysical Presumptions," *Philosophical Psychology* 13, no. 3 (2000): 277-297.

[3] Pascal Boyer, *Religion Explained: The Evolutionary Origins of Religious Thought* (New York: Basic Books, 2001).

[4] Scott Atran, *In Gods We Trust: The Evolutionary Landscape of Religion* (New York: Oxford University Press, 2002), 101.

and Scott Atran, intuitive concepts were recalled more often than counterintuitive concepts, but a few counterintuitive concepts dispersed in a belief set of several intuitive concepts had the highest rate of memory recall after a temporary delay and the lowest rate of memory erosion over time.[5] Thus, counterintuitive concepts seem to work best when they are embedded in stories that contain a considerable amount of intuitive concepts.

At the level of an individual belief, counterintuitive concepts are more memorable, but if too many counterintuitive concepts dominate a specific religious narrative, it may make it difficult to remember and transmit to others. Retention and transmission of counterintuitive concepts are affected by other variables as well. Attempting to recall counterintuitive concepts in the presence of contradictory contextual variables decreases retention, while relevant context fosters increased retention.[6] This suggests that the ability to remember certain types of concepts is not primarily a result of the properties of the concept itself, but requires additional factors to facilitate retention. Thus, contextual variables present during the encoding of the concept and the knowledge base of the person attempting to retain the concept will have a significant effect on the ability to retain the counterintuitive material.[7]

The counterintuitive hypothesis provides important evidential support for the realization that the formation of religious beliefs, like most aspects of human cognition, is not free from certain kinds of constraints.[8] Human creativity is not a cognitive free for all, but works within the limitations of human cognitive functioning. In fact, it is actually those cognitive limitations that allow for creativity to flourish and create with a purpose in mind. Unconstrained cognitive creativity would simply result in a disorderly assemblage of several disconnected thoughts, which would be unidentifiable under the term creative. Creativity is based on elements of thought that are already well understood and then re-arranging those elements in new and provocative ways without ever severing the original connections to known quantities.

In a similar sense, religious beliefs are not disconnected from the contexts and concrete problems of human existence. There are certainly religious beliefs that are far from center and can seem quite strange when viewed from an outside perspective. However, if a religious belief is too far removed from the everyday

---

[5] Ara Norenzayan and Scott Atran, "Cognitive and Emotional Processes in the Cultural Transmission of Natural and Nonnatural Beliefs," in *The Psychological Foundations of Culture*, ed. M. Schaller and C. Crandall (Hillsdale: Erlbaum, 2002), 149-179.

[6] Lauren O. Gonce and others, "Role of Context in the Recall of Counterintuitive Concepts," *Journal of Cognition and Culture* 6, no. 3-4 (2006): 521-547.

[7] M. Afzal Upal and others, "Contextualizing Counterintuitiveness: How Context Affects Comprehension and Memorability of Counterintuitive Concepts," *Cognitive Science* 31 (2007): 415-439.

[8] Michael H. Kelly and Frank C. Keil, "The More Things Change ... : Metamorphoses and Conceptual Structure," *Cognitive Science* 9 (1985): 403-416.

objects of human cognitive processing its survival seems highly unlikely. The same cognitive systems that process information about weight, distance, emotion, lying, categorization, and a myriad of other domains are the same systems that process information about religion. Thus, it seems obvious that the majority of religious beliefs would not be *disconnected* from the natural world, but instead highly integrated with the natural world. Religious beliefs may be abstract, aesthetic, and highly imaginative, but they still either started from or actively engage aspects of the natural world. Thus, the counterintuitive hypothesis describes initial conditions involved in the formation of religious beliefs. Religious beliefs are formed and transmitted based on the partial constraints imposed by the different categories in which religious reasoning occurs.

Hyperactive Agency Detection

The idea of God concepts being related to the general cognitive domain of agency detection originally began in the work of Stewart Gutherie, who claimed that human beings usually process ambiguous stimuli through the attribution of anthropomorphic or animistic explanations.[9] Justin Barrett modified this claim slightly to suggest that supernatural concepts are closely associated with an excessive identification of agents in the world, which is a product of a mental tool he called the hyperactive agency detection device (HADD).[10] It was evolutionarily advantageous to over-detect agents in the natural world rather under-detecting other agents who may be potential predators. This is also related to a classic psychological study in which agency is inferred to inanimate objects such as geometrical shapes that appear to be chasing each other.[11] Thus, the architecture of human cognition is primed for finding agents in the world and it is a relatively easy cognitive adjustment to conceptualize agents according to supernatural properties.

HADD is the aspect of cognition that processes the agency aspects of religious beliefs, while the counterintuitive properties connect religious beliefs to general features of the natural world making them easier to process and remember. In addition, theory of mind seems to be related to the functions of HADD and has become a primary cognitive function used to explain religious beliefs, especially

---

[9] Stewart Guthrie, "A Cognitive Theory of Religion," *Current Anthropology* 21, no. 2 (1980): 181-203; Stewart Guthrie, *Faces in the Clouds: A New Theory of Religion* (Oxford: Oxford University Press, 1993); Benson Saler, "Anthropomorphism and Animism: On Stewart E. Guthrie, *Faces in the Clouds* (1993)," in *Contemporary Theories of Religion: A Critical Companion*, ed. Michael Stausberg (New York: Routledge, 2009), 39-52.

[10] Justin L. Barrett, "Exploring the Natural Foundations of Religion," *Trends in Cognitive Sciences* 4, no. 1 (2000): 29-34.

[11] Fritz Heider and Mary-Ann Simmel, "An Experimental Study of Apparent Behavior," *American Journal of Psychology* 57 (1944): 243-249.

beliefs in supernatural agents and gods.[12] Theory of mind enables easy acquisition of supernatural concepts because it is used to infer the potential intentions of any agent, including animals, ghosts, or even God. During childhood, theory of mind seems to include a default setting that infers superhuman properties to many different types of intentional agents. Thus, supernatural concepts, as processed by theory of mind, simply exploit the natural tendency to identify the intentions of any inanimate object.

Theory of mind is a basic cognitive function that develops around the age of five and plays an important role in interpreting the intentions, thoughts and beliefs of others.[13] Prior to age five, children have difficulty believing that persons can have false beliefs or beliefs that are different from their own, but this later develops into a generalized ability to understand and infer the thoughts of others.[14] A popular experiment used to assess this ability is taking a box of crackers, showing it to group of children, and then asking them what they think is inside.[15] The children answer "crackers" and are then shown that the box actually contains rocks. When asked what their parents would think is in the box, most three to four-year-olds answer "rocks" while most five-year-olds answer "crackers" realizing that their parents will be fooled by not being able to see the contents of the box.

This experiment has interesting consequences when applied to the concept of God. In a study with American Protestant children, 5-year-olds still realized that their parents would be unaware of the true contents of the cracker box, but God would know that rocks were in the box.[16] In a similar study with Mayan children, children demonstrated a similar outcome in differentiating between the cognitive abilities of their mothers and God.[17] In another experiment using occluded visual displays, all ages assumed that God had a form of "omniscience" that enabled the correct identification of any type of occluded display.[18] Younger children would assume that mothers had a similar ability while older children would begin to make

---

[12] Justin L. Barrett, *Why Would Anyone Believe in God?* (Walnut Creek: AltaMira Press, 2004).

[13] Simon Baron-Cohen, *Mindblindness: An Essay on Autism and Theory of Mind* (Cambridge: The MIT Press, 1997); Martin J. Doherty, *Theory of Mind: How Children Understand Others' Thoughts and Feelings* (New York: Psychology Press, 2008).

[14] H. Wellman, D. Cross, and J. Watson, "Meta-Analysis of Theory of Mind Development: The Truth About False-Belief," *Child Development* 72 (2001): 655-684.

[15] Daniel T. Levin and Melissa R. Beck, *Thinking and Seeing: Visual Metacognition in Adults and Children* (Cambridge: The MIT Press, 2004).

[16] Justin L. Barrett, R. A. Richert, and A. Driesenga, "God's Beliefs Versus Mother's: The Development of Non-Human Agent Concepts," *Child Development* 71 (2001): 50-65.

[17] Nicola Knight and others, "Children's Attributions of Beliefs to Humans and God: Cross-Cultural Evidence," *Cognitive Science* 28, no. 1 (2004): 117-126.

[18] Justin L. Barrett, R. A. Newman, and R. A. Richert, "When Seeing Does Not Lead to Believing: Children's Understanding of the Importance of Background Knowledge for Interpreting Visual Displays," *Journal of Cognition and Culture* 3 (2003): 91-108.

a distinction between the cognitive abilities of mothers (prone to false beliefs) and God (not prone to false beliefs).

A possible concern for theologians is the notion that the over-detection of agents by the HADD is a cognitive error, thus belief in gods is simply the misuse of a cognitive default, which promotes beliefs in supernatural agents that are not really present.[19] However, religious beliefs cannot be causally reduced to the processing of any one aspect of human cognition. As I have argued in previous chapters, human cognition, especially at the level of individual beliefs, is dependent upon a number of internal and external variables that are emergent and impossible to reduce to the functions of one aspect of cognition. As discussed in Chapter 4, theory of mind may be better described as an emergent feature of cognition rather than a domain-specific cognitive module.

Attributing agency and assessing the actual presence of an agent are two very different human behaviors. Although it is easy to misattribute agency to sounds around the house, most adults simply investigate the sounds to assess the validity of their initial cognitive suspicions. As Justin Barrett explains, the use of HADD is one cognitive feature among many that is used to assess the validity of a particular belief.

> If HADD worked alone in determining when or where we discovered the existence of agents, we would never be able to tell definitively when it was wrong. ... Other cognitive mechanisms, including our abilities to consider evidence reflectively, can override HADD or any other single cognitive mechanism that tries to generate a belief. ... As HADD and the other cognitive mechanisms that promote belief in god do not work alone to generate beliefs, their accuracy cannot be evaluated in isolation.[20]

Thus, HADD is a cognitive device that is a necessary condition for some aspects of supernatural concepts and religious beliefs, but it is not a sufficient condition for evaluating the legitimacy of theistic belief.

Emotion and Religion

The counterintuitive hypothesis and agency detection are helpful starting points for understanding the initial conditions involved in the formation of religious beliefs. One important factor that needs to be added is the role of emotional processing in cognition generally and religious belief specifically. It is becoming clear that a rigid distinction between cognition and emotion is no longer a viable description of

---

[19] Paul Bloom, "Is God an Accident?," *Atlantic Monthly*, December 2005; Richard Dawkins, *The God Delusion* (Boston: Houghton Mifflin Harcourt, 2006).

[20] Justin L. Barrett, "Is the Spell Really Broken? Bio-Psychological Explanations of Religion and Theistic Belief," *Theology and Science* 5, no. 1 (2007): 68.

how humans process information.[21] One of the primary assumptions of the social and affective neurosciences is that emotion is not secondary to cognition, but provides adaptive responses and relevant content for human cognition.[22] An early criticism of the counterintuitive hypothesis was the failure to address the emotional and motivational aspects of religious belief.[23] Even if supernatural agents are counterintuitive, what is it that motivates religious beliefs and causes the high levels of emotionality that are usually associated with rituals and individual experiences?

This is often called the Mickey Mouse problem.[24] There are many types of concepts that seem to meet the standard for counterintuitive properties and also utilize the HADD device in terms of understanding these concepts as agents. Mickey Mouse and Santa Claus are prime examples. Both are counterintuitive in that they retain certain general properties of naturally occurring persons and animals, yet these properties are slightly violated in terms of a talking mouse and a man from the North Pole who rides in a sleigh. Obviously, agency is another important aspect of these characters; Santa Claus could not deliver presents if he was unable to perform certain actions for an intended purpose. Yet, neither of these characters is worshipped or understood in religious terms. What is it about religion that engages the devotional, sacrificial, and emotional aspects of human nature? Boyer argues that religion activates an additional suite of human thoughts and behaviors that include social relationships, communal rituals, group identity, and heightened emotional states.[25] Thus, it is important to add human affect and emotion to our list of initial conditions involved in the formation of religious beliefs.

Emotion is an important aspect of religious beliefs and behaviors. Many philosophers and theologians argue that religion should be primarily defined in terms of its experiential and existential qualities, which are usually understood in terms of emotional processes and events. Friedrich Schleiermacher argued that the heart of religion is a feeling of absolute dependence upon something greater than the individual isolated self.[26] Rudolph Otto considered religion to be a numinous, non-sensory experience that terrifies and fascinates those whom experience it.[27] Martin Buber identified two different ways of relating to the world

---

[21] Luiz Pessoa, "On the Relationship between Emotion and Cognition," *Nature Reviews Neuroscience* 9 (2008): 148-158.

[22] Ralph Adolphs and Michael Spezio, "Social Cognition," in *The Handbook of Neuroscience for the Behavioral Sciences*, ed. G. G. Bernston and J. T. Cacioppo (New York: Wiley and Sons, 2009).

[23] Ilkka Pyysiäinen, *How Religion Works: Toward a New Cognitive Science of Religion* (Leiden: Brill 2003), 77.

[24] Atran, *In Gods We Trust*, 14.

[25] Boyer, *Religion Explained*, 90.

[26] Friedrich Schleiermacher, *On Religion: Speeches to Is Cultured Despisers*, trans. John Oman (New York: Harper & Row, 1958).

[27] Rudolph Otto, *The Idea of the Holy*, trans. J. W. Harvey (Oxford: Oxford University Press, 1969).

and God.[28] The I-It relation was the scientific objective stance, which Buber felt was distant and analytical. This stance separated the individual from what he or she was trying to understand; it was the categorization of an object at the expense of actually experiencing it. The I-Thou relation was the type of stance necessary for relating to God, which was a reciprocal relationship of the other. Buber likened this stance to experiencing God because the stance allowed for mutual interaction and affect between partners in this type of relationship; God was not categorized but experienced and both partners impacted the other. The classic definition of religious experience in the psychology of religion comes from the work of William James, who primarily identified religion with individual, solitary experiences.

> Religion, therefore, as I now ask you arbitrarily to take it, shall mean for us the feelings, acts, and experiences of men in their solitude, so far as they apprehend themselves to stand in relation to whatever they may consider the divine.[29]

However, to limit religion to individual experiences misses a great deal of important aspects of religious beliefs, which include several different social and relational functions.

Emotion is an important aspect of different forms of religious beliefs, rituals, and behaviors. Many different forms of religious rituals trigger high levels of emotional arousal, which may play an important role in their cultural transmission and sustainability over time.[30] Different forms of religious ritual may include having a feast and drinking wine with the community or restraining from food for a given amount of time. Other rituals include loud music, rhythmic drums and dancing or mind-altering drugs and other forms of altered states of consciousness. Emotional and physiological arousal play an important role in these types of activities, which would obviously involve different parts of the brain that specifically deal with emotion, affect, and arousal.

Neuroscience and Emotion

Much of the recent research in cognitive neuroscience has focused on aspects of the social or emotional brain.[31] Some of the specific cortical and subcortical

---

[28] Martin Buber, *I and Thou*, trans. Ronald Gregor Smith (New York: Scribner Classics, 1958/2000).

[29] William James, *The Varieties of Religious Experience* (New York: Modern Library, 1902/1999), 36.

[30] E. Thomas Lawson and Robert N. McCauley, *Rethinking Religion: Connecting Cognition and Culture* (Cambridge: Cambridge University Press, 1990).

[31] Christopher Frith and Daniel Wolpert, eds., *The Neuroscience of Social Interaction: Decoding, Imitating, and Influencing the Actions of Others* (New York: Oxford University Press, 2004); Richard Lane and Lynn Nadel, eds., *Cognitive Neuroscience of Emotion* (New York: Oxford University Press, 2000); Joseph LeDoux, *The Emotional Brain:*

areas under research are the ventromedial prefrontal cortex, somatosensory cortex, cingulate, insula, amygdala, hippocampus, and the hypothalamus.[32] Each of these areas provides a unique function for processing emotion-related information. The amygdala is most often associated with emotional reactions, specifically the fear response. In research with non-human primates, damage or ablation of the amygdala caused severe deficits in processing emotionally relevant information, especially in regard to fear.[33] Damage to the central nucleus of the amygdala was shown to interfere with several aspects of fear, including freezing behavior, autonomic responses and reflexive readiness.[34] Damage to the amygdala in humans shows a similar pattern of inability to process auditory emotional information and to analyze the emotional facets of facial expressions.[35] A direct pathway from the thalamus to the amygdala enables quick processing of fearful stimuli, an important factor in the fight or flight response.

The amygdala also plays an important role in emotional memory, especially encoding the implicit, mostly unconscious, emotional valence of particular memories, while the hippocampus (a seahorse shaped structure located in the temporal lobe) processes information relevant to conscious, narrative, and temporal aspects of memory.[36] Although the hippocampus does not store memories, it plays an important role in encoding explicit aspects of memory, possibly due to the pyramidal neuronal cells located throughout the structure.[37] The role of the hippocampus was most clearly demonstrated in the case of H.M., who lost the ability to make new memories after bilateral removal of the medial temporal lobe, including the hippocampus.[38]

Another area of the brain important for emotional processing is the cingulate cortex, which lies just above the corpus callosum in the interior of the longitudinal fissure.[39] Various areas of the cingulate become activated during recall of emotional

---

The Mysterious Underpinnings of Emotional Life (New York: Touchstone, 1996); Jaak Panksepp, *Affective Neuroscience: The Foundations of Human and Animal Emotions* (New York: Oxford University Press, 1998).

[32] Louis Cozolino, *The Neuroscience of Human Relationships: Attachment and the Developing Social Brain* (New York: W. W. Norton & Co., 2006), 51.

[33] H. Kluver and P. C. Bucy, "Preliminary Analysis of the Temporal Lobes in Monkeys," *Archives of Neurology and Psychiatry* 42 (1939): 979-1000.

[34] Joseph LeDoux, "Emotion: Clues from the Brain," *Annual Review of Psychology* 46 (1995): 209-235.

[35] Ralph Adolphs and others, "Impaired Recognition of Emotion in Facial Expression Following Bilateral Damage to the Human Amygdala," *Nature* 372 (1994): 669-672; S. K. Scott and others, "Impaired Auditory Recognition of Fear and Anger Following Bilaeral Amygdala Lesions," *Nature* 385 (1997): 254-257.

[36] Endel Tulving, *Elements of Episodic Memory* (Oxford: Clarendon Press, 1983).

[37] Carlson, *Physiology of Behavior*, 416.

[38] Kolb and Whishaw, *Human Neuropsychology*, 357-360.

[39] Ibid., 51.

memories and it also has a role in attachment, including mothering instincts such as consoling and nursing.[40] Damage to the cingulate leads to a decrease in empathy and related maternal behaviors as well as problems in maintaining emotional stability.[41] The cingulate plays a role in integrating attentional and emotional aspects of current caretaking tasks in order to facilitate the development of attunement to the needs of the infant.[42]

The somatosensory cortex lies just behind the lateral fissure that separates the frontal lobe from the parietal lobe and is primarily associated with sensory functions of different areas of body, which are topographically mapped on the surface.[43] Thus, different areas of the somatosensory cortex correspond to sensory inputs from the hands, face, lips, genitals, etc. At the base of the somatosensory cortex is the insular cortex (insula), which is hidden in the Sylvian fissure between the frontal and temporal lobes.[44]

J. R. Augustine argues that the insula integrates information from different parts of the limbic system with the frontal, parietal, and temporal cortices.[45] The insula appears to play a role in linking body states with expressions of awareness, emotion, and behavior. In conjunction with the cingulate, the insula makes us aware of our internal somatosensory states and provides a channel for reflecting on our emotional experiences. A. Bartels and S. Zeki suggest that the insula is involved in a variety of emotions from feelings of disgust to love.[46] The hypothalamus is located just under the thalamus at the top of the brainstem and is most often associated with the autonomic nervous system, which increases levels of arousal to ready the person for action.[47] It is linked with several social and emotional behaviors, including the regulation of sexual behavior and aggression, eating, sleeping, temperature regulation, and movement.[48] These and other areas of the brain play an important role in the emotional aspects of religious beliefs and rituals. One theory that attempts to describe different cognitive and emotional processes involved in religious belief is the modes theory.

---

[40] Cozolino, *Neuroscience of Relationships*, 104.

[41] L. Brothers, "Brain Mechanisms of Social Cognition," *Journal of Psychopharmacology* 10 (1996): 2-8.

[42] H. Yamaski, K. S. LaBar, and G. McCarthy, "Dissociable Prefrontal Brain Systems for Attention and Emotion," *Proceedings of the National Academy of Sciences, USA* 99 (2002): 11447-11451.

[43] Carlson, *Physiology of Behavior*, 82.

[44] Kolb and Whishaw, *Human Neuropsychology*, 286.

[45] J. R. Augustine, "Circuitry and Functional Aspects of the Insular Lobe in Primates, Including Humans," *Brain Research Reviews* 22 (1996): 229-244.

[46] A. Bartels and S. Zeki, "The Neural Basis of Romantic Love," *NeuroReport* 11 (2000): 3829-3834.

[47] Carlson, *Physiology of Behavior*, 87.

[48] Kolb and Whishaw, *Human Neuropsychology*, 48; Cozolino, *Neuroscience of Relationships*, 57.

Emotion and the Modes Theory

Harvey Whitehouse identifies two distinct modes of religiosity, the doctrinal and imagistic mode. The doctrinal mode is primary concerned with rituals that emphasize recitation, repetition, and verbal transmission of important beliefs and values.[49] The doctrinal mode typically tries to convey religious meanings that are more abstract and complex and typically encoded in semantic forms of human memory. This creates a more intense cognitive load on general features of human memory and thus requires the more lengthy forms of repetition and routine to transmit the information to other persons. Some Protestant Christian services may be illustrative of this mode in that familiar hymns, repetitive rituals, and abstract sermons are used to convey the important doctrines for the church.

The imagistic mode focuses on rituals that occur only rarely, but are typically highly emotionally arousing for the participants.[50] The imagistic mode typically encodes in memory systems that are more focused on episodic memories, which combine into long-term autobiographical memories and narratives. Many of these rituals may produce flash bulb memories, which are memories of such intense emotional arousal that they become permanently etched on the psyche. The explosion of the *Challenger* space shuttle or the destruction of the World Trade Center on 9/11 is often cited as intense experiences, which produced lasting memories. Religious initiation rituals, which may be violent or traumatic or highly ecstatic rituals and altered states of consciousness, serve as examples of the imagistic mode. The intensity of the experience creates group cohesion, which means that direct forms of leadership and organization are not as necessary for the success of the religious practice.

Whitehouse argues that neither mode is an accurate representation of any one religion, but each mode acts as a pole along a continuum of religious practice and ritual. However, the close association between cognition and emotion, currently affirmed in the cognitive neurosciences, questions these poles as accurate representations of the divergent factors involved in religious belief, experience, and ritual. For the imagistic mode, flashbulb memory seems to be an unreliable form of memory and several studies have demonstrated significant errors and distortions for memories of highly emotional, public events usually characterized as flash-bulb types of events.[51] For the doctrinal mode, it would seem to fall prey to the same sorts of limitations described by the Mickey Mouse problem. Without

---

[49] Harvey Whitehouse, *Modes of Religiosity: A Cognitive Theory of Religious Transmission* (Walnut Creek: AltaMira Press, 2004), 66-69.

[50] Ibid., 70-74.

[51] U. Neiesser and N. Harsch, "Phantom Flashbulbs: False Recollection of Hearing News About the *Challenger*," in *Affect and Accuracy of Recall: Studies Of "Flashbulb" Memories*, ed. E. Winograd and U. Neiesser (Cambridge: Cambridge University Press, 1992); J. M. Talaricho and D. C. Rubin, "Confidence, Not Consistency, Characterizes Flashbulb Memories," *Psychological Science* 14 (2003): 455-461.

a sense of emotionality, typical cognitive beliefs do little to actually motivate behaviors that include devotion and sacrifice. Thus, for any set of religious beliefs, both the cognitive and emotional content would be highly relevant to understanding the formation of religious beliefs and their role in directing human action. As the next section clearly demonstrates, emotionality is an important aspect of daily decision-making.

Emotion and Decision-making

Connections from the emotional centers of the brain (including the amygdala, somatosensory and insular cortices) to the ventromedial sector of the prefrontal cortex have a profound effect on decision-making.[52] Antonio Damasio argues that the states of emotional arousal in the body (somatic markers) influence aspects of decision-making as processed by the prefrontal cortex.[53] Thus, emotions (both positive and negative) have a dramatic affect on the ways information is processed and the initiation of action. The connection between emotion and decision-making was originally conceived by a re-examination of the fascinating story of Phineas Gage.

Gage was a medical marvel who survived an accident in 1848 while working on the railway system in New England. He was in charge of detonating large portions of dirt and rock that were blocking the intended route of the railway, using an iron rod tamper and explosive powder.[54] While attempting to set one of the detonations, Gage forgot to put sand into the hole as a buffer between the iron rod and the explosive material being tamped. When the rod hit the powder it exploded like a rocket, shooting right through his eye socket and out the top of his head. Remarkably, Gage survived the accident and never lost consciousness, but he was never quite the same. Gage had an amazing recovery and, in two months, he seemed to be functioning normally. He could talk, see, hear, walk, and move about without any problem, but he began to make poor vocational and social decisions.[55] Something in the accident had caused a radical adjustment in his character; a new self had emerged that was a ghostly shadow of the former Phineas Gage.

A re-examination of the damage to Gage's skull showed that the iron rod had damaged the orbital region of the frontal cortex.[56] Damasio found that the damage was mainly in an area of the orbital prefrontal cortex known as the ventromedial prefrontal region. Patients with damage to the ventromedial prefrontal area

---

[52] Antoine Bechara, Hanna Damasio, and Antonio Damasio, "Emotion, Decision Making and the Orbitofrontal Cortex," *Cerebral Cortex* 10 (2000): 295-307.

[53] Antonio Damasio, *Descartes' Error: Emotion, Reason, and the Human Brain* (New York: Quill, 1994), 174.

[54] Ibid., 3-4.

[55] Ibid., 11.

[56] Ibid., 22-23.

have similar behavioral and decision-making problems as Gage with deficits in social and personal decision-making.[57] "These patients seem to have 'myopia' for the future in that they are oblivious to the consequences of their actions and are guided only by immediate prospects."[58] Research on persons with similar prefrontal damage that occurred before the age of 16 months showed that these subjects exhibited many of the behavior problems of adult onset of prefrontal damage, but were in some ways even worse. Here is a description of one case:

> Her behavior became progressively disruptive, so much so that, by age fourteen, she required placement in the first of several treatment facilities. Her teachers considered her to be intelligent and academically capable, but she routinely failed to complete assigned tasks. Her adolescence was marked by disruptive behavior in school and at home.[59]

In this particular case, the behavior of this patient continued to decline, leading to more social and moral failures.

These deficits are difficult to detect by standard psychological tests, so Damasio and his colleagues developed a different assessment called the gambling task. This is a game involving four decks of cards, $2000 in facsimile money, and the monitoring of the tester.[60] Damasio describes the main facets of the gambling task.

> The subjects are told that (1) the goal of the task is to maximize profit on the loan of play money, (2) they are free to switch from any deck to another at any time, and as often as wished; but (3) they are not told in advance how many card selections must be made.[61]

The four decks are labeled A, B, C, and D; decks A and B involve the highest amount of monetary value, but also the highest risk for the player, while decks C and D involve the least amount of monetary value, but also less risk to the player.[62]

---

[57] Antoine Bechra, Daniel Tanel, and Hanna Damasio "Characterization of the Decision-Making Deficit of Patients with Ventromedial Prefrontal Cortex Lesions," *Brain*, 123 (2000): 2189.

[58] Ibid.

[59] Steven W. Anderson and others, "Impairment of Social and Moral Behavior Related to Early Damage in Human Prefrontal Cortex," *Nature Neuroscience* 2 (1999): 1034.

[60] Antonio Damasio, "The Somatic Marker Hypothesis and Possible Functions of the Prefrontal Cortex" in *The Prefrontal Cortex: Cognitive and Executive Functions*, ed. A. C. Roberts, T. W. Robbins, and L. Weiskrantz (Oxford: Oxford University Press, 1998), 45.

[61] Ibid.

[62] Damasio, *Descartes' Error*, 213.

The test mirrors the ability to inhibit certain behaviors for a greater gain in the long run. Most normal patients, while preferring decks A and B at first, eventually realize that they will make more money by sticking with decks C and D. Damasio describes the unconscious "hunches" of the normal person.

> I suspect that before and beneath the conscious hunch there is a non conscious process gradually formulating a prediction for the outcome of each move, and gradually telling the mindful player, at first softly but then even louder, that punishment or reward is about to strike if a certain move is carried out.[63]

Patients with ventromedial damage continue to pick from the disadvantageous decks A and B and ultimately require loans to continue playing the game. They do not have the hunch or feeling that decks A and B are ultimately more risky and provide less pay off than the other two decks. Damasio's research demonstrates the role of emotional processes in decision-making suggesting a larger role for emotion in cognition. Additionally, emotional processes seem to be related to attachment, which plays an important role in human development and is often associated with concepts of God.

God as Attachment Figure

Attachment theory is based on the work of Konrad Lorenz, an ethologist who studied the parent-offspring behaviors of geese.[64] Lorenz hypothesized that birds would follow the first thing that moved in front of them, which would typically be the mother goose; but Lorenz managed to get the offspring to follow him instead. This behavioral response is called imprinting; the offspring *imprints* the moving object as a mother and begins to follow her wherever she goes. Attachment theory drew a great deal from Lorenz's seminal work, but its primary importance was its application to the behavior of children. John Bowlby suggested that the nature of the relational bond between the mother and child determined the emotional well-being of children. This relational bond was established according to instinctual responses that helped to establish a binding dynamic between mother and child.[65] The attachment behavior system developed as an evolutionary adaptation by providing a system of proximity-seeking behaviors.

Although instinctual responses set up some of the initial parameters of attachment, it was the nature of the relationship that determined the quality of attachment between mother and child.

---

[63] Ibid, 214.

[64] Konrad Lorenz, "Der Kumpan in Der Umvelt Des Vogels [Companionship in Bird Life]," *Journal of Ornithology* 83 (1935): 137-213.

[65] John Bowlby, "The Nature of the Child's Tie to His Mother," *International Journal of Psycho-Analysis* 39 (1958): 351.

Based on repeated experience, infants and children develop a set of expectations and beliefs—a schema, in cognitive terms—about the availability and responsiveness of their primary caregivers which guides future behavioral, emotional, and cognitive responses in social interactions.[66]

For Bowlby, instinctual responses and relational feedback worked together to form a particular set of expectations that guided future behavior. Mary Ainsworth proposed that different types of attachment relationships formed different types of attachment between mother and child. For example, secure infants tended to cry when their mothers left the room, but would vocalize and move towards the mother when she returned. Nonattached infants did not cry when their mothers left or respond when their mothers returned. Insecurely attached children would cry excessively when their mothers left and cling to them when they returned.

Attachment experiences coalesce into an internal working model (IWM) that contains a specific schema or set of expectations about attachment-related features of relationships.[67] Kim Bartholomew developed a four-group model of attachment style and behavior based on IWMs of self and other: secure, preoccupied, dismissing, and fearful.[68] Each of the attachment styles was situated according to models of the self (positive or negative) and models of the other (positive or negative) as well as dependence (high or low) and avoidance (high or low). Secure persons were positive on models of the self and other and low on dependence and avoidance. Preoccupied persons held a negative opinion of the self, which led to a high level of dependence. Dismissing persons held a negative view of other persons and tended to be independent and denied the need for attachment. Fearful persons had a negative view of the self and other and tended to avoid attachments. The three-group and four-group model showed considerable concurrent validity when compared to each other.[69]

Interestingly, IWMs constrain future relationships while also being malleable according to current relational interactions. Ambivalent women tended to seek out avoidant men because the relationship would confirm their own views of themselves and the nature of relationship.[70] Current relationships can also affect IWMs for

---

[66] Lee A. Kirkpatrick, *Attachment, Evolution, and the Psychology of Religion* (New York: The Guilford Press, 2005), 38.

[67] Inge Bretherton and Kristine A. Munholland, "Internal Working Models: A Construct Revisited," in *Handbook of Attachment: Theory, Research, and Clinical Applications*, ed. Jude Cassidy and Phillip R. Shaver (New York: The Guilford Press, 1999).

[68] Kim Bartholomew, "Avoidance of Intimacy: An Attachment Perspective," *Journal of Social and Personal Relationships* 7 (1990): 147-178.

[69] Judith A. Feeney, "Adult Romantic Attachment and Couple Relationships," in *Handbook of Attachment: Theory, Research, and Clincial Applications*, ed. Cindy Hazan and Phillip R. Shaver (New York: The Guilford Press, 1999), 362.

[70] Lee A. Kirkpatrick and K. E. Davis, "Attachment Style, Gender, and Relationship Stability: A Longitudinal Analysis," *Journal of Personality and Social Psychology* 66

better or worse. Persons who have ambivalent feelings about a relationship may alter their views when current relational experiences disconfirm expectations about the partner. Similarly, securely attached individuals can be affected in a negative way by relational experiences which are hurtful or emotionally abusive to the person.[71] This research is important on two counts: First, it emphasizes the importance of relationships, both past and present, in the development of the self and romantic partnerships. Second, it shows that IWMs of attachment are present throughout the lifespan and constrain other types of attachment relationships.

Regulatory Systems in Attachment

Regulatory processes jumpstart the relational processes of attachment in many mammalian species from the beginning of the lifespan onwards. Research on the rat brain and heart-rate control shows that when rat pups were separated from their mother, there was a decrease in heart rate and later difficulties in heart rate regulation.[72] The rat pups use the heartbeat of the mother as a type of external cue to regulate their own heartbeats. Similar research suggests that rat pups rely on the mother for several types of biological regulation, including neurochemical, metabolic, sleep, endocrine, and immune regulation.[73] In fact, when most mammals are separated from their primary attachment figures there are rapid changes in levels of arousal, blood pressure, growth hormones, behavioral reactivity, sucking, and sleep patterns.[74] Several areas of physiological regulation rely on feedback from primary caregivers to establish optimal levels of biological arousal.

Outsourcing feedback mechanisms of regulation seems to be a normal part of mammalian development in order to establish the correct levels and maintenance of physiological states.

(1994): 502-512.

[71] Judith A. Feeney, "Adult Attachment and Relationship-Centered Anxiety: Responses to Physical and Emotional Distancing," in *Attachment Theory and Close Relationships*, ed. J. A. Simpson and W. S. Rholes (New York: Guilford Press, 1998); Judith A. Feeney, P. Noller, and V. J. Callan, "Attachment Style, Communication and Satisfaction in the Early Years of Marriage," in *Advances in Personal Relationships: Vol. 5. Attachment Processes in Adulthood*, ed. Kim Bartholomew and D. Perlman (London: Jessica Kingsley, 1994); M. Senchak and K. E. Leonard, "Attachment Styles and Marital Adjustment among Newlywed Couples," *Journal of Social and Personal Relationships* 9 (1992): 51-64.

[72] Myron A. Hofer, "Survival and Recovery of Physiologic Functions after Early Maternal Separation in Rats," *Physiology and Behavior* 15, no. 5 (1975): 475-480.

[73] Myron A. Hofer, "Early Social Relationships: A Psychobiologist's View," *Child Development* 58, no. 3 (1987): 633-647.

[74] Myron A. Hofer, "Hidden Regulators: Implications for a New Understanding of Attachment, Separation, and Loss," in *Attachment Theory: Social, Developmental, and Clinical Perspectives*, ed. S. Goldberg, R. Muir, and J. Kerr (Hillsdale: Analytic Press, 1995).

> A number of scientists now believe that somatic concordances like these are not just normal but necessary for mammals. The mammalian nervous system depends for its neurophysiologic stability on a system of interactive coordination, wherein steadiness comes from synchronization with nearby attachment figures.[75]

These biological regulation programs are constrained according to the interactions between primary caregivers and offspring. Their particular configuration develops through feedback and internalization of those regulatory parameters that are operative during optimal functioning of physiological arousal. These programs are dependent upon external parameters that "write" the particular maintenance programs into neuronal patterns, which are eventually used by the offspring on their own, independent of their primary caregivers.

In human infants, the development of the mechanisms and the organization of the brain are dependent upon two variables: (1) genetically coded prescriptions for the development of particular structures and (2) environmental influences.[76]

> The nervous system was once thought to unfold into maturity in accordance with the instructions in its DNA, much as a person alone in a room might, with a set of directions ... But as we now know most of the nervous system needs exposure to crucial experiences to drive its healthy growth.[77]

Just holding an infant helps the hypothalamus to regulate body temperature, and a brief separation from the attachment figure may result in abnormal hypothalamic-pituitary-adrenal responses.[78] Prolonged separations can have a detrimental effect on homeostatic regulatory responses in the infant.[79] Attachment behaviors contribute to the proper regulation of several neurochemicals that are a part of the central nervous system, including catecholamines, dopamine and noradrenaline.[80] These neurochemicals help in the maintenance of several homeostatic processes, including energy metabolism, blood flow, and stress functions. They also play a

---

[75] Thomas Lewis, Fari Amini, and Richard Lannon, *A General Theory of Love* (New York: Vintage Books, 2000).

[76] N. A. Fox, S. D. Calkins, and M. A. Bell, "Neural Plasticity and Development in the First Two Years of Life: Evidence from Cognitive and Socioemotional Domains of Research," *Development and Psychopathology* 6 (1994): 677-696.

[77] Lewis, Amini, and Lannon, *Theory of Love*, 89.

[78] Louis Cozolino, *The Neuroscience of Human Relationships: Attachment and the Developing Social Brain* (New York: W. W. Norton & Co., 2006), 102.

[79] Ibid., 115.

[80] Allan Schore, "Effects of a Secure Attachment Relationship on Right Brain Development, Affect Regulation, and Infant Mental Health," *Infant Mental Health Journal* 22, no. 1-2 (2001): 7-66.

role in activating proteins at the correct time in order to coordinate the activation of developmental processes.

Certain regulatory functions present in the right brain of the infant are important not only for physiological homeostasis, but also for mental health. These mechanisms are dependent on experience and differences between positive and negative attachments that affect the present and future mental health of the infant.

> In a series of contributions I have proposed that the maturation of these adaptive right brain regulatory capacities is experience dependent, and that this experience is embedded in the attachment relationship between the infant and primary caregiver. But it is important to point out that this experience can either positively or negatively influence the maturation of brain structure, and therefore, the psychological development of the infant. This developmental psychoneurobiological model clearly suggests direct links between secure attachment, development of efficient right brain regulatory functions, and adaptive infant mental health, as well as between traumatic attachment, inefficient right brain regulatory function, and maladaptive infant mental health.[81]

Impairments in the regulatory functions of the right hemisphere greatly influence the development of mental disorders such as post-traumatic stress disorder (PTSD).[82] Without proper interactional processes, the right brain does not develop the optimal resources for resiliency during traumatic events, making it more susceptible to PTSD and other mental disorders, either in frequency of occurrence or severity of symptoms.

These regulatory programs begin to form the early parameters of IWMs of attachment. Programs of regulation emerge as a result of the complex interplay between internal modes of regulation and the top-down constraints of the attachment environment in which the infant is embedded. Early regulatory programs are not primarily a by-product of adaptations, but of the regulatory systems and the environment working together. An IWM of attachment will also include a lot more information on relationships in addition to the parameters set by regulatory processes. An IWM of attachment is partially constituted by the coordinated activation of several areas of the brain devoted to emotional processing.

From Damasio's research, it seems clear that emotional states influence the types of decisions that are made in social and moral contexts. Emotional and somatic states act as pre-conscious hunches that direct our decisions in particular directions. The unconscious emotional aspects of IWMs have a similar effect by providing certain hunches or gut-level emotional markers that influence decision-making in relationships. An IWM activates several facets of the emotional

---

[81] Ibid., 10.

[82] Allan Schore, "Dysregulation of the Right Brain: A Fundamental Mechanism of Traumatic Attachment and the Psychopathogenesis of Posttraumatic Stress Disorder," *Australian and New Zealand Journal of Psychiatry* 36 (2002): 9-30.

brain that directs our actions and perceptions of current situations. Much of this processing is below the level of conscious awareness, yet it greatly constraints our perceptions and actions. Based on this research, several psychologists have argued that there is relationship between attachment and concepts of God, which has been an active research program in psychology of religion for decades.

God Concepts and Attachment Relationships

Sigmund Freud originally suggested a relationship between the image of the parent and the image of God.[83] Freud asserted that the concept of God was a projection or idealization of the parental figure, especially the father. Based on his work, Ana-Maria Rizzuto developed a qualitative study to determine the convergence between concepts of parents and concepts of God.[84] A personal concept of God is based on the object representation of parental figures in interaction with personal experiences and understanding of the self. Similar to the work of Rizzuto, Lee Kirkpatrick claims that God acts as an attachment figure in religion, especially in the Christian tradition.[85] Persons turn to God as a source of comfort during distress more than as a guide for morals.[86]

According to Bowlby, three classes of stimuli are particularly relevant for activating the attachment system: (1) Fearful or distressing events, (2) illness or injury, and (3) separation from attachment figures.[87] Not surprisingly, R. W. Hood, B. Spilka, B. Hunsberger, and R. Gorsuch developed a similar list of situations in which persons turn to God during times of distress.[88] Prayer is a good example of proximity seeking behavior; it is clearly an expression of the desire to connect with God and seek comfort and solace during times of distress.[89] Speaking in tongues or *glossolalia* is a special type of prayer language to God that for outside observers can often resemble infant babbling or other child-like forms of language.[90] Persons often raise their arms and heads toward God in a stance

---

[83] Sigmund Freud, *The Psychopathology of Everyday Life*, trans. Anthea Bell (New York: Penguin Books, 2002).

[84] Ana-Maria Rizzuto, *The Birth of the Living God: A Psychoanalytic Study* (Chicago: University of Chicago Press, 1979).

[85] Kirkpatrick, *Evolution, Religion*, 16.

[86] K. I. Pargament and J. Hahn, "God and the Just World: Causal and Coping Attributions to God in Health Situations," *Journal for the Scientific Study of Religion* 25 (1986): 193-207.

[87] Bowlby, *Nature of the Child's Tie*, 350.

[88] R. W. Hood, Jr. and others, *The Psychology of Religion: An Empirical Approach*, 2nd edn. (New York: Guilford Press, 1996).

[89] Kirkpatrick, *Evolution, Religion*, 59.

[90] W. E. Oates, "A Sociopsychological Study of Glossolalia," in *Glossolalia: Tongue Speaking in Biblical, Historical, and Psychological Perspective*, ed. F. Stagg, E. G. Hinson, and W. E. Oates (New York: Abingdon, 1967).

very similar to infants when they are seeking to be picked up by their parents. Descriptions of this experience often involve metaphors of a child reaching out to their father for security and love.[91]

Many theologians have described God in terms analogous to a parent or secure base through which life is explored and experienced. Friedrich Schleiermacher speaks of religious experience as a "feeling of absolute dependence," while contemporary devotional writer Henri Nouwen speaks of God as both a mother and father figure.[92] In *The Return of the Prodigal Son*, Nouwen recounts his devotional experience with Rembrandt's painting *Return of the Prodigal Son*:

> As soon as I recognized the difference between the two hands of the father, a new world of meaning opened up for me. The father is not simply a great patriarch. He is mother as well as father. He holds, and she caresses. He confirms and she consoles. He is, indeed, God, in whom both manhood and womanhood, fatherhood and motherhood, are fully present. That gentle caressing right hand echoes for me the words of the prophet Isaiah: "Can a woman forget her baby at the breast, feel no pity for the child she has borne? Even if these were to forget, I shall not forget you. Look, I have engraved you on the palms of my hands."[93]

N. L. Collins and S. J. Read speculate that IWMs of attachment form a hierarchical structure with a general model that informs different types of attachment relationships such as parent, peer, and God.[94] If this is true, Kirkpatrick argues that there should be a correspondence between individual differences in attachment styles and their concept of God.[95] Several studies of adolescents and children support this conclusion. K. Tammimnen found that children who reported a close relationship with their parents perceived God as close, caring, and forgiving.[96]

---

[91] J. P. Kildahl, *The Psychology of Speaking in Tongues* (New York: Harper & Row, 1972).

[92] Henri J. M. Nouwen, *Return of the Prodigal Son: A Story of Homecoming* (New York: Doubleday, 1994); Friedrich Schleiermacher, *On Religion: Speeches to Is Cultured Despisers*, trans. John Oman (New York: Harper & Row, 1958).

[93] Henri J. M. Nouwen, *Return of the Prodigal Son: A Story of Homecoming* (New York: Doubleday, 1994), 99.

[94] N. L. Collins and S. J. Read, "Cognitive Representations of Attachment: The Structure and Function of Working Models," in *Advances in Personal Relationships: Vol. 5. Attachment Processes in Adulthood*, ed. Kim Bartholomew and D. Perlman (London: Jessica Kingsley, 1994).

[95] Lee A. Kirkpatrick, "An Attachment-Theoretical Approach to the Psychology of Religion," *International Journal for the Psychology of Religion* 2, no. 1 (1992): 3-28; Lee A. Kirkpatrick and Phillip R. Shaver, "Attachment Theory and Religion: Childhood Attachments, Religious Beliefs, and Conversion," *Journal for the Scientific Study of Religion* 29 (1990): 315-334.

[96] K. Tamminen, *Religious Development in Childhood and Adolescence* (Helsinki: Suomalainen Tiedeakatemia, 1991).

In several studies, during adolescence, individual differences in perceptions of parents were related to differences in perceptions of God.[97]

As discussed earlier, an IWM of attachment also affects the perceptions of the self and other. This same phenomenon extends to concepts of God, in that there is a relationship between perceptions of the self, other, and God. Kirkpatrick performed a study using 1300 undergraduate students over a two-year period comparing their orientation towards romantic relationships with their level of religiosity.[98] Those students with high positive accounts of self and other tended to be more religious than others. This also corresponds with research that links positive images of God as loving and caring with higher levels of self-esteem and positive views of the self and other.[99] Interestingly, further analysis showed that models of the self were most closely related to images of God while positive models of the other were related to an image of God as personal and secure.

Critiques of God and Attachment

The relationship between attachment and concepts of God has received little attention in the cognitive science of religion, except in the case of critique. Most of the literature generated in this research paradigm has focused on ways to conceptualize religious beliefs based on a wide range of religions in many different cultures, whereas most of the research on attachment and concepts of God has focused on the Judeo-Christian tradition. In contrast, the cognitive science of religion has made a concerted effort to investigate the broad categories of human cognition that constrain the formation and transmission of religious beliefs that would be applicable in a wide range of religious traditions.

In many cultures, concepts of god are far removed from notions of a benevolent parental attachment figure. Pre-Columbian Maya and Mexican religious cultures featured deities who were mainly objects of fear, while the village goddess of a rural area of India is mainly worshiped to avoid incurring her wrath, which included devouring human bones.[100] In addition, snake worship is an important aspect of many religious traditions, including the Christian concept of Satan, with connections to ideas of reincarnation or more fearful notions of snake-like gods who many be intent on harming others.[101] The concept

---

[97] Kirkpatrick, *Attachment, Evolution*, 104-105.

[98] Lee A. Kirkpatrick, "God as a Substitute Attachment Figure: A Longitudinal Study of Adult Attachment Style and Religious Change in College Students," *Personality and Social Psychology Bulletin* 24 (1998): 961-973.

[99] Kirkpatrick, *Attachment, Evolution*, 108.

[100] Scott Atran, *In Gods We Trust: The Evolutionary Landscape of Religion* (New York: Oxford University Press, 2002); H Whitehead, *The Village Gods of South India* (Madras: Asia Education Services, 1921/1988).

[101] N. Gerrard, "The Serpent-Handling Religions of West Virginia," *Trans-Action* 5 (1968): 22-28; J. Henderson and M. Oakes, *The Wisdom of the Serpent* (Princeton: Princeton

of God as attachment figure is most appropriate in monotheistic religions such as Christianity, Judaism, and Islam, whereas this concept may not apply to the same extent in other religions.

Barrett argues that Theory of Mind and HADD are more basic cognitive programs used to conceptualize God in contrast to the "anthropomorphism hypothesis" that is so prevalent in the psychology of religion.[102] The anthropomorphism hypothesis argues that persons first conceptualize a person (or attachment figure) and then project that image onto a conceptualization of God. Barrett claims that it is more likely that superhuman or supernatural beliefs come first followed by more accurate identification and differentiation of what types of agents (such as attachment figures) are representative of the religious concept of God. Rather than developing a concept of a father than projecting it onto a supernatural agent, it appears that persons, especially children, presume supernatural properties to be present in certain types of religious beliefs and only later differentiate between gods, parents, and other types of attachment figures. Thus, supernatural properties are the leading factor involved in the formation of religious beliefs rather than attachment qualities, which would limit the feasibility of attachment as an early contributor to the evolution of religious beliefs.

A recent study of nominated religious exemplars from three monotheistic religions (Islam, Judaism, and Christianity) demonstrated that the representation of the divine is far removed from concepts usually associated with attachment such as parents.[103] The study used latent semantic analysis (LSA), a computational program that analyses text, to assess the similarities in meanings assigned to God, self, parent, romantic partner, and best friend during a structured interview. For all three religious traditions, God was not linked with meanings derived for parents. For the Jewish participants, God was associated with best friend; in the Muslim participants, God was associated with the self as well as best friend; and in the Christian sample, God was associated with the self and partially with best friend and romantic partner.

In a follow up study conducted by Van Slyke, Reimer, and Dueck, once again, it was shown that representations for God were distant from representations for parent in all three monotheistic religions.[104] Both the compensation and correspondence hypothesis assume that representations of God and parent are closely associated in cognitive schemas of attachment. Our analysis used a structured interview

---

University Press, 1990); B. Munkur, *The Cult of the Serpent* (Albany: State University of New York Press, 1983).

[102] Barrett, *Why Would Anyone*, 76.

[103] Kevin S. Reimer and others, "Varieties of Religious Cognition: A Computational Approach to Self-Understanding in Three Monotheist Contexts," *Zygon* 45, no. 1 (2010): 75-90.

[104] James A. Van Slyke, Kevin S. Reimer, and Alvin C. Dueck, "Correspondence, Compensation, or Something Else? Limitations for Attachment in Religious Cognition of Monotheist Exemplars," *Journal of Cognition and Culture* (in submission).

that included questions about the self, others, and critical life events that had an impact on their spiritual identity including childhood memories. The interview was used to extract meanings of various cognitive representations such as the self, God, and parent, which served as approximations of the cognitive structure of schemas of attachment. For our analysis, although God was close to attachment representations of the self, the parental concept was far removed for each of the three groups of monotheistic exemplars.

Based on these critiques, it would seem that attachment plays a much more limited role in the formation of religious beliefs and concepts than is commonly assumed in the psychology of religion. With the preponderance of evidence that attachment research has generated in the psychology of religion it would seem that there is still some role for attachment in explaining religion, but that role can only be understood in relation to several other factors involved in the evolution of religion. Most likely, attachment plays a role in belief formation only after a sufficient amount of experience, obviously attachment related, has occurred in an individual. Secondly, it may be difficult to differentiate the causal role of attachment from other relational experiences. For most of the evolution of humanity, attachment relationships occurred in the context of many other social relationships. The idea of a nuclear family living in isolation from the rest of the community does not seem to be a part of the general evolutionary direction of primates.

By the time of the origins of religion in primitive cultures, social relationships probably played as important a role in the evolution of religion as attachment relationships and may have played a substantially greater role. However, the transition from attachment-based to group-based social relationships and the corresponding emotional processes play a vital role in the evolution and formation of religious beliefs. From this perspective it follows that we can add different types of relational dynamics based on social feedback to the initial conditions based on cognitive and emotional processes.

Consequently, the explanation for religious beliefs can expand from internal cognitive factors to relational and social factors based on feedback mechanisms present in groups and cultures. Social forms of cognition are not merely the result of cultural rules and values that are simply learned by children and new members. Rather, the human brain was uniquely formed through evolution to process social and emotional information very easily and quickly integrate important aspects of social functioning into a general understanding of expected behavior. As the evidence on the neuroscience of both emotion and attachment demonstrates, human persons are primed to be in relationships with each other, both to our gain and peril. Attachment relationships were the jumpstart mechanism that fostered other types of social relationships in the evolution of human psychology.

Religion and Group Processes

Attachment seems to be related to the evolutionary process of kin selection, which argues that an organism will help another organism based on the degree of genetic relatedness between them.[105] Several studies in evolutionary psychology have shown that helping behavior is often directed toward one's relatives in contrast to other persons. During one experiment subjects were given monetary rewards that were distributed to themselves, their close relatives, or a children's charity, according to the amount of time they could remain in an uncomfortable position.[106] Overwhelmingly, subjects would endure the most discomfort for themselves and their closest relatives. In another experiment, grandparents were shown to be discriminating in the amount of investment shown to grandchildren based on genetic certainty and inheritance was usually distributed based on the degree of genetic relatedness.[107]

In human nature, there is a substantial motivation to care for our relatives even at a cost to ourselves. This seems to be one of the bases for the evolution of pro-sociality and altruism in human nature. Kin selection is not necessarily altruism, but it is a step from self-interest to a larger concern for the needs of another. Attachment and the corresponding social bonds it facilitates is an important step in the emergence of pro-sociality and altruism in the human species. Human social and emotional concern expanded from primary attachment figures to other immediate relatives. However, later developments in human nature and group relationships expanded this concern even farther to concerns for other tribe members, allies, and even friends.

Reciprocal altruism and indirect reciprocity are two theories that have been used to describe the evolution of pro-sociality, cooperation, and altruism. Reciprocal altruism claims that acts which benefit another will be offered as long as there is a reasonable expectation that the benefit will be returned at a later time.[108] In general, three conditions must hold for reciprocal altruism to occur: reasonable chance of meeting the recipient of altruism again, must be able to recognize cheats and those who honestly engage in reciprocation, and the ratio for "cost to donor/benefit to receiver must be low" or at least a higher degree of certainty for reciprocation.[109]

---

[105] W. D. Hamilton, "The Genetical Evolution of Social Behaviour," *Journal of Theoretical Biology* 7 (1964): 1-16; Mary J. West-Eberhard, "The Evolution of Social Behavior by Kin Selection," *Quarterly Review of Biology* 50 (1975): 1-33.

[106] R. I. M. Dunbar, *Grooming, Gossip, and the Evolution of Language* (London: Faber and Faber, 1996).

[107] H. A. Euler and B. Weitzel, "Discriminating Grandparental Solicitude as Reproductive Strategy," *Human Nature* 7 (1996): 39-59; Martin S. Smith, Bradley J. Kish, and Charles B. Crawford, "Inheritance of Wealth as Human Kin Investment," *Ethology and Sociobiology* 8, no. 3 (1987): 171-182.

[108] Robert L. Trivers, "The Evolution of Reciprocal Altruism," *Quarterly Review of Biology* 46 (1971): 35-57.

[109] John Cartwright, *Evolution and Human Behavior: Darwinian Perspectives on Human Nature* (Cambridge: The MIT Press, 2008), 200.

Examples of this type of reciprocal altruism have been demonstrated in vampire bats and baboons.[110]

Another factor involved in the evolution of pro-sociality is indirect reciprocity, which is the role of reputation in receiving cooperation and help from others.[111] Even if a person does not get direct benefits from helping another, forming a reputation as an honest helper can help in the long run for receiving benefits from others. Using computational programs that model these types of indirect reciprocal relationships, it was found that cooperation could spread in a population of players if there was an ability to observe and keep track of those who helped and those who did not even if the giver and receiver of help never met up again directly.[112] During the evolution of humans, group sizes grew to levels where cooperation could not function effectively based solely on kin selection or direct forms of reciprocity.[113] Yet, there are important advantages to larger group sizes in terms of pooling economic resources, larger numbers of potential mates, and defending against outside attackers.

Neuroeconomics

Research in the emerging field of neuroeconomics demonstrates that several areas of the brain may be specialized for judging reciprocal exchange, which suggests that forms of direct and indirect reciprocity may have played an important role in the evolution of human cognition. Social decision-making has become one of the major areas of research in neuroeconomics, which attempts to set up economic games that are played by subjects using real money and investigates the neural mechanisms used during the games.[114] Historically, the dominate paradigm in economic game theory was that persons will make their decisions in economic games based on rational principles and their own self-interest.[115] However, several studies are calling this picture of economic decision-making into question.

Persons often make decisions based on reputational preferences and the social consequences of the strategies used by other players in the game. For example, in

---

[110] R. I. M. Dunbar, "Determinants and Evolutionary Consequences of Dominance among Female Gelada Baboons," *Behavioral Ecology and Sociobiology* 7 (1980): 253-265; G. S. Wilkinson, "Food Sharing in Vampire Bats," *Scientific American* 262 (1990): 76-82.

[111] R. D. Alexander, *The Biology of Moral Systems* (New York: Aldine de Gruyter, 1987).

[112] Martin A. Nowak and Karl Sigmund, "Evolution of Indirect Reciprocity by Image Scoring," *Nature* 393 (1998): 573-576.

[113] R. I. M. Dunbar, *Grooming, Gossip, and the Evolution of Language* (London: Faber and Faber, 1996).

[114] Ernst Fehr and Colin Camerer, "Social Neuroeconomics: The Neural Circuitry of Social Preferences," *Trends in Cognitive Sciences* 11, no. 10 (2007): 419-427.

[115] Colin Camerer and Ernst Fehr, "When Does 'Economic Man' Dominate Social Behavior?," *Science* 311 (2006): 47-52.

the prisoner's dilemma game, participants prefer mutually cooperative strategies to unilateral defection although defection results in higher monetary payoffs.[116] This preference may be linked to the reward systems of the ventral striatum that have been associated with the experience of mutual cooperation between human partners.[117] Participants also prefer to punish persons who are acting unfairly in the game even if the punishment takes away from their overall monetary gain. One study associated this type of punishment with the dorsal striatum, which was strongly activated during a real punishment condition in contrast to a symbolic one.[118]

This research suggests that economic games involve several neural processes involved in social and emotional cognition. In one study, participants played economic games with confederate fair and unfair players. When the confederates were administered a brief electrical shock, the confederate fair players elicited an empathetic response in the participants, which was measured by activation in the anterior cingulate and anterior insula. The confederate unfair players elicited a desire for revenge in the participants, which was measured by activation in the nucleus accumbens and orbital frontal cortex.[119] Research by Paul Zak and colleagues has shown that the neuromodulator oxytocin (also associated with maternal behaviors) can increase generosity in humans through its effects on reward, emotion, and social areas of the brain.[120] In the ultimatum game, generosity was increased by 80 percent over placebo in participants who were infused intranasally with oxytocin and the participants who were generous left the game with less money.

Costly Signaling Theory

Costly signaling theory proposes that religious morality and belief systems may serve as a proxy for detecting trustworthy persons. The potential for cooperation and alliance in a partner is measured by their commitment to religious beliefs and values, which function as predictors for reciprocal exchange. The more an individual is able to adopt or perform certain religious rituals and behaviors, especially at a cost to themselves, the more likely that same person will incur

---

[116] Fehr and Camerer, "Social Neuroeconomics," 421.

[117] James K. Rilling and others, "A Neural Basis for Social Cooperation," *Neuron* 35 (2002): 395-405; James K. Rilling and others, "Opposing Bold Responses to Reciprocated and Unreciprocated Altruism in Putative Reward Pathways," *Neuroreport* 15, no. 16 (2004): 2439-2543.

[118] Dominique J. de Quervain and others, "The Neural Basis of Altruistic Punishment," *Science* 305 (2004): 1254-1258.

[119] Tania Singer and others, "Empathetic Neural Responses are Modulated by the Perceived Fairness of Others," *Nature* 439 (2006): 466-469.

[120] Paul Zak, Angela Stanton, and Shelia Ahmadi, "Oxytocin Increases Generosity in Humans," *PLoS One* 2, no. 11 (2007): e1128.

similar costs necessary for the fair exchange of other types of commodities. Costly signaling theory builds on the insights of reciprocal altruism and indirect reciprocity and suggests that the evolution of religion may be related to the types of display behaviors that indicate trust and reciprocation.

Several areas of research indicate that religion provides certain assurances to various problems in social life for different communities. Among the Utila people, men prefer women who show a certain level of religious piety as potential marriage partners.[121] These men, however, do not frequently attend religious services themselves because they spend a significant amount of time working and fishing, but they use the religious piety of potential female partners as an estimate of their ability to remain faithful during the long periods of separation. During poor economic conditions in the 1990s, Muslims contributed greater amounts of monetary resources to religious institutions as a means to insure against individual financial collapses among households.[122] This led to increases in religious intensity and between-group violence such that religious commitment served as an indication of group commitment and fidelity. Thus, religious identity insured the potential for possible economic relief from the religious institutions if the need arose.

In a comparative study of different communes during the nineteenth century, religious communities were far more likely to outlive similar secular communities across time; for any given year, religious communities were four times as likely to survive in comparison to secular communities.[123] Religious communes impose many more types of costly religious requirements in contrast to secular communes. As a consequence of these requirements, higher levels of religious commitment were correlated with higher levels of longevity in religious communities.[124] Among members of an Israeli kibbutz, males with higher levels of participation in religious practices were more likely to be altruistic in their decision-making during common-goods resource games.[125]

---

[121] Joseph Bulbulia, "Meme Infection or Religious Niche Construction?: An Adaptationist Alternative to the Cultural Maladaptationist Hypothesis," *Method and Theory in the Study of Religion* 20 (2008): 92.

[122] Daniel L. Chen, "Islamic Resurgence and Social Violence During the Indonesian Financial Crisis," in *Institutions and Norms in Economic Development*, ed. K. Konrad and M. Gradstein (Cambridge: The MIT Press, 2006).

[123] Richard Sosis, "Religion and Intragroup Cooperation: Preliminary Results of a Comparative Analysis of Utopian Communities," *Cross-Cultural Research* 34, no. 1 (2000): 70-87.

[124] Richard Sosis and Eric R. Bressler, "Cooperation and Commune Longevity: A Test of the Costly Signaling Theory of Religion," *Cross-Cultural Research* 37, no. 2 (2003): 11-39.

[125] Richard Sosis and Bradley J. Ruffle, "Religious Ritual and Cooperation: Testing for a Relationship on Israeli Religious and Secular Kibbutzim," *Current Anthropology* 44, no. 5 (2003): 713-722.

It is difficult to know the extent of the effect of religion on pro-sociality or if some other variable is embedded in religious communal functions that can account for these changes in behavior. Although religious persons often report a higher-level of concern for others, empirical analysis often demonstrates that religious persons are no more willing to help others than non-religious persons.[126] Other types of non-religious stimuli can also be used to induce cooperation among persons. In one neuroeconomic study, eyespots on a computer screen increased the level of monetary offers during the dictator game.[127] A similar effect was demonstrated when an image of a pair of eyes was placed above a box used to collect money for drinks during a university party, which increased the amount of contributions collected for the drinks.[128]

Supernatural agents seem to have a similar effect to the use of images of eyes in pro-social behavior. It was suggested to one group of university students that the ghost of a dead graduate student resided in a classroom, which decreased the levels of cheating on a test.[129] This same effect was demonstrated in three-year-old children, who were told that "Princess Alice" was in the room with them watching their actions, which decreased cheating behavior in the form of opening a "forbidden box" that was placed in the room.[130] Supernatural agents have obvious connections to religious beliefs and could be possible candidates for directing social behaviors. Other experiments have tried to assess religious concepts themselves, to determine their ability to promote certain types of pro-social behaviors.

When religious concepts are implicitly activated, participants give more money to anonymous subjects during the dictator game.[131] To prime religious concepts, participants were given sentences that they had to unscramble and drop an extraneous word.[132] Sentences contained target words such as spirit, divine,

---

[126] C. D. Batson and others, "Religious Prosocial Motivation: Is It Altruistic or Egoistic?," *Journal of Personality and Social Psychology* 57 (1989): 873-884; C. D. Batson, P. A. Schoenrade, and L. W. Ventis, *Religion and the Individual: A Social-Psychological Perspective* (Oxford: University Press, 1993).

[127] K. J. Haley and D. M. T. Fessler, "Nobody's Watching? Subtle Cues Affect Generosity in an Anonymous Economic Game," *Evolution and Human Behavior* 26 (2005): 245-256.

[128] M. Bateson, D. Nettle, and G. Roberts, "Cues of Being Watched Enhance Cooperation in a Real-World Setting," *Biology Letters* 2 (2006): 412-414.

[129] J. M. Bering, K. McLeod, and T. K. Shakelford, "Reasoning About Dead Agents Reveals Possible Adaptive Trends," *Human Nature* 16 (2005): 360-381.

[130] J. M. Bering and B. D. Parker, "Children's Attributions of Intentions to an Invisible Agent," *Developmental Psychology* 42, no. 2 (2006): 253-262.

[131] Azim F. Shariff and Ara Norenzayan, "God Is Watching You: Priming God Concepts Increases Prosocial Behavior in an Anonymous Economic Game," *Psychological Science* 18, no. 9 (2007): 803-809.

[132] T. K. Scrull and R. S. Wyer, "The Role of Category Accessibility in the Interpretation of Information About Persons: Some Determinants and Implications," *Journal of Personality and Social Psychology* 37 (1979): 1660-1672.

God, sacred, or prophet, which acted as primes for religious concepts. After unscrambling the sentences, participants played a two-person dictator game where they were given $10 and could decide how much they wanted to give to an anonymous stranger. The only person who would know about their decision would be the other participant in the game who was actually a confederate researcher. With religious concept priming, participants gave considerably more during the game with an average of $4.22, while non-primed participants gave $1.82.[133] In a related study, religious primes were shown to decrease cheating on subsequent tasks.[134]

Religion is a very complex variable to analyze and there is probably a type of continuum between general factors involved in pro-sociality regardless of religious affiliation and those factors that are more explicitly dependent upon religious beliefs and values. During the 2006 Lebanon war, many Israeli women read psalms from the Hebrew Bible to deal with stress and conditions of uncertainty. Psalm recitation was shown to effectively decrease levels of stress and anxiety during conditions where there was little ability for direct control over the situation, as is usually the case in times of war.[135] Interestingly, psalm recitation did not diminish stress and anxiety for a related group of Israeli women who were not currently dealing with the uncertainties that exist during times of war. According to this study, for religious rituals to have an effect, it requires a level of uncertainty as a type of contextual variable that sets up the conditions for religious rituals as reducers of stress and anxiety.

Religious prosociality may have extended reciprocity relationships beyond kin selection and individual monitoring to large-scale cooperative communities.[136] "Belief in morally concerned gods may stabilize prosocial norms even in the absence of social monitoring mechanisms."[137] Interestingly, a qualitative analysis of 186 different societies demonstrated that cultures with larger numbers of persons were most often associated with morally concerned gods.[138] The western worldview typically assumes that an important function of supernatural agency is morality, but many smaller-scale cultures do not place the same type of emphasis on supernatural agents as monitors of behavior. And this follows from the evidence, smaller scale cultures and self-monitor relationships much easier than

---

[133] Shariff and Norenzayan, "God is Watching You," 804.

[134] Brandon Randolph-Seng and Michael E. Nielsen, "Honesty: One Effect of Primed Religious Representations," *International Journal for the Psychology of Religion* 17, no. 4 (2007): 303-315.

[135] Richard Sosis, "Psalms and Coping with Uncertainty: Religious Israeli Women's Responses to the 2006 Lebanon War," *American Anthropologist* 113 (2011): 40-55.

[136] Ara Norenzayan and Azim F. Shariff, "The Origin and Evolution of Religious Prosociality," *Science* 322 (2008): 58-62.

[137] Ibid., 61.

[138] Frans L. Roes and Michel Raymond, "Belief in Moralizing Gods," *Evolution and Human Behavior* 24 (2003): 126-135.

larger ones. A related issue is the role of group-level vs. individual-level selection in the evolution of religion. There is considerable debate on the legitimacy of group-level selection, but there may be good reasons for considering it another level of evolutionary processes involved in the formation of religious belief and practice.

Group Selection, Religion, and Sexual Morality

Until recently, the primary component of evolutionary change was assumed to be at the level of individual differences, which were the result of differences in phenotypes that lead to relative fitness. Thus, the term "selfish gene" became a common phrase indicating the genetic factors that cause the formation of a particular phenotype, which enhances survival and reproduction in competition with other organisms.[139] However, in the history of the theory of evolution, groups were thought to be possible candidates as potential loci of evolutionary adaptation, but poor theoretical and empirical development lead many biologists to discredit this view, especially in the work of G. C. Williams.[140] Recently, there has been a revival of sorts in looking to groups and multiple levels of possible evolutionary change rather than focusing solely on the individual differences between and within species.

Group selection can be defined as a form of selection that occurs along a particular vector that includes multiple processes working at various levels of selection.[141] Thus, individual vs. group selection is not a zero sum game between two competing processes; both contribute, in varying degrees, to the evolution of some particular trait. The difficulty that arises in defining group selection is that any apparent trait that benefits the group is seemingly a deficit for the individual. In the case of a sentinel (an animal that warns a group of potential danger), it would seem to be a deficit to the sentinel to warn others because it also singles out the warning caller as potential prey.[142] Individual level foragers would have a higher level of fitness in comparison to the sentinels; the fitness of the foragers

---

[139] Richard Dawkins, *The Selfish Gene* (Oxford: Oxford University Press, 1976).

[140] G. C. Williams, *Adaptation and Natural Selection: A Critique of Some Current Evolutionary Thought* (Princeton: Princeton University Press, 1966); David Sloan Wilson, "Human Groups as Adaptive Units: Toward a Permanent Consensus," in *The Innate Mind: Culture and Cognition*, ed. Peter Carruthers, Stephen Laurence, and Stephen Stich (Oxford: Oxford University Press, 2007).

[141] David Sloan Wilson, "Group-Level Evolutionary Processes," in *The Oxford Handbook of Evolutionary Psychology*, ed. Robin Dunbar and Louise Barrett (Oxford: Oxford University Press, 2007).

[142] P. A. Bednekoff, "Mutualism among Safe, Selfish Sentinels: A Dynamic Game," *American Naturalist* 150 (1997): 373-392; David Sloan Wilson, "Human Groups as Adaptive Units: Toward a Permanent Consensus," in *The Innate Mind: Culture and Cognition*, ed. Peter Carruthers, Stephen Laurence, and Stephen Stich (Oxford: Oxford University Press, 2007), 85.

(who benefit from the calls, yet do not inherit the same level of danger) would be slightly higher than the sentinels over time.

However, P. A. Bednekoff found that over time the absolute level of fitness for both sentinels and foragers was actually the same, yet he referred to this as "selfish" or "safe" behavior for sentinels.[143] As David Sloan Wilson points out, what is clearly an example of group-level selection becomes reinterpreted according to the constraints of individual-level selection, reflecting an apparent bias in empirical interpretation.[144] To counter this form of bias, Wilson and Elliott Sober constructed a working definition of group selection. For group selection to occur there must be different groups in a population and those groups must vary in regard to the presence of a particular trait. The trait enables a difference in fitness in comparison to other groups in that the trait makes the group more likely to survive and reproduce.[145] Additionally, the trait that makes one group more fit than others must be able to override the potential differences in traits at work in the group.

Aspects of morality may have evolved at the group level in addition to the individual level factors that were involved in the evolution of *homo sapiens* and religion. For example, aspects of the evolution of religious sexual values could be explained as a consequence of the evolution of social mechanisms that enhance cooperation and cohesion at the group level. Sexual mating is greatly constrained by the social situations that exist in both human and nonhuman primate cultures. Humans are a highly cooperative species and any sexual preferences must have been exercised within a particular group. Sexual selection occurs mainly between individuals as both males and females use particular strategies to enhance their reproductive potential both in terms of their chances for mating and the quality of potential mates. However, these strategies must have been exercised in particular groups and the strategies could not have been isolated from corresponding issues such as coalitions, economy, and food. Thus, it seems highly probable that at the group level those social structures that could help to effectively manage sexual selection among its members would have a slight advantage over other groups lacking those resources.

Recent research demonstrates a link between different aspects of religion and mating strategies. Religious attendance may be linked to a particular mating strategy, which focuses on a higher probability of fertility and the promotion of monogamy. In a recent survey of over 21,000 United States residents, sexual behaviors were the strongest predictors of attendance at different religious institutions.[146] Moral views about sexuality were more strongly linked to religious attendance in comparison to other moral issues. Mating strategies provide a strong

---

[143] Bednekoff, "Mutualism."

[144] Wilson, "Group-level Evolutionary Processes," 86.

[145] Elliott Sober and David Sloan Wilson, *Unto Others: The Evolution and Psychology of Unselfish Behavior* (Cambridge: Harvard University Press, 1998), 26.

[146] Jason Weeden, Adam B. Cohen, and Douglas T. Kenrick, "Religious Attendance as Reproductive Support," *Evolution and Human Behavior* 29 (2008): 327-334.

predictor for religious affiliation in comparison to personality or other behavioral traits. Another study demonstrated that religious affiliation and commitment increases in the presence of other same-sex mating competitors. Higher levels of religiosity were reported after looking at mating pools of attractive people of the same sex in contrast to pools of the opposite sex.[147]

The seeds for human sexual morality, promoted in some form or another by most religions, evolved as a consequence of both individual and group-level selection. This is not to say that sexuality or religion is reducible to these two forms of selection, but that many of the initial processes in the formation of these aspects of human nature required both forms of selection. In fact, it is probably the case that there was a highly complex interaction between several different factors in the evolution of sexual morality and religion including cultural evolution.[148] The foundations for the emergence of religious sexual morality obviously included individual differences in sexual selection that occurred throughout the evolution of the human species. Cognitive adaptations identified by evolutionary psychology such as the waist-to-hip ratio, facial symmetry, and perceived status obviously inform aspects of human sexuality.[149] Yet, some of the most distinctive aspects of human behavior are social and hierarchical relationships, which indicate that human sexual preferences must have been exercised primarily in social groupings.

Therefore, at the group level, those social norms that benefit the group by managing individual sexual mate preferences and relationships would most likely lead to a higher level of fitness in comparison to groups that did not manage mate selection strategies as well. The early appearance of religion in human history makes is a very likely candidate for a special role in the formation of such social norms. And, in fact, religion may have evolved as a consequence of the need to manage human relationships through social norms, of which religion has always played an important role. Many of the functions of the human brain and cognition evolved as a consequence of problems posed by complex social relationships.[150]

Morality evolved at the group level as a system of beliefs and practices that regulated behavior in early hunter-gather societies.[151] Religion can be defined as a

---

[147] Jessica Yexin Li and others, "Mating Competitors Increase Religious Beliefs," *Journal of Experimental Social Psychology* 46, no. 2 (2010): 428-431.

[148] Robert Boyd and Peter J. Richerson, *The Origin and Evolution of Cultures* (Oxford: Oxford University Press, 2005).

[149] David Buss, *The Evolution of Desire*, revised edn. (New York: Basic Books, 2003), 25; 28-31; Devendra Singh, "Adaptive Significance of Female Physical Attractiveness: Role of Waist-to-Hip Ratio," *Journal of Personality and Social Psychology* 65, no. 2 (1993): 293-307; Randy Thornhill and Steven W. Gangestad, "Facial Attractiveness," *Trends in Cognitive Sciences* 3, no. 12 (1999): 452-460.

[150] R. I. M. Dunbar, "The Social Brain Hypothesis," *Evolutionary Anthropology* 6 (1998).

[151] David Sloan Wilson, *Darwin's Cathedral: Evolution, Religion, and the Nature of Society* (Chicago: University of Chicago Press, 2002), 25.

set of sacred symbols that motivates different forms of behavior in terms of both regulation and encouragement of behaviors that benefit the group.[152] In terms of sexuality, religion has obviously played an important role in regulating the sexual behavior of humans living in groups. Religious doctrines often target marriage and sexuality as primary locations of behavioral regulation and many competing interests including mate preference, the possibility of mate poaching and retention, and certainty of paternity have shaped human sexual desire.[153] However, religion is certainly not an exclusively positive influence on sexual behavior; there are several indications that suggest that religious leaders use their power and prestige as a way to gain sexual access to a wider variety of partners.[154] Religion and sexuality have a complex relationship between each other that includes both positive and negative consequences.

Conclusion

Many factors were involved in the evolution and formation of religious beliefs and behaviors. Several different causal factors, studied at multiple levels in the hierarchy of science, contributed to the emergence of cognitive and social aspects of religion. Cognitive constraints, such as counterintuitiveness and agency detection, play an important role in the formation of religious concepts and beliefs. However, as demonstrated in Chapters 2 and 3, several emergent and top-down factors play an important role in the formation of cognitive representations of religious beliefs. Thus, religious beliefs cannot be exhaustively or reductively explained as by-products of cognitive constraints. Aspects of religious beliefs are by-products, while other properties are constituted according to feedback processes that occur in the social contexts in which religious beliefs develop.

In addition to cognitive factors, religious beliefs also include different motivational and inspirational factors that are based in the arousal and emotional systems of the brain. Different areas of the brain are specialized for processing emotional information and may constrain different aspects of cognition. Additionally, the social and affective neurosciences have shown that emotion plays an important functional role in different types of adaptive behaviors and decision-making. Classic definitions of religion from the psychology and philosophy of religion have focused on the experiential and phenomenological aspects of religious belief and experience, which are most likely processed by the emotional and social areas of the brain.

The emotional aspects of the brain and human cognition are the initial conditions necessary for attachment, yet attachment involves relational factors

---

[152] Ibid., 227.

[153] David Buss, "Sex, Marriage, and Religion: What Adaptive Problems Do Religious Phenomena Solve?," *Psychological Inquiry* 13, no. 3 (2002): 201-238.

[154] Ibid., 202.

that go beyond a by-product theory of religion. Attachment is the relational dynamic that develops between offspring and primary caregivers, which is based in several specialized regions of the brain. Attachment plays an important role in parental nurturance and providing for the basic needs of the offspring, as well as regulating arousal and psychological well-being. Concepts of God are often associated with concepts of parents and primary caregivers, which are often based on the type of attachment relationship (secure or insecure) between child and parent. Recent research has called into question the extent to which attachment affects the formation of religious beliefs and behaviors, which suggests that larger social factors are involved in different aspects of religious belief and behavior.

Attachment was a precursor to other types of social mechanisms that enabled group cohesion, cooperation, and pro-sociality. Kin selection, indirect reciprocity, and reciprocal altruism are two important processes that occurred in the evolution of *homo sapiens* that enabled the possibility of altruism and different types of social relationships that could benefit the group. Neuroeconomics has shown that persons are especially proficient at making decisions in regard to reciprocal relationships, cooperation, and even generosity, which involves regions of the brain, specialized for processing this type of information. Thus, aspects of religious belief and commitment evolved as a signal to indicate trustworthiness and reliability in reciprocal relationships. Several empirical studies demonstrate that religion plays a role in different forms of pro-social behavior, though it is difficult to ascertain the extent of this effect. Religion may have played an important role in extending pro-social relationships based on individual transactions to larger cooperative communities.

The final type of process involved in the evolution and formation of religion is at the group level. Religious beliefs, values, and norms may have given the groups that possessed them a selective advantage over others in terms of group cohesion, monitoring of behavior, and motivating pro-sociality. I argued that religion might have played an important role in monitoring sexual selection at the individual level by providing moral rules and values that constrained and promoted different types of sexual behavior. Those groups who used religion to successfully navigate the sometimes difficult aspects of mate selection, retention, and parenting may have had an advantage over those groups that did not have the same types of social constraints and motivations. Group selection is another level of empirical investigation that studies the causal factors involved in the emergence of religious thought and behavior. Ultimately, a number of different causal factors (cognitive, emotional, and social) were involved in the evolution of religion and continue to play an important role in many different aspects of religious concepts, beliefs, and behaviors.

Postscript

The cognitive science of religion provides many important insights into the function, formation, and transmission of religion. This book is primarily a critique of one aspect of this field, the standard model of cognition and reduction used by some researchers and proponents in their investigation and evaluation of religion. It is not my intention to advocate the elimination of cognitive and evolutionary explanations of religion. On the contrary, I highly endorse the use of science to help explain and investigate different aspects of religion. My critique focuses on some of the larger interpretations that have been given in regard to religion offered by the standard model and commonly associated with the cognitive science of religion. Some of the debates are more philosophical in nature, which is why I used the concepts of emergence and top-down constraints to help illuminate some problems in reductive accounts of religion. However, some of the debates are more scientific in nature and involve conflicting views on how cognition works and the role of cognitive adaptations in explaining thoughts and behaviors.

My hope is that this book will contribute to discussion and debate within the cognitive science of religion, as well as the larger religious studies and theological community. Part of this will be accomplished through empirical investigation and the development of new methods and theories that study religion from the perspective of cognitive science. The other part will be the development of better philosophical and theological models for understanding the role of cognitive and evolutionary science in explaining religion. This is obviously a difficult task, but hopefully the cognitive science of religion can continue to contribute to the immensely complex social, political, and personal phenomena, known as religion.

Bibliography

Adolphs, Ralph, and Michael Spezio. "Social Cognition." In *The Handbook of Neuroscience for the Behavioral Sciences*, ed. G. G. Bernston and J. T. Cacioppo, Vol. 2, 923-939. New York: Wiley and Sons, 2009.

Adolphs, Ralph, Daniel Tranel, Hanna Damasio, and Antonio Damasio. "Impaired Recognition of Emotion in Facial Expression Following Bilateral Damage to the Human Amygdala." *Nature* 372 (1994): 669-672.

Alexander, R. D. *The Biology of Moral Systems*. New York: Aldine de Gruyter, 1987.

Alligood, Kathleen T., Tim Sauer, and James A. Yorke. *Chaos: An Introduction to Dynamical Systems*. New York: Springer-Verlag, 1996.

Anderson, Janice C., and Stephen D. Moore, eds. *Mark and Method: New Approaches in Biblical Studies*. Minneapolis: Fortress Press, 2008.

Anderson, Steven W., Antoine Bechara, Hanna Damasio, Daniel Tranel, and Antonio Damasio. "Impairment of Social and Moral Behavior Related to Early Damage in Human Prefrontal Cortex." *Nature Neuroscience* 2 (1999): 1032-1037.

Antonini, A., and M. P. Stryker. "Development of Individual Geniculocortical Arbors in Cat Striate Cortex and Effects of Bionocular Impulse Blockade." *Journal of Neuroscience* 13 (1993): 3549-3573.

Aronson, Ronald. "The New Atheists." *The Nation*, June 25, 2007.

Association, American Psychiatric. *Diagnostic and Statistical Manual of Mental Disorders*. 4th edn. Washington: American Psychiatric Association, 2000.

Atran, Scott. *In Gods We Trust: The Evolutionary Landscape of Religion*. New York: Oxford University Press, 2002.

Augustine, J. R. "Circuitry and Functional Aspects of the Insular Lobe in Primates, Including Humans." *Brain Research Reviews* 22 (1996): 229-244.

Ayala, Francisco J. "Introduction." In *Studies in the Philosophy of Biology: Reduction and Related Problems*, ed. Francisco J. Ayala and Theodosius Dobzhansky. Berkeley and Los Angeles: University of California Press, 1974.

Ayala, Francisco J., and Theodosius Dobzhansky, eds. *Studies in the Philosophy of Biology: Reduction and Related Problems*. Berkeley and Los Angeles: University of California Press, 1974.

Bailergeon, R. "Representing the Existence and Location of Hidden Objects: Object Permanence in Six and Eight Month Old Infants." *Cognition* 23 (1986): 21-41.

Barbour, Ian. *Religion and Science: Historical and Contemporary Issues*. San Francisco: Harper San Francisco, 1997.

Baron-Cohen, Simon. *Mindblindness: An Essay on Autism and Theory of Mind*. Cambridge: The MIT Press, 1997.

Barrett, Justin L. "Theological Correctness: Cognitive Constraint and the Study of Religion." *Method and Theory in the Study of Religion* 11 (1999): 325-339.

———. "Exploring the Natural Foundations of Religion." *Trends in Cognitive Sciences* 4, no. 1 (2000): 29-34.

———. "Bringing Data to Mind: Empirical Claims of Lawson and McCauley's Theory of Religious Ritual." In *Religion as Human Capacity: A Festschrift in Honor of E. Thomas Lawson*, ed. T. Light and B. C. Wilson, 265-288. Cambridge: Cambridge University Press, 2004.

———. *Why Would Anyone Believe in God?* Walnut Creek: AltaMira Press, 2004.

———. "Cognitive Science of Religion: What Is It and Why Is It?" *Religion Compass* 1, no. 6 (2007): 768-786.

———. "Is the Spell Really Broken? Bio-Psychological Explanations of Religion and Theistic Belief." *Theology and Science* 5, no. 1 (2007): 57-72.

Barrett, Justin L., and Frank C. Keil. "Conceptualizing a Non-Natural Entity: Anthropomorphism in God Concepts." *Cognitive Psychology* 31 (1996): 219-247.

Barrett, Justin L., R. A. Newman, and R. A. Richert. "When Seeing Does Not Lead to Believing: Children's Understanding of the Importance of Background Knowledge for Interpreting Visual Displays." *Journal of Cognition and Culture* 3 (2003): 91-108.

Barrett, Justin L., and M. Nyhof. "Spreading Nonnatural Concepts." *Journal of Cognition and Culture* 1 (2001): 69-100.

Barrett, Justin L., R. A. Richert, and A. Driesenga. "God's Beliefs Versus Mother's: The Development of Non-Human Agent Concepts." *Child Development* 71 (2001): 50-65.

Bartels, A., and S. Zeki. "The Neural Basis of Romantic Love." *NeuroReport* 11 (2000): 3829-3834.

Bartholomew, Kim. "Avoidance of Intimacy: An Attachment Perspective." *Journal of Social and Personal Relationships* 7 (1990): 147-178.

Bateson, M., D. Nettle, and G. Roberts. "Cues of Being Watched Enhance Cooperation in a Real-World Setting." *Biology Letters* 2 (2006): 412-414.

Batson, C. D., K. C. Oleson, S. P. Weeks, S. P. Healy, P. Jennings, and T. Brown. "Religious Prosocial Motivation: Is It Altruistic or Egoistic?" *Journal of Personality and Social Psychology* 57 (1989): 873-884.

Batson, C. D., P. A. Schoenrade, and L. W. Ventis. *Religion and the Individual: A Social-Psychological Perspective*. Oxford: University Press, 1993.

Bechara, Antoine, Hanna Damasio, and Antonio Damasio. "Emotion, Decision Making and the Orbitofrontal Cortex." *Cerebral Cortex* 10 (2000): 295-307.

Bechtel, William. *Mental Mechanisms: Philosophical Perspectives on Cognitive Neuroscience*. New York: Routledge, 2008.

Bechtel, William, and Adele Abrahamsen. "Explanation: A Mechanist Alternative." *Studies in History and Philosophy of Biological and Biomedical Sciences* 36 (2005): 421-441.

Bedau, Mark A. "Downward Causation and Autonomy in Weak Emergence." In *Emergence: Contemporary Readings in Philosophy and Science*, ed. Mark A. Bedau and Paul Humphreys. Cambridge: The MIT Press, 2008.

Bedau, Mark A., and Paul Humphreys, eds. *Emergence: Contemporary Readings in Philosophy and Science*. Cambridge: The MIT Press, 2008.

Bednekoff, P. A. "Mutualism among Safe, Selfish Sentinels: A Dynamic Game." *American Naturalist* 150 (1997): 373-392.

Bergson, Henry. *Creative Evolution*. Translated by Arthur Mitchell. New York: Dover, 1911/1998.

Bering, J. M., K. McLeod, and T. K. Shakelford. "Reasoning About Dead Agents Reveals Possible Adaptive Trends." *Human Nature* 16 (2005): 360-381.

Bering, J. M., and B. D. Parker. "Children's Attributions of Intentions to an Invisible Agent." *Developmental Psychology* 42, no. 2 (2006): 253-262.

Blackmore, Susan. *The Meme Machine*. Oxford: Oxford University Press, 1999.

Bloom, Paul. "Is God an Accident?" *Atlantic Monthly*, December 2005, 1-8.

Bourgeois, J. P., P. S. Goldman-Rakic, and P. Rakic. "Synaptogenesis in the Prefrontal Cortex of Rhesus Monkeys." *Cerebral Cortex* 4 (1994): 78-96.

Bowlby, John. "The Nature of the Child's Tie to His Mother." *International Journal of Psycho-Analysis* 39 (1958): 350-373.

Boyd, Robert, and Peter J. Richerson. *The Origin and Evolution of Cultures*. Oxford: Oxford University Press, 2005.

Boyer, Pascal. "Natural Epistemology or Evolved Metaphysics?: Developmental Evidence for Early-Developed, Intuitive, Category-Specific, Incomplete, and Stubborn Metaphysical Presumptions." *Philosophical Psychology* 13, no. 3 (2000): 277-297.

———. *Religion Explained: The Evolutionary Origins of Religious Thought*. New York: Basic Books, 2001.

———. "Religious Thought and Behavior as by-Products of Brain Function." *Trends in Cognitive Sciences* 7, no. 3 (2003): 119-124.

———. "A Reductionistic Model of Distinct Modes of Religious Transmission." In *Mind and Religion: Psychological and Cognitive Foundations of Religiosity*, ed. Harvey Whitehouse and Robert N. McCauley, 3-30. Walnut Creek: AltaMira Press, 2005.

Boyer, Pascal, and Clark Barrett. "Evolved Intuitive Ontology: Integrating Neural, Behavioral and Developmental Aspects of Domain Specificity." In *Handbook of Evolutionary Psychology*, ed. David Buss, 96-118. Hoboken: John Wiley & Sons, Inc., 2005.

Boyer, Pascal, and Charles Ramble. "Cognitive Templates for Religious Concepts: Cross-Cultural Evidence for Recall of Counter-Intuitive Representations." *Cognitive Science* 25 (2001): 535-564.

Brelsford, Theodore. "Lessons for Religious Education from Cognitive Science of Religion." *Religious Education* 100, no. 2 (2005): 174-191.

Bretherton, Inge, and Kristine A. Munholland. "Internal Working Models: A Construct Revisited." In *Handbook of Attachment: Theory, Research, and*

Clinical Applications, ed. Jude Cassidy and Phillip R. Shaver. New York: The Guilford Press, 1999.
Brigandt, Ingo, and Alan Love. "Reductionism in Biology." In *The Stanford Encyclopedia of Philosophy*, ed. Edward N. Zalta. Stanford: The Metaphysics Research Lab, 2008.
Brothers, L. "Brain Mechanisms of Social Cognition." *Journal of Psychopharmacology* 10 (1996): 2-8.
Brown, Warren S., Nancey Murphy, and H. Newton Maloney, eds. *Whatever Happened to the Soul?: Scientific and Theological Portraits of Human Nature*. Minneapolis: Fortress Press, 1998.
Buber, Martin. *I and Thou*. Translated by Ronald Gregor Smith. New York: Scribner Classics, 1958/2000.
Bulbulia, Joseph. "Meme Infection or Religious Niche Construction?: An Adaptationist Alternative to the Cultural Maladaptationist Hypothesis." *Method and Theory in the Study of Religion* 20 (2008): 67-107.
———. "Religion as Evolutionary Cascade: On Scott Atran, *in Gods We Trust* (2002)." In *Contemporary Theories of Religion: A Critical Companion*, ed. Michael Stausberg, 156-172. New York: Routledge, 2009.
Bulkeley, Kelly. "Review of Religion Explained: The Evolutionary Origins of Religious Thought, by Pascal Boyer and How Religion Works: Towards a New Cognitive Science of Religion, by Ilkka Pyysiäinen." *Journal of the American Academy of Religion* 71, no. 3 (2003): 671-674.
Buller, David J. *Adopting Minds: Evolutionary Psychology and the Persistent Quest for Human Nature*. Cambridge: The MIT Press, 2005.
Buss, David. "Sex, Marriage, and Religion: What Adaptive Problems Do Religious Phenomena Solve?" *Psychological Inquiry* 13, no. 3 (2002): 201-238.
———. *The Evolution of Desire*. Revised ed. New York: Basic Books, 2003.
———. "The Evolution of Human Mating." *Acta Psychologica Sinica* 39 (2007): 502-512.
———. ed. *The Handbook of Evolutionary Psychology*. New Jersey: John Wiley & Sons, Inc., 2005.
Buss, David, and Todd K. Shackelford. "Attractive Women Want It All: Good Genes, Economic Investment, Parenting Proclivities, and Emotional Commitment." *Evolutionary Psychology* 6, no. 1 (2008): 134-146.
Camerer, Colin, and Ernst Fehr. "When Does 'Economic Man' Dominate Social Behavior?" *Science* 311 (2006): 47-52.
Campbell, Donald. "'Downward Causation' in Hierarchically Organized Biological Systems." In *Studies in the Philosophy of Biology: Reduction and Related Problems*, ed. Francisco J. Ayala and Theodosius Dobzhansky, 179-186. Berkeley and Los Angeles: University of California Press, 1974.
Carlson, Neil R. *Physiology of Behavior*. 6th edn. Boston: Allyn and Bacon, 1998.
Carnap, Rudolph. *The Logical Structure of the World and Pseudoproblems in Philosophy*. Chicago: Open Court, 1928/2003.

Cartwright, John. *Evolution and Human Behavior: Darwinian Perspectives on Human Nature*. Cambridge: The MIT Press, 2008.
Cary, Phillip. *Augustine's Invention of the Inner Self: The Legacy of a Christian Platonist*. Oxford: Oxford University Press, 2000.
Caston, Victor. "Epiphenomenalism, Ancient and Modern." *Philosophical Review* 106 (1997): 309-363.
Chen, Daniel L. "Islamic Resurgence and Social Violence During the Indonesian Financial Crisis." In *Institutions and Norms in Economic Development*, ed. K. Konrad and M. Gradstein, 179-200. Cambridge: The MIT Press, 2006.
Churchland, Patricia. *Brain-Wise: Studies in Neurophilosophy*. Cambridge: MIT Press, 2002.
Churchland, Paul M. *A Neurocomputational Perspective: The Nature of Mind and the Structure of Science*. Cambridge: The MIT Press, 1993.
―――. *The Engine of Reason, the Seat of the Soul: A Philosophical Journey into the Brain*. Cambridge: The MIT Press, 1996.
―――. *Neurophilosophy at Work*. New York: Cambridge University Press, 2007.
Cimino, Aldo, and Andrew W. Delton. "On the Perception of Newcomers: Toward an Evolved Psychology of Intergenerational Coalitions." *Human Nature* 21 (2010): 186-202.
Clark, Andy. *Being There: Putting Brain, Body, and World Together Again*. Cambridge: The MIT Press, 1997.
Clayton, Philip. *Mind and Emergence: From Quantum to Consciousness*. Oxford: Oxford University Press, 2004.
Clayton, Philip, and Paul Davies, eds. *The Re-Emergence of Emergence: The Emergentist Hypothesis from Science to Religion*. Oxford: Oxford University Press, 2006.
Collins, N. L., and S. J. Read. "Cognitive Representations of Attachment: The Structure and Function of Working Models." In *Advances in Personal Relationships: Vol. 5. Attachment Processes in Adulthood*, ed. Kim Bartholomew and D. Perlman. London: Jessica Kingsley, 1994.
Cosmides, Leda, and John Tooby. "Introduction to Evolutionary Psychology." In *The Cognitive Neurosciences* ed. Michael Gazzaniga. Cambridge The MIT Press, 1995.
―――. "Introduction to Evolutionary Psychology." In *The Cognitive Neurosciences* ed. Michael Gazzaniga, 1163-1166. Cambridge The MIT Press, 1995.
―――. "Evolutionary Psychology: A Primer" www.psych.ucsb.edu/research/cep/primer.html (accessed August 2004).
―――. "Neurocognitive Adaptations Designed for Social Exchange." In *Evolutionary Psychology Handbook*, ed. David Buss. New York: Wiley, 2005.
Cottrell, G. W. "Extracting Features from Faces Using Compression Networks: Face, Identity, Emotions, and Gender Recognition Using Holons." In *Connectionists Models: Proceedings of the 1990 Summer School*, ed. D. Touretzky, Jeffrey L.

Elman, Terrence J. Sejnowski and G. Hinton. San Mateo: Morgan Kauffman, 1991.
Cozolino, Louis. *The Neuroscience of Human Relationships: Attachment and the Developing Social Brain*. New York: W. W. Norton & Co., 2006.
d'Holbach, Paul Henry Thiry Baron. *System of Nature, or, the Laws of the Moral and Physical World*. 2 Vols. London, 1797.
Dailey, M. N., G. W. Cottrell, C. Padgett, and Ralph Adolphs. "EMPATH: A Neural Network That Categorizes Facial Expressions." *Journal of Cognitive Neuroscience* 14, no. 8 (2002): 1158-1173.
Damasio, Antonio. *Descartes' Error: Emotion, Reason, and the Human Brain*. New York: Quill, 1994.
Darwin, Charles. *The Origin of the Species*. London: John Murray, 1859.
Dawkins, Richard. *The Selfish Gene*. Oxford: Oxford University Press, 1976.
_____. *The God Delusion*. Boston: Houghton Mifflin Harcourt, 2006.
Day, Matthew. "Rethinking Naturalness: Modes of Religiosity and Religion in the Round." In *Mind and Religion: Psychological and Cognitive Foundations of Religiosity*, ed. Harvey Whitehouse and Robert N. McCauley. Walnut Creek: AltaMira Press, 2005.
de Quervain, Dominique J., Urs Fischbacher, Valerie Treyer, Melanie Schellhammer, Ulrich Schnyder, Alfred Buck, and Ernst Fehr. "The Neural Basis of Altruistic Punishment." *Science* 305 (2004): 1254-1258.
Deacon, Terrence. *The Symbolic Species: The Co-Evolution of Language and the Brain*. New York: W. W. Norton & Co., Inc., 1997.
_____. "Multilevel Selection in a Complex Adaptive System: The Problem of Language Origins." In *Evolution and Learning: The Baldwin Effect Reconsidered*, ed. Bruce H. Weber and David J. Depew. Cambridge: The MIT Press, 2003.
_____. "Three Levels of Emergent Phenomena." In *Evolution & Emergence: Systems, Organisms, Persons*, ed. Nancey Murphy and William R. Stoeger, SJ, 88-112. Oxford: Oxford University Press, 2007.
Dennett, Daniel. *Consciousness Explained*. Boston: Little, Brown and Company, 1991.
_____. *Darwin's Dangerous Idea: Evolution and the Meanings of Life*. New York: Simon and Schuster: A Touchstone Book, 1995.
_____. *Breaking the Spell: Religion as a Natural Phenomenon*. New York: Viking, 2006.
Depew, David J. "Baldwin and His Many Effects." In *Evolution and Learning: The Baldwin Effect Reconsidered*, ed. Bruce H. Weber and David J. Depew. Cambridge: The MIT Press, 2003.
Descartes, Rene. "Meditations (1641)." In *The Essential Descartes*, ed. Margaret D. Wilson. New York: Meridian, 1969.
_____. "Discourse (1637)." In *Discourse on Method and Related Writings* ed. Desmond M. Clarke. London: Penguin Books, 1999.

di Pellegrino, G., L. Fadiga, L. Fogassi, V. Gallese, and G. Rizzolatti. "Understanding Motor Events: A Neurophysiological Study." *Experimental Brain Research* 91, no. 1 (1992): 176-180.

Doherty, Martin J. *Theory of Mind: How Children Understand Others' Thoughts and Feelings*. New York: Psychology Press, 2008.

Donald, Merlin. *Origins of the Modern Mind: Three Stages in the Evolution of Culture and Cognition*. Cambridge: Harvard University Press, 1991.

_____. "Imitation and Mimesis." In *Perspectives on Imitation: From Neuroscience to Social Science*, ed. Susan L. Hurley and Nick Chater, Vol. 2, 283-300. Cambridge: The MIT Press, 2005.

Dretske, Fred. "Mental Events as Structuring Causes of Behavior." In *Mental Causation*, ed. John Heil and Alfred Mele, 121-136. Oxford: Clarendon Press, 1995.

Dunbar, R. I. M. "Determinants and Evolutionary Consequences of Dominance among Female Gelada Baboons." *Behavioral Ecology and Sociobiology* 7 (1980): 253-265.

_____. *Grooming, Gossip, and the Evolution of Language*. London: Faber and Faber, 1996.

_____. "The Social Brain Hypothesis." *Evolutionary Anthropology* 6 (1998): 178-190.

Edelman, Gerald M. *Neural Darwinism: The Theory of Neuronal Group Selection*. New York: Basic Books, 1987.

_____. *Bright Air, Brilliant Fire*. New York: Basic Books, 1992.

Edelman, Gerald M., and Giulio Tononi. *A Universe of Consciousness: How Matter Becomes Imagination*. New York: Basic Books, 2000.

Euler, H. A., and B. Weitzel. "Discriminating Grandparental Solicitude as Reproductive Strategy." *Human Nature* 7 (1996): 39-59.

Feeney, Judith A. "Adult Attachment and Relationship-Centered Anxiety: Responses to Physical and Emotional Distancing." In *Attachment Theory and Close Relationships*, ed. J. A. Simpson and W. S. Rholes. New York: Guilford Press, 1998.

_____. "Adult Romantic Attachment and Couple Relationships." In *Handbook of Attachment: Theory, Research, and Clinical Applications*, ed. Cindy Hazan and Phillip R. Shaver. New York: The Guilford Press, 1999.

Feeney, Judith A., P. Noller, and V. J. Callan. "Attachment Style, Communication and Satisfaction in the Early Years of Marriage." In *Advances in Personal Relationships: Vol. 5. Attachment Processes in Adulthood*, ed. Kim Bartholomew and D. Perlman. London: Jessica Kingsley, 1994.

Fehr, Ernst, and Colin Camerer. "Social Neuroeconomics: The Neural Circuitry of Social Preferences." *Trends in Cognitive Sciences* 11, no. 10 (2007): 419-427.

Feldman, M. W., and K. N. Laland. "Gene-Culture Coevolutionary Theory." *Trends in Evolution and Ecology* 11 (1996): 453-457.

Feuerbach, Ludwig. *The Essence of Religion*. Translated by Alexander Loos. Amherst: Prometheus Books, 1873/2004.

Feyerabend, Paul. *Against Method*. London: Verso, 1975/1988.
Flanagan, Owen. *The Science of the Mind*. 2nd edn. Cambridge: The MIT Press, 1991.
Fox, N. A., S. D. Calkins, and M. A. Bell. "Neural Plasticity and Development in the First Two Years of Life: Evidence from Cognitive and Socioemotional Domains of Research." *Development and Psychopathology* 6 (1994): 677-696.
Freud, Sigmund. *The Psychopathology of Everyday Life*. Translated by Anthea Bell. New York: Penguin Books, 1901/2002.
_____. *The Future of an Illusion*. New York: Norton, 1961.
_____. *The Psychopathology of Everyday Life*. Translated by Anthea Bell. New York: Penguin Books, 2002.
Friedlander, M. J., K. A. C. Martin, and D. Wassenhove-McCarthy. "Effects of Monocular Visual Deprivation on Geniculocortical Innervation of Area 18 in Cat." *Journal of Neuroscience* 11 (1991): 3268-3288.
Frith, Christopher, and Daniel Wolpert, eds. *The Neuroscience of Social Interaction: Decoding, Imitating, and Influencing the Actions of Others*. New York: Oxford University Press, 2004.
Fuster, Joaquín M. *The Prefrontal Cortex: Anatomy, Physiology, and Neuropsychology of the Frontal Lobe*. New York: Raven Press, 1997.
_____. *Cortex and Mind*. Oxford: Oxford University Press, 2003.
Gerrard, N. "The Serpent-Handling Religions of West Virginia." *Trans-Action* 5 (1968): 22-28.
Gibbs, Raymond W. *Embodiment and Cognitive Science*. Cambridge: Cambridge University Press, 2005.
Giedd, J. N. "Structural Magnetic Resonance Imaging of the Adolescent Brain." *Annals of the New York Academy of Sciences* 1021 (2004): 105-109.
Globus, A., M. R. Rosenzweig, E. L. Bennett, and M. C. Diamond. "Effects of Differential Experience on Dendritic Spine Counts in Rat Cerebral Cortex." *Journal of Comparative and Physiological Psychology* 82 (1973): 175-181.
Globus, A., and A. B. Scheibel. "The Effect of Visual Deprivation on Cortical Neurons: A Golgi Study." *Experimental Neurology* 19 (1967): 331-345.
Gonce, Lauren O., M. Afzal Upal, D. Jason Slone, and Ryan D. Tweney. "Role of Context in the Recall of Counterintuitive Concepts." *Journal of Cognition and Culture* 6, no. 3-4 (2006): 521-547.
Gordon, Deborah. *Ants at Work: How an Insect Society Is Organized* New York: Free Press, 1999.
Gould, Stephen J., and Richard C. Lewontin. "The Spandrels of San Marco and the Panglossian Paradigm: A Critique of the Adaptationist Programme." *Proceedings of the Royal Society of London* 205, no. 1161 (1979): 581-598.
Gould, Stephen. J. "Exaptation: A Crucial Tool for Evolutionary Psychology." *Journal of Social Issues* 47 (1991): 43-46.
Green, Joel. "Bodies—That Is, Human Lives: A Re-Examination of Human Nature in the Bible." In *Whatever Happened to the Soul? Scientific and Theological*

Portraits of Human Nature, ed. Warren S. Brown, Nancey Murphy, and H. Newton Maloney. Minneapolis: Fortress Press, 1998.

———. *Body, Soul, and Human Life: The Nature of Humanity in the Bible* Studies in Theological Interpretation. Grand Rapids: Baker Academic, 2008.

———. ed. *What About the Soul?: Neuroscience and Christian Anthropology*. Nashville: Abingdon Press, 2004.

Grenz, Stanley J. *Theology for the Community of God*. Grand Rapids and Vancouver: Wm. B. Eerdmans and Regent College, 2000.

Griffiths, Paul J. "'Faith Seeking Explanation.' Review of *Religion Explained: The Evolutionary Origins of Religious Thought*, by Pascal Boyer." *First Things*, no. 119 (2002).

Grossman, E. D., and R. Blake. "Brain Activity Evoked by Inverted and Imagined Biological Motion." *Vision Research* 41 (2001): 1475-1482.

Grossman, E. D., M. Donnelly, R. Price, D. Pickens, V. Morgan, G. Neighbor, and R. Blake. "Brain Areas Involved in Perception of Biological Motion." *Journal of Cognitive Neuroscience* 12 (2000): 711-720.

Guthrie, Stewart. "A Cognitive Theory of Religion." *Current Anthropology* 21, no. 2 (1980): 181-203.

———. *Faces in the Clouds: A New Theory of Religion*. Oxford: Oxford University Press, 1993.

Haley, K. J., and D. M. T. Fessler. "Nobody's Watching? Subtle Cues Affect Generosity in an Anonymous Economic Game." *Evolution and Human Behavior* 26 (2005): 245-256.

Hallam, J. C. T., and M. Malcolm. "Behaviour: Perception, Action and Intelligence—the View from Situated Robots." *Philosophical Transactions: Physical Sciences and Engineering* 349, no. 1689 (1994): 29-42.

Hamilton, W. D. "The Genetical Evolution of Social Behaviour." *Journal of Theoretical Biology* 7 (1964): 1-16.

Hankinson, R. James. "Galen." In *The Cambridge Dictionary of Philosophy*, ed. Robert Audi. Cambridge: Cambridge University Press, 1999.

Haught, John. "The Darwinian Universe: Isn't There Room for God?" *Commonweal* 129, no. 2 (2002).

Hebb, Donald O. *The Organization of Behavior*. New York: Wiley, 1949.

Heider, F., and S. Simmel. "An Experimental Study of Apparent Behavior." *American Journal of Psychology* 77 (1944): 243-259.

Heider, Fritz, and Mary-Ann Simmel. "An Experimental Study of Apparent Behavior." *American Journal of Psychology* 57 (1944): 243-249.

Henderson, J., and M. Oakes. *The Wisdom of the Serpent*. Princeton: Princeton University Press, 1990.

Hinde, Robert A. "Modes Theory: Some Theoretical Considerations." In *Mind and Religion: Psychological and Cognitive Foundations of Religiosity*, ed. Harvey Whitehouse and Robert N. McCauley. Walnut Creek: Alta Mira Press, 2005.

Hofer, Myron A. "Survival and Recovery of Physiologic Functions after Early Maternal Separation in Rats." *Physiology and Behavior* 15, no. 5 (1975): 475-480.

———. "Early Social Relationships: A Psychobiologist's View." *Child Development* 58, no. 3 (1987): 633-647.

———. "Hidden Regulators: Implications for a New Understanding of Attachment, Separation, and Loss." In *Attachment Theory: Social, Developmental, and Clinical Perspectives*, ed. S. Goldberg, R. Muir and J. Kerr. Hillsdale: Analytic Press, 1995.

Hood, R. W., Jr., B. Spilka, B. Hunsberger, and R. Gorsuch. *The Psychology of Religion: An Empirical Approach*. 2nd edn. New York: Guilford Press, 1996.

Intraub, H. "The representation of visual scenes." *Trends in Cognitive Sciences*, 1(6) (1997).

James, William. *Principles of Psychology*. New York: Henry Holt, 1890.

———. *The Varieties of Religious Experience*. New York: Modern Library, 1902/1999.

Jeeves, Malcolm ed. *From Cells to Souls—and Beyond: Changing Portraits of Human Nature*. Grand Rapids: Wm. B. Eerdmans, 2004.

Jensen, Jeppe Sinding. "Religion as the Unintended Product of Brain Functions in the 'Standard Cognitive Science of Religion Model': On Pascal Boyer, *Religion Explained* (2001) and Ilkka Pyysiäinen, *How Religion Works* (2003)." In *Contemporary Theories of Religion: A Critical Companion*, ed. Michael Stausberg, 129-155. New York: Routledge, 2009.

Johansson, Gunnar. "Visual Perception of Biological Motion and a Model for Its Analysis." *Perception and Psychophysics* 14 (1973): 201-211.

Johnson, Mark H., and John Morton. *Biology and Cognitive Development: The Case of Face Recognition*. Oxford: Blackwell, 1991.

Johnson, Steven. *Emergence: The Connected Lives of Ants, Brains, Cities, and Software*. New York: Scribner, 2001.

Juarrero, Alicia. *Dynamics in Action: Intentional Behavior as a Complex System*. Cambridge: The MIT Press, 1999.

Kelly, Michael H., and Frank C. Keil. "The More Things Change...: Metamorphoses and Conceptual Structure." *Cognitive Science* 9 (1985): 403-416.

Kildahl, J. P. *The Psychology of Speaking in Tongues*. New York: Harper & Row, 1972.

Kim, Jaegwon. "Being Realistic About Emergence." In *The Re-Emergence of Emergence: The Emergentist Hypothesis from Science to Religion*, ed. Philip Clayton and Paul Davies. Oxford: Oxford University Press, 2006.

Kinsbourne, Marcel. "Imitation as Entrainment: Brain Mechanisms and Social Consequences." In *Perspectives on Imitation: From Neuroscience to Social Science*, ed. Susan L. Hurley and Nick Chater, Vol. 2, 163-172. Cambridge: The MIT Press, 2005.

Kirkpatrick, Lee A. "An Attachment-Theoretical Approach to the Psychology of Religion." *International Journal for the Psychology of Religion* 2, no. 1 (1992): 3-28.

―――――. "God as a Substitute Attachment Figure: A Longitudinal Study of Adult Attachment Style and Religious Change in College Students." *Personality and Social Psychology Bulletin* 24 (1998): 961-973.

―――――. *Attachment, Evolution, and the Psychology of Religion*. New York: The Guilford Press, 2005.

Kirkpatrick, Lee A., and K. E. Davis. "Attachment Style, Gender, and Relationship Stability: A Longitudinal Analysis." *Journal of Personality and Social Psychology* 66 (1994): 502-512.

Kirkpatrick, Lee A., and Phillip R. Shaver. "Attachment Theory and Religion: Childhood Attachments, Religious Beliefs, and Conversion." *Journal for the Scientific Study of Religion* 29 (1990): 315-334.

Kluver, H., and P. C. Bucy. "Preliminary Analysis of the Temporal Lobes in Monkeys." *Archives of Neurology and Psychiatry* 42 (1939): 979-1000.

Knight, Nicola, Paulo Sousa, Justin L. Barrett, and Scott Atran. "Children's Attributions of Beliefs to Humans and God: Cross-Cultural Evidence." *Cognitive Science* 28, no. 1 (2004): 117-126.

Koechlin, Etienne, Chrystele Ody, and Frederique Kouneiher. "The Architecture of Cognitive Control in the Human Prefrontal Cortex." *Science* 302, no. 5648 (2003): 1181-1185.

Kolb, Bryan, and Ian Q. Whishaw. *Fundamentals of Human Neuropsychology*. 4th edn. New York: Worth Publishers Incorporated, 1995.

Krentz, Edgar. *The Historical-Critical Method*. Eugene: Wipf and Stock, 2002.

Kuhn, Thomas. *The Structure of Scientific Revolutions*. Chicago: Chicago University Press, 1962.

Küppers, Bernd-Olaf. "Understanding Complexity." In *Chaos and Complexity: Scientific Perspectives on Divine Action*, ed. Robert John Russell, Nancey Murphy, and Arthur Peacocke. Berkeley and Vatican City State: The Center for Theology and the Natural Sciences and Vatican Observatory Publications, 1995.

Kurzban, Robert. "The Social Psychophysics of Cooperation: Nonverbal Communication in a Public Goods Game." *Journal of Nonverbal Behavior* 25, no. 4 (2001): 241-259.

Kurzban, Robert, John Tooby, and Leda Cosmides. "Can Race Be Erased? Coalitional Computation and Social Categorization." *Proceedings of the National Academy of Sciences* 98, no. 26 (2001): 15387.

Lane, Richard, and Lynn Nadel, eds. *Cognitive Neuroscience of Emotion*. New York: Oxford University Press, 2000.

Lassek, William D., and Steven J. C. Gaulin. "Waist-Hip Ratio and Cognitive Ability: Is Gluteofemoral Fat a Privileged Store of Neurodevelopmental Resources?" *Evolution and Human Behavior* 29 (2008): 26-34.

Lawson, E. Thomas, and Robert N. McCauley. *Rethinking Religion: Connecting Cognition and Culture*. Cambridge: Cambridge University Press, 1990.

LeDoux, Joseph. "Emotion: Clues from the Brain." *Annual Review of Psychology* 46 (1995): 209-235.

_____. *The Emotional Brain: The Mysterious Underpinnings of Emotional Life*. New York: Touchstone, 1996.

Lee, Desmond, ed. *Wittgenstein's Lectures Cambridge 1930-1932*. Oxford: Blackwell, 1980.

Levin, Daniel T., and Melissa R. Beck. *Thinking and Seeing: Visual Metacognition in Adults and Children*. Cambridge: The MIT Press, 2004.

Lewes, George Henry. *Problems of Life and Mind*. Vol. 2. London: Kegan, Paul, Trench, Turbner & Co., 1872.

Lewis, Thomas, Fari Amini, and Richard Lannon. *A General Theory of Love*. New York: Vintage Books, 2000.

Li, Jessica Yexin, Adam B. Cohen, Jason Weeden, and Douglas T. Kenrick. "Mating Competitors Increase Religious Beliefs." *Journal of Experimental Social Psychology* 46, no. 2 (2010): 428-431.

Lieberman, Debra, John Tooby, and Leda Cosmides. "The Architecture of Human Kin Detection." *Nature* 445 (2007): 727-731.

Lieberman, Phillip. *On the Origins of Language: An Introduction to the Evolution of Human Speech*. New York: Macmillan, 1975.

Lorenz, Konrad. "Der Kumpan in Der Umvelt Des Vogels [Companionship in Bird Life]." *Journal of Ornithology* 83 (1935): 137-213.

MacIntyre, Alasdair. *After Virtue: A Study in Moral Theory*. Notre Dame: University of Notre Dame Press, 1981.

_____. *Whose Justice? Which Rationality?* Notre Dame: University of Notre Dame Press, 1988.

MacKay, Donald M. *Behind the Eye*, ed. Valerie MacKay. Oxford: Blackwell, 1991.

Marr, David. *Vision: A Computational Investigation into the Human Representation and Processing of Visual Information*. San Francisco: Freeman, 1982.

Matlin, Margaret W. *Cognition*. 6th edn. Hoboken: John Wiley & Sons, 2005.

McCauley, Robert N. "Reduction: Models of Cross-Scientific Relations and Their Implications for the Psychology-Neuroscience Interface." In *Handbook of the Philosophy of Science: Philosophy of Psychology and Cognitive Science*, ed. Paul Thagard, 105-158. Amsterdam: Elsevier, 2007.

McCauley, Robert N., and William Bechtel. "Explanatory Pluralism and the Heuristic Identity Theory." *Theory and Psychology* 11 (2001): 738-761.

McClendon, James Wm., Jr., and James M. Smith. *Convictions: Defusing Religious Relativism*. Valley Forge: Trinity Press International, 1994.

McLaughlin, Brian P. "Philosophy of Mind." In *The Cambridge Dictionary of Philosophy*, ed. Robert Audi. Cambridge: Cambridge University Press, 1999.

Meltzoff, Andrew N. "Understanding the Intentions of Others: Re-Enactment of Intended Acts by 18-Month-Old Children." *Developmental Psychology* 31 (1995): 838-850.

---------. "Imitation and Other Minds: The 'Like Me' Hypothesis." In *Perspectives on Imitation: From Neuroscience to Social Science*, ed. Susan L. Hurley and Nick Chater, Vol. 2, 55-78. Cambridge: The MIT Press, 2005.
Meltzoff, Andrew N., and M. Keith Moore. "Imitation of Facial and Manual Gestures by Human Neonates." *Science* 198 (1977): 75-78.
---------. "Newborn Infants Imitate Adult Facial Gestures." *Child Development* 54 (1983): 702-709.
---------. "Imitation in Newborn Infants: Exploring the Range of Gestures Imitated and the Underlying Mechanisms." *Developmental Psychology* 25 (1989): 954-962.
Mill, John Stuart. *A System of Logic*. 8th edn. London: Longmans, Green, Reader, and Dyer, 1943.
Miller, Greg. "Growing Pains for *f*MRI." *Science* 320 (2008): 1412-1414.
Montague, P. Read, and Steven Quartz. "Computational Approaches to Neural Reward and Development." *Mental Retardation and Developmental Disabilities Research Reviews* 5 (1999): 86-99.
Morowitz, Harold J. *The Emergence of Everything: How the World Became Complex*. Oxford: Oxford University Press, 2002.
Munkur, B. *The Cult of the Serpent*. Albany: State University of New York Press, 1983.
Murphy, Nancey. *Theology in the Age of Scientific Reasoning*. Ithaca: Cornell University Press, 1990.
---------. "Human Nature: Historical, Scientific, and Religious Issues." In *Whatever Happened to the Soul? Scientific and Theological Portraits of Human Nature*, ed. Warren S. Brown, Nancey Murphy and H. Newton Maloney. Minneapolis: Fortress Press, 1998.
---------. "Supervenience and the Downward Efficacy of the Mental: A Nonreductive Physicalist Account of Human Action." In *Neuroscience and the Person: Scientific Perspectives on Divine Action*, ed. Robert John Russell, Nancey Murphy, Theo C. Meyering, and Michael Arbib. Vatican City State and Berkeley: Vatican Observatory Publications and the Center for Theology and the Natural Sciences, 1999.
---------. *Bodies and Souls or Spirited Bodies?* Cambridge: Cambridge University Press, 2006.
---------. "Naturalism and Theism as Competing Traditions." In *29th International Wittgenstein Symposium*. Kirchber am Wechel, Austria: Austrian Ludwig Wittgenstein Society, 2006.
---------. "Reductionism: How Did We Fall into It and Can We Emerge from It?" In *Evolution & Emergence: Systems, Organisms, Persons*, ed. Nancey Murphy and William R. Stoeger, SJ, 19-39. Oxford: Oxford University Press, 2007.
Murphy, Nancey, and Warren S. Brown. *Did My Neurons Make Me Do It? Philosophical and Neurobiological Perspectives on Moral Responsibility and Free Will* Oxford: Oxford University Press, 2007.

Murphy, Nancey, and George F. R. Ellis. *On the Moral Nature of the Universe: Theology, Cosmology, and Ethics*. Minneapolis: Fortress Press, 1996.

Murphy, Nancey, and William R. Stoeger SJ, eds. *Evolution & Emergence: Systems, Organisms, Persons*. Oxford: Oxford University Press, 2007.

Nagel, Ernst. *The Structure of Science*. New York/Indianapolis: Harcourt, Brace and World/Hackett, 1961/1979.

Neiesser, U., and N. Harsch. "Phantom Flashbulbs: False Recollection of Hearing News About the *Challenger*." In *Affect and Accuracy of Recall: Studies Of "Flashbulb" Memories*, ed. E. Winograd and U. Neiesser, 9-31. Cambridge: Cambridge University Press, 1992.

Nietzsche, Friedrich. *Genealogy of Morals*. Translated by Walter Kaufmann. New York: Random House, 1966.

Nieuwenhuys, R., H. J. Donkelaar, and C. Nicholson. *The Central Nervous System of Vertebrates*. New York: Springer, 1997.

Noë, Alva, Luiz Pessoa, and Evan Thompson, "Beyond the Grand Illusion: What Change Blindness Really Teaches Us About Vision." *Visual Cognition* 7 (2000).

Norenzayan, Ara, and Scott Atran. "Cognitive and Emotional Processes in the Cultural Transmission of Natural and Nonnatural Beliefs." In *The Psychological Foundations of Culture*, ed. M. Schaller and C. Crandall, 149-170. Hillsdale: Erlbaum, 2002.

Norenzayan, Ara, and Azim F. Shariff. "The Origin and Evolution of Religious Prosociality." *Science* 322 (2008): 58-62.

Nouwen, Henri J. M. *Return of the Prodigal Son: A Story of Homecoming*. New York: Doubleday, 1994.

Nowak, Martin A., and Karl Sigmund. "Evolution of Indirect Reciprocity by Image Scoring." *Nature* 393 (1998): 573-576.

Oates, W. E. "A Sociopsychological Study of Glossolalia." In *Glossolalia: Tongue Speaking in Biblical, Historical, and Psychological Perspective*, ed. F. Stagg, E. G. Hinson and W. E. Oates. New York: Abingdon, 1967.

Oppenheim, Paul, and Hillary Putnam. "The Unity of Science as a Working Hypothesis." In *Concepts, Theories, and the Mind-Body Problem*, ed. Herbert Feigel, Michael Scriven, and Grover Maxwell, Vol. 2, 3-36. Minneapolis: University of Minnesota Press, 1958.

Otto, Rudolph. *The Idea of the Holy*. Translated by J. W. Harvey. Oxford: Oxford University Press, 1969.

Oviedo, Lluis. "Is a Complete Biocognitive Account of Religion Feasible?" *Zygon* 43, no. 1 (2008): 103-126.

Panksepp, Jaak. *Affective Neuroscience: The Foundations of Human and Animal Emotions*. New York: Oxford University Press, 1998.

Pargament, K. I., and J. Hahn. "God and the Just World: Causal and Coping Attributions to God in Health Situations." *Journal for the Scientific Study of Religion* 25 (1986): 193-207.

Peacocke, Arthur. *Theology for a Scientific Age: Being and Becoming—Natural and Divine*. Oxford: Basil Blackwell, 1990. Reprint, Minneapolis: Fortress Press, 1993.

Pessoa, Luiz "On the Relationship between Emotion and Cognition." *Nature Reviews Neuroscience* 9 (2008): 148-158.

Peterson, Gregory R. "Species of Emergence." *Zygon* 41, no. 3 (2006): 689-712.

_____. "Theology and the Science Wars: Who Owns Human Nature?" *Zygon* 41, no. 4 (2006): 853-862.

Petit, T. L., J. C. LeBoutillier, A. Gregorio, and H. Libstug. "The Pattern of Dendritic Development in the Cerebral Cortex of the Rat." *Brain Research* 469 (1988): 209-219.

Piaget, Jean. *The Psychology of the Child*. Paris Presses Universitaires de France, 1966.

Pierce, Charles Sanders. "Logic as Semiotic: The Theory of Signs." In *Philosophical Writings of Pierce*, ed. Justus Buchler. New York: Dover Publications, Inc., 1955.

Pinker, Steven. *The Language Instinct: How the Mind Creates Language*. New York: William Morrow, 1994.

_____. *How the Mind Works*. New York: W. W. Norton & Co., 1997.

Pojman, Louis P. "The Pre-Socratics." In *Classics of Philosophy*, ed. Louis P. Pojman and Lewis Vaughn, 3-12. New York: Oxford University Press, 2011.

Polkinghorne, John. "Some of the Truth." *Science* 28 (2001): 2400.

Popper, Karl, and John Eccles. *The Self and Its Brain*. New York: Springer-Verlag, 1977.

Pyysiäinen, Ilkka. *How Religion Works: Toward a New Cognitive Science of Religion*. Leiden: Brill 2003.

Quartz, Steven R. "Toward a Developmental Evolutionary Psychology: Genes, Development, and the Evolution of the Human Cognitive Architecture." In *Evolutionary Psychology: Alternative Approaches*, ed. Steven J. Scher and Frederick Rauscher, 185-210. New York: Springer Publishing Co., 2002.

Quartz, Steven R., and Terrence J. Sejnowski. "The Neural Basis of Cognitive Development: A Constructivist Manifesto." *Behavioral and Brain Sciences* 20 (1997): 537-596.

_____. *Liars, Lovers, and Heroes: What the New Brain Science Reveals About How We Become Who We Are*. New York: William Morrow & Company, 2002.

Rakic, Pasko, J. P. Bourgeois, M. F. Eckenhoff, N. Zecevic, and P. S. Goldman-Rakic. "Concurrent Overproduction of Synapses in Diverse Regions of the Primate Cerebral Cortex." *Science* 232 (1986): 232-235.

Randolph-Seng, Brandon, and Michael E. Nielsen. "Honesty: One Effect of Primed Religious Representations." *International Journal for the Psychology of Religion* 17, no. 4 (2007): 303-315.

Reimer, Kevin S., Alvin C. Dueck, Garth Neufeld, Sherry Steenwyk, and Tracy Sidesinger. "Varieties of Religious Cognition: A Computational Approach to

Self-Understanding in Three Monotheist Contexts." *Zygon* 45, no. 1 (2010): 75-90.

Rilling, James K., David A. Gutman, Thorsten R. Zeh, Giuseppe Pagnoni, Gregory S. Berns, and Clinton D. Kilts. "A Neural Basis for Social Cooperation." *Neuron* 35 (2002): 395-405.

Rilling, James K., Alan G. Sanfey, Jessica A. Aronson, Leigh E. Nystrom, and Jonathan D. Cohen. "Opposing BOLD Responses to Reciprocated and Unreciprocated Altruism in Putative Reward Pathways." *Neuroreport* 15, no. 16 (2004): 2539-2543.

Rizzolatti, G., and M. Arbib. "Language within Our Grasp." *Trends in Neurosciences* 21 (1998): 188-194.

Rizzolatti, G., L. Fodiga, L. Fogassi, and V. Gallese. "Premotor Cortex and the Recognition of Motor Actions." *Cognitive Brain Research* 3 (1996): 131-141.

Rizzolatti, G., L. Fogassi, and V. Gallese. "Neurophsyiological Mechanisms Underlying the Understanding and Imitation of Action." *Nature Reviews Neuroscience* 2, no. 9 (2001): 661-670.

Rizzolatti, G. "The Mirror Neuron System and Imitation." In *Perspectives on Imitation: From Neuroscience to Social Science*, ed. Susan Hurley and Nick Chater, Vol. 1, 55-76. Cambridge: The MIT Press, 2005.

Rizzuto, Ana-Maria. *The Birth of the Living God: A Psychoanalytic Study*. Chicago: University of Chicago Press, 1979.

Roes, Frans L., and Michel Raymond. "Belief in Moralizing Gods." *Evolution and Human Behavior* 24 (2003): 126-135.

Rorty, Richard. *Philosophy and the Mirror of Nature*. Princeton: Princeton University Press, 1979.

Rumelhart, D. E., J. L. McClelland, and PDP Research Group. *Parallel Distributed Processing: Explorations in the Microstructure of Cognition*. 2 vols. Cambridge: The MIT Press, 1986.

Ruse, Michael. "Methodological Naturalism under Attack." In *Intelligent Design Creationism and Its Critics: Philosophical, Theological, and Scientific Perspectives*, ed. Robert T. Pennock. Cambridge: The MIT Press, 2001.

Russell, Bertrand. *Logical Atomism*. Chicago: Open Court, 1918/1985.

Russell, Robert John. "Special Providence and Genetic Mutation: A New Defense of Theistic Evolution." In *Evolutionary and Molecular Biology*, ed. Robert John Russell, William R. Stoeger SJ and Francisco J. Ayala, 191-224. Berkeley and Vatican City State: Vatican Observatory Publications and Center for Theology and the Natural Sciences, 1998.

Saler, Benson. "Anthropomorphism and Animism: On Stewart E. Guthrie, *Faces in the Clouds* (1993)." In *Contemporary Theories of Religion: A Critical Companion*, ed. Michael Stausberg, 39-52. New York: Routledge, 2009.

Savage-Rumbaugh, Sue. *Ape Language: From Conditioned Response to Symbol*. New York: Columbia University Press, 1986.

Savage-Rumbaugh, Sue, and Roger Lewin. *Kanzi: The Ape at the Brink of the Human Mind*. New York: Wiley, 1994.

Savage-Rumbaugh, Sue, Duane Rumbaugh, and Sally Boysen. "Symbolization, Language and Chimpanzees: A Theoretical Re-Evaluation Based on Initial Language Acquisition Processes in Four Young Pan Troglodytes." *Brain and Language* 6 (1978): 265.

Schade, J. P., and W. B. van Groenigen. "Structural Organization of the Human Cerebral Cortex I: Maturation of the Middle Frontal Gyrus." *Acta Anatomica* 47 (1961): 72-111.

Schleiermacher, Friedrich. *On Religion: Speeches to Is Cultured Despisers.* Translated by John Oman. New York: Harper & Row, 1958.

Schore, Allan. "Effects of a Secure Attachment Relationship on Right Brain Development, Affect Regulation, and Infant Mental Health." *Infant Mental Health Journal* 22, no. 1-2 (2001): 7-66.

———. "Dysregulation of the Right Brain: A Fundamental Mechanism of Traumatic Attachment and the Psychopathogenesis of Posttraumatic Stress Disorder." *Australian and New Zealand Journal of Psychiatry* 36 (2002): 9-30.

Scott, S. K., A. W. Young, A. J. Calder, D. J. Hellawell, J. P. Aggleton, and M. Johnson. "Impaired Auditory Recognition of Fear and Anger Following Bilateral Amygdala Lesions." *Nature* 385 (1997): 254-257.

Scrull, T. K., and R. S. Wyer. "The Role of Category Accessibility in the Interpretation of Information About Persons: Some Determinants and Implications." *Journal of Personality and Social Psychology* 37 (1979): 1660-1672.

Selfridge, O. "Pattern Recognition and Modern Computers." In *Proceedings of the Western Joint Computer Conference*. Los Angeles, CA: Institute of Electrical and Electronics Engineers, 1955.

Sellars, Roy Wood. *Philosophy of Physical Realism*. New York: Macmillian, 1932.

Senchak, M., and K. E. Leonard. "Attachment Styles and Marital Adjustment among Newlywed Couples." *Journal of Social and Personal Relationships* 9 (1992): 51-64.

Seyfarth, Robert, Dorothy Cheney, and Peter Marler. "Monkey Responses to Three Different Alarm Calls: Evidence of Predator Classification and Semantic Communication." *Science* 210 (1980): 801-803.

Shariff, Azim F., and Ara Norenzayan. "God Is Watching You: Priming God Concepts Increases Prosocial Behavior in an Anonymous Economic Game." *Psychological Science* 18, no. 9 (2007): 803-809.

Silberstein, Michael, and John McGeever. "The Search for Ontological Emergence." *Philosophical Quarterly* 49 (1999).

Simons, D. J., and D. T. Levin. "Change Blindness." *Trends in Cognitive Sciences*, 1(7) (1997).

Simonds, R. J., and A. B. Scheibel. "The Postnatal Development of the Motor Speech Area: A Preliminary Study." *Brain and Language* 37 (1989): 42-58.

Singer, Tania, Ben Seymour, John P. O'Doherty, Klaas E. Stephan, Raymond J. Dolan, and Chris D. Frith. "Empathetic Neural Responses Are Modulated by the Perceived Fairness of Others." *Nature* 439 (2006): 466-469.

Singh, Devendra. "Adaptive Significance of Female Physical Attractiveness: Role of Waist-to-Hip Ratio." *Journal of Personality and Social Psychology* 65, no. 2 (1993): 293-307.

Skinner, B. F. *Beyond Freedom and Dignity*. New York: Knopf, 1971.

Slone, D. Jason. *Theological Incorrectness: Why Religious People Believe What They Shouldn't*. Oxford: Oxford University Press, 2004.

Smith, Edward, and Stephen Kosslyn. *Cognitive Psychology: Mind and Brain*. Upper Saddle River: Pearson Prentice Hall, 2007.

Smith, Martin S., Bradley J. Kish, and Charles B. Crawford. "Inheritance of Wealth as Human Kin Investment." *Ethology and Sociobiology* 8, no. 3 (1987): 171-182.

Sober, Elliott, and David Sloan Wilson. *Unto Others: The Evolution and Psychology of Unselfish Behavior*. Cambridge: Harvard University Press, 1998.

Sørensen, Jesper. "Religion, Evolution, and an Immunology of Cultural Systems." *Evolution and Cognition* 10, no. 1 (2004): 61-73.

Sosis, Richard. "Religion and Intragroup Cooperation: Preliminary Results of a Comparative Analysis of Utopian Communities." *Cross-Cultural Research* 34, no. 1 (2000): 70-87.

──────. "Psalms and Coping with Uncertainty: Religious Israeli Women's Responses to the 2006 Lebanon War." *American Anthropologist* (forthcoming).

Sosis, Richard, and Candace Alcorta. "Signaling, Solidarity, and the Sacred: The Evolution of Religious Behavior." *Evolutionary Anthropology* 12 (2003): 264-274.

Sosis, Richard, and Eric R. Bressler. "Cooperation and Commune Longevity: A Test of the Costly Signaling Theory of Religion." *Cross-Cultural Research* 37, no. 2 (2003): 11-39.

Sosis, Richard, and Bradley J. Ruffle. "Religious Ritual and Cooperation: Testing for a Relationship on Israeli Religious and Secular Kibbutzim." *Current Anthropology* 44, no. 5 (2003): 713-722.

Spelke, Elizabeth. "Principles of Object Perception." *Cognitive Science* 14 (1990): 29-56.

Sperber, Dan. *Explaining Culture: A Naturalistic Approach*. Oxford: Blackwell Publishers, 1996.

Sperry, Roger W. *Science and Moral Priority: Merging Mind, Brain, and Human Values*. New York: Columbia University Press, 1983.

Talaricho, J. M., and D. C. Rubin. "Confidence, Not Consistency, Characterizes Flashbulb Memories." *Psychological Science* 14 (2003): 455-461.

Tamminen, K. *Religious Development in Childhood and Adolescence*. Helsinki: Suomalainen Tiedeakatemia, 1991.

Thornhill, Randy, and Steven W. Gangestad. "Facial Attractiveness." *Trends in Cognitive Sciences* 3, no. 12 (1999): 452-460.

Tomasello, Michael. *The Cultural Origins of Human Cognition*. Cambridge: Harvard University Press, 1999.

──────. *Origins of Human Communication*. Cambridge: The MIT Press, 2008.

Tomasello, Michael, and Malinda Carpenter. "Intention Reading and Imitative Learning." In *Perspectives on Imitation: From Neuroscience to Social Science*, ed. Susan L. Hurley and Nick Chater, Vol. 2, 133-148. Cambridge: The MIT Press, 2005.

Tooby, John, and Leda Cosmides. "The Past Explains the Present: Emotional Adaptations and the Structure of Ancestral Environments." *Ethology and Sociobiology* 11 (1990): 375-424.

──────. "The Psychological Foundations of Culture." In *The Adapted Mind: Evolutionary Psychology and the Generation of Culture*, ed. Jerome H. Barkow, Leda Cosmides and John Tooby, 19-136. New York: Oxford University Press, 1992.

──────. "Mapping the Evolved Functional Organization of the Mind and Brain." In *The Cognitive Neurosciences*, ed. Michael Gazzaniga. Cambridge: The MIT Press, 1995.

Tooby, John, and Irven DeVore. "The Reconstruction of Hominid Evolution through Strategic Modeling." In *The Evolution of Human Behavior: Primate Models*, ed. W. G. Kinzey. Albany: SUNY Press, 1987.

Trivers, Robert L. "The Evolution of Reciprocal Altruism." *Quarterly Review of Biology* 46 (1971): 35-57.

Tulving, Endel. *Elements of Episodic Memory*. Oxford: Clarendon Press, 1983.

Turing, Alan. "On Computable Numbers, with an Application to the Entscheidungsproblem." In *Proceedings of the London Mathematical Society*, 42, 230-265. London, 1937.

──────. "Computing Machinery and Intelligence." *Mind* 49, no. 236 (1950): 433-460.

Upal, M. Afzal, Lauren O. Gonce, Ryan D. Tweney, and D. Jason Slone. "Contextualizing Counterintuitiveness: How Context Affects Comprehension and Memorability of Counterintuitive Concepts." *Cognitive Science* 31 (2007): 415-439.

Valverde, Facundo. "Apical Dendritic Spines of the Visual Cortex and Light Deprivation in the Mouse." *Experimental Brain Research* 3 (1967): 337-352.

──────. "Rate and Extent of Recovery from Dark Rearing in the Visual Cortex of the Mouse." *Brain Research* 33 (1971): 1-11.

Van Gulick, Robert. "Who's in Charge Here? And Who's Doing All the Work?" In *Mental Causation*, ed. John Heil and Alfred Mele. Oxford: Clarendon, 1995.

──────. "Reduction, Emergence and Other Recent Options on the Mind/Body Problem." *Journal of Consciousness Studies* 8, no. 9-10 (2001): 1-34.

Van Slyke, James A., Kevin S. Reimer, and Alvin C. Dueck. "Correspondence, Compensation, or Something Else? Limitations for Attachment in Religious Cognition of Monotheist Exemplars." *Journal of Cognition and Culture* (in submission).

Warren, R. M., and R. P. Warren. "Auditory Illusions and Confusions." *Scientific American* 223, no. 6 (1970): 30-36.

Wedin, Michael V. "Aristotle." In *The Cambridge Dictionary of Philosophy*, ed. Robert Audi. Cambridge: Cambridge University Press, 1999.

Weeden, Jason, Adam B. Cohen, and Douglas T. Kenrick. "Religious Attendance as Reproductive Support." *Evolution and Human Behavior* 29 (2008): 327-334.

Wellman, H., D. Cross, and J. Watson. "Meta-Analysis of Theory of Mind Development: The Truth About False-Belief." *Child Development* 72 (2001): 655-684.

West-Eberhard, Mary J. "The Evolution of Social Behavior by Kin Selection." *Quarterly Review of Biology* 50 (1975): 1-33.

White, Graham. "Medieval Theories of Causation." In *The Stanford Encyclopedia of Philosophy*, ed. Edward N. Zalta. Stanford: The Metaphysics Research Lab, 2009.

Whitehead, H. *The Village Gods of South India*. Madras: Asia Education Services, 1921/1988.

Whitehouse, Harvey. *Modes of Religiosity: A Cognitive Theory of Religious Transmission*. Walnut Creek: AltaMira Press, 2004.

Wilkinson, G. S. "Food Sharing in Vampire Bats." *Scientific American* 262 (1990): 76-82.

Williams, G. C. *Adaptation and Natural Selection: A Critique of Some Current Evolutionary Thought*. Princeton: Princeton University Press, 1966.

Wilson, David Sloan. "Adaptive Genetic Variation and Human Evolutionary Psychology." *Ethology and Sociobiology* 15 (1994): 219-235.

_____. *Darwin's Cathedral: Evolution, Religion, and the Nature of Society*. Chicago: University of Chicago Press, 2002.

_____. "Group-Level Evolutionary Processes." In *The Oxford Handbook of Evolutionary Psychology*, ed. Robin Dunbar and Louise Barrett. Oxford: Oxford University Press, 2007.

_____. "Human Groups as Adaptive Units: Toward a Permanent Consensus." In *The Innate Mind: Culture and Cognition*, ed. Peter Carruthers, Stephen Laurence, and Stephen Stich. Oxford: Oxford University Press, 2007.

Wilson, Edward O. *Sociobiology: The New Synthesis*. Cambridge: Harvard University Press, 1975.

Wimsatt, William. "Reductionism, Levels of Organization, and the Mind-Body Problem." In *Consciousness and the Brain*, ed. A. Globus, G. Maxwell, and I. Savodnik, 199-267. New York: Plenum Press, 1976.

Wittgenstein, Ludwig. *Philosophical Investigations*. Translated by G. E. M. Anscombe. 3rd edn. New York: Macmillan, 1958.

Yamaski, H., K. S. LaBar, and G. McCarthy. "Dissociable Prefrontal Brain Systems for Attention and Emotion." *Proceedings of the National Academy of Sciences, USA* 99 (2002): 11447-11451.

Zak, Paul, Angela Stanton, and Shelia Ahmadi. "Oxytocin Increases Generosity in Humans." *PLoS One* 2, no. 11 (2007): e1128.

Index

ant colony behavior 47-8
attachment theory 134-43
   critiques 141-3
   God concepts 139-41
   regulatory systems 136-9
Atran, Scott 3 n12, 5-6, 25, 122-3,
     127 n24, 141 n100

Barrett, Justin L. 5-8, 28, 62-3, 94, 124-6,
     142
Bechtel, William 19, 28-9
Bowlby, John 134-5, 139
Boyer, Pascal 1-3, 5-6, 8-11, 16, 25-6,
     32-4, 122, 127
Brown, Warren S. 15 n39, 24 n75-7, 71,
     75-6, 113-14
Buss, David 10 n22, 93 n6, 94 n11,
     96 n23&26, 152 n149, 153 n153

Campbell, Donald 117
Churchland, Patricia S. 23 n72, 81 n62
Churchland, Paul M. 21 n61, 81 n61,
     84 n68, 87-9
Clark, Andy 43-5, 72, 75
cognitive scaffolding 72-4
cognitive science of religion
   definition of 2-4, 5-6
   hypotheses 6-9
computational modeling 81-4
Cosmides, Leda 10 n22-3, 43 n45, 92-99
costly signaling theory 9, 146-50
counterintuitive hypothesis 8-9, 31-8, 58-9,
     122-4, 126-7
cultural epidemiology 10, 34-6, 38

Dawkins, Richard 25-6, 34, 126 n19,
     150 n139
Deacon, Terrence 45-7, 50-51, 77, 107-18
Dennett, Daniel C. 25 n80, 34, 36
Descartes, Rene 36, 88

Donald, Merlin 101-4

emergence
   cognition 42-51
   definition 16-19
   historical factors 39-41
   neuroscience 51-8
   three aspects
     feedback 44-7
     initial conditions 42-4
     pattern formation 47-51
   weak vs. strong 18
emotion
   decision-making 132-4
   neuroscience 128-30
   religion 126-8
evolutionary psychology 10, 43-4, 92-101,
     144, 152
   critiques 98-101
   hypotheses 96-8
   Swiss Army knife 10, 94-5

Gage, Phineas 132-4
group selection 4, 9, 150-54

hyperactive agency detection device
     (HADD) 7, 124-6

imitation 101-7

Johnson, Steven 17 n47, 47-8
Juarrero, Alicia 19-20, 45 n53, 73 n39,
     78-9, 84-5, 114

Lawson, E. Thomas 5, 7-8, 128 n30

McCauley, Robert N. 5, 7-8, 22-3, 28-9,
     128 n30
MacKay, Donald M. 70-71
Meltzoff, Andrew 101-4, 106-7

mirror neurons 101-2
modes of religiosity hypothesis 8, 131-2
Murphy, Nancey 15, 18, 24 n75-7, 26 n83, 29-30, 71, 75-6, 88, 113-14

neuroeconomics 145-6, 154, 158
neural constructivism 54-7
nerual darwinism 57-8
Norenzayan, Ara 122-3, 148-9

old or young woman illusion 86

parallel distributed processing (PDP) 83
Peacocke, Arthur 28-30
Pierce's theory of signs 108-10
Pyysiainen, Ilkka 1, 35, 127 n23

Quartz, Steven R. 49 n64, 52-7, 69, 99-101

reduction
    causal 12, 15-18, 35
    eliminative 21
    epistemological 12-15, 21
    historical factors 13-15
    inter vs. intra 22-5
    methodological 14
Religion Explained 1-2, 6, 25

Sejnowski, Terrence J. 52-7, 99-101
shared intentions 103-7

Slone, D. Jason 62-64, 74 n41
somatic markers 132-4
Sosis, Richard 3 n10, 147 n123-5, 149 n135
Sperber, Dan 10 n24, 34 n11, 35 n14, 37 n20
Sperry, Roger W. 40-41
standard model 3-4, 9-13, 43, 47
    causal reduction 16
    critiques 11-12, 37-8, 51, 119
    reduction 11
symbolic mind 107-18
    co-evolution 116-18
    learning a language 115-16
    neuroanatomy 111-13

theological correctness/incorrectness 62-5
theory of mind 28, 105, 119, 124-6, 142
Tomasello, Michael 103-5
Tooby, John 10 n22&23, 43 n45, 92-9
top-down
    causation 17, 20-21, 61, 77-80, 117-18
    constraints 4-5, 12, 16, 19-21, 30, 61, 65-8, 71, 77-81, 90-92, 105, 108, 114, 117-19, 155
    processing 20, 65-8, 81, 90

Whitehouse, Harvey 5, 8-9, 131-2
Wilson, David Sloan 3 n9, 98 n34, 150-53
Wittgenstein, Ludwig 38